Gavin Ambrose and Paul Harris

The Fundamentals of Creative Design

AVA Publishing SA
Switzerland

An AVA Book

Published by AVA Publishing SA
rue du Bugnon 7
CH-1299 Crans-près-Céligny
Switzerland
Tel: +41 786 005 109
Email: enquiries@avabooks.ch

Distributed by Thames and Hudson (ex-North America)
181a High Holborn
London WC1V 7QX
United Kingdom
Tel: +44 20 7845 5000
Fax: +44 20 7845 5055
Email: sales@thameshudson.co.uk
www.thamesandhudson.com

Distributed by Sterling Publishing Co., Inc.
in USA
387 Park Avenue South
New York, NY 10016-8810
Tel: +1 212 532 7160
Fax: +1 212 213 2495
www.sterlingpub.com

in Canada
Sterling Publishing
c/o Canadian Manda Group
One Atlantic Avenue, Suite 105
Toronto, Ontario M6K 3E7

English Language Support Office
AVA Publishing (UK) Ltd.
Tel: +44 1903 204 455
Email: enquiries@avabooks.co.uk

ISBN 2-88479-023-3

10 9 8 7 6 5 4 3 2 1

Design by Gavin Ambrose and Paul Harris

Production and separations by AVA Book Production Pte. Ltd., Singapore
Tel: +65 6334 8173
Fax: +65 6334 0752
Email: production@avabooks.com.sg

Acknowledgements

Special thanks to Natalia Price-Cabrera – who devised the original concept for this project – Laura Owen and Brian Morris at AVA Publishing, without whose enthusiasm, support and belief this project would not have been realised; to the many contributors whose dedication has made this such a special project to work on; and to Xavier Young for his care and attention in photographing the collected work.

Photographs on pages 11, 12, 13, 16, 17, 21 (top), 22 (bottom), 25, 34, 35, 48, 59, 68, 115 by Xavier Young
Tel: +44 (0)20 713 5502

Photographs on pages 69 and 168 by Richard Learoyd
Tel: +44 (0)7958 390 133

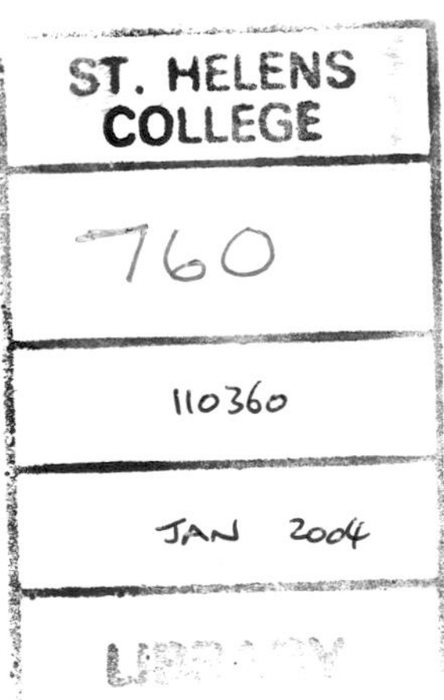

The Fundamentals of Creative Design

Bell Gothic 1938 Mergenthaler

This book is set in Bell Gothic, which was originally commissioned for the Bell Telephone Company. Noted for its space-saving capabilities, the font is of a relatively thin cut.

contents

introduction

CREATIVE DESIGN IS IN SOMETHING OF A GOLDEN AGE. NEVER BEFORE HAVE THE OPPORTUNITIES AND OUTLETS BEEN SO BROAD AS SOCIETY CONTINUES TO BECOME VISUALLY RICHER AND MORE ADVENTUROUS AND TECHNOLOGICAL DEVELOPMENTS CONTINUE TO ADVANCE THE FRONTIERS OF THE VISUAL WORLD. WE LIVE IN A MEDIA-RICH AGE, ONE IN WHICH WE ARE BOMBARDED FROM ALL SIDES BY FINELY TARGETED NICHE PRODUCTS AND SERVICES, EACH STRIVING TO GRAB OUR ATTENTION THROUGH THE ARTISTRY OF THE GRAPHIC DESIGNER. WE ARE SURROUNDED BY THEIR OUTPUT IN BOTH PRINT AND ELECTRONIC FORMAT FROM ADVERTISING BILLBOARDS, SHAMPOO BOTTLES AND MAGAZINES TO TELEVISION AND THE INTERNET.

WITH SO MUCH VYING FOR OUR ATTENTION, GETTING NOTICED IN THE VISUAL MORASS AND QUICKLY CREATING A GOOD IMPRESSION IS BECOMING INCREASINGLY DIFFICULT. AT THE SAME TIME, TECHNOLOGY IS DEMOCRATISING CREATIVE DESIGN AND MAKING IT EASIER FOR NON-DESIGNERS TO PRODUCE CREDIBLE WORK. AS A CONSEQUENCE, A SOLID GRASP OF CREATIVE DESIGN FUNDAMENTALS IS OF PARAMOUNT IMPORTANCE TO PRODUCE EFFECTIVE AND EYE-CATCHING DESIGNS, A SOUND FOUNDATION FROM WHICH CREATIVITY CAN FLOURISH.

THE FUNDAMENTALS OF CREATIVE DESIGN IS INTENDED AS A GUIDE TO EQUIP PEOPLE ENGAGED IN DESIGN WITH THE LONG ESTABLISHED TENETS THAT UNDERPIN BOTH PRINT AND DIGITAL DESIGN. PROVIDING CONCISE, ILLUSTRATED EXPLANATIONS OF THE FUNDAMENTALS, ENHANCED WITH EXAMPLES OF THEIR PRACTICAL APPLICATION THROUGH EXAMPLES OF CONTEMPORARY DESIGN PROJECTS, THIS BOOK OFFERS A UNIQUE RESOURCE TO ALL DESIGN PRACTITIONERS, STUDENTS AND MEMBERS OF THE GENERAL PUBLIC WITH AN INTEREST IN DESIGN.

how to get the most out of this book

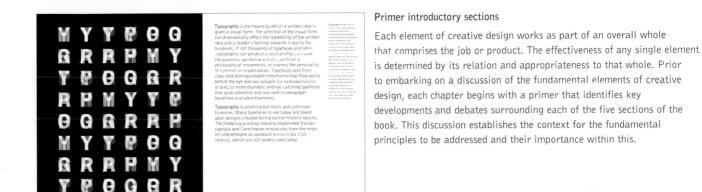

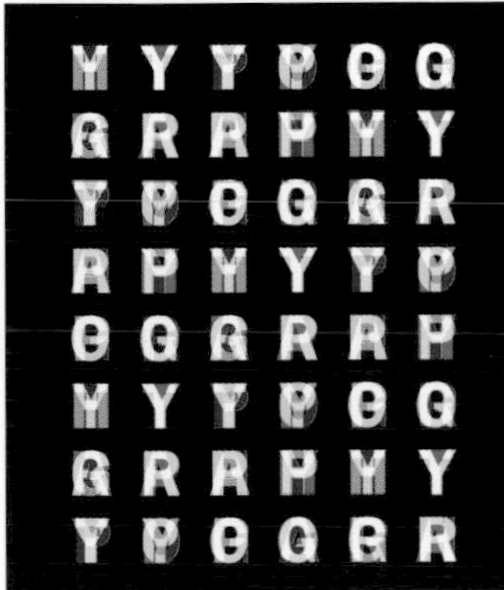

Typography is the means by which a written idea is given a visual form. The selection of the visual form can dramatically affect the readability of the written idea and a reader's feelings towards it due to the hundreds, if not thousands of typefaces available. Typography can produce a neutral effect or rouse the passions, symbolise artistic, political or philosophical movements, or express the personality of a person or organisation. Typefaces vary from clear and distinguishable letterforms that flow easily before the eye and are suitable for extended blocks of text, to more dramatic and eye-catching typefaces that grab attention and are used in newspaper headlines and advertisements.

Typography is anything but static and continues to evolve. Many typefaces in use today are based upon designs created during earlier historic epochs. The fledgling printing industry established Roman capitals and Carolingian minuscules from the reign of Charlemagne as standard forms in the 15th century, which are still widely used today.

Primer introductory sections

Each element of creative design works as part of an overall whole that comprises the job or product. The effectiveness of any single element is determined by its relation and appropriateness to that whole. Prior to embarking on a discussion of the fundamental elements of creative design, each chapter begins with a primer that identifies key developments and debates surrounding each of the five sections of the book. This discussion establishes the context for the fundamental principles to be addressed and their importance within this.

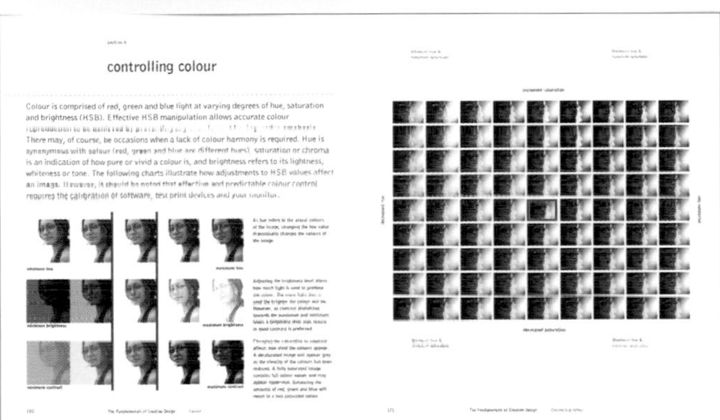

controlling colour

Colour is comprised of red, green and blue light at varying degrees of hue, saturation and brightness (HSB). Effective HSB manipulation allows accurate colour reproduction to be achieved by ... There may, of course, be occasions when a lack of colour harmony is required. Hue is synonymous with colour (red, green and blue are different hues), saturation or chroma is an indication of how pure or vivid a colour is, and brightness refers to its lightness, whiteness or tone. The following charts illustrate how adjustments to HSB values affect an image. However, it should be noted that effective and predictable colour control requires the calibration of software, test print devices and your monitor.

Fundamentals

Getting the fundamentals correct is the first step towards successful design but to do so requires an understanding of why they are important. The fundamental rules pages outline the key principles of contemporary design practice. Each rule is concisely explained and illustrated with a detailed diagrammatic illustration enabling the reader to understand both theoretically and visually the principles discussed. Through the use of examples, the reader will see the fundamental principles in action and the visual impact that they can achieve.

hulton archive

Practical applications

There is no better way to acquire an understanding of the fundamental principles of creative design than to see them at work in a real life application. The examples that follow the fundamentals are taken from actual projects created by contemporary designers and have been chosen to highlight the practical application of the fundamental principles discussed in this book. The choices and decisions made by the designers are discussed to give the reader an insight into the creative process of professional designers and why they make the decisions they do.

A0
1188 x 840mm

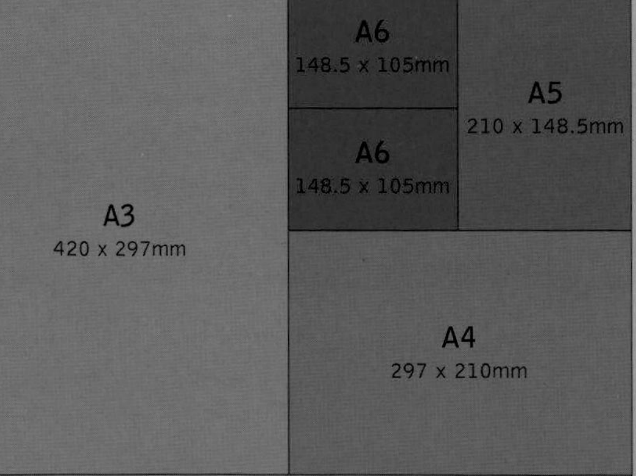

A1
840 x 594mm

A2
594 x 420mm

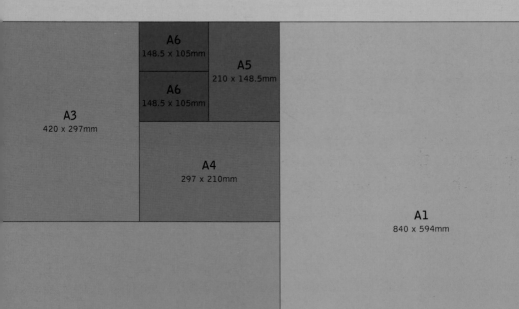

Format is the shape and size of the final product whether it is a book, magazine, brochure, or package. Format selection is an area that is often neglected due to the ISO (International Organization for Standardization) series of paper sizes, based on a rectangle with sides in a ratio of 1:1.4142. This series provides a benchmark range of proportionally related paper sizes that, in effect, means that a designer does not have to give his or her full consideration to format. The existence of a standard range of sizes gives a degree of uniformity for all involved in print production. However, the design brief may call for something different.

Format selection is typically embroiled in the practical considerations such as who the target audience is, the nature of the information to be presented and the budget as non-standard paper sizes will be more expensive to print and finish. That said, a creative approach to format selection can produce dramatic results. With a variety of folding options available the designer has additional creative possibilities that can have a pronounced affect on the resulting product whether it is an annual report or a magazine insert.

Format concerns the physical dimensions of the product and the space one has to present the graphic elements of a design. This section will explore how the shapes, sizes and fold patterns can be used in the creative design process to achieve differentiation. Format is predominantly concerned with print media though certain aspects can be applied to the design of website panels, pop-up boxes and other on screen components.

ISO paper sizes

Standard paper sizes provide a convenient and efficient means for designers, printers and others involved in printing and publishing to communicate product specifications and keep costs down. Standardised paper sizes can be traced back to 14th-century Bologna in Italy where the outlines for four paper sizes were given to guide local paper manufacturers.

1

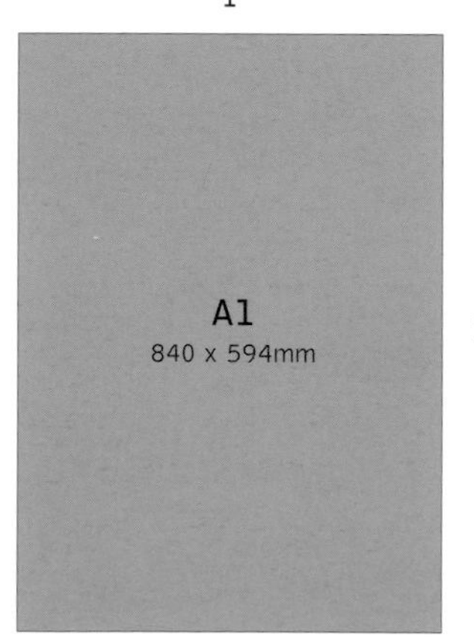

1.61803

1.61803

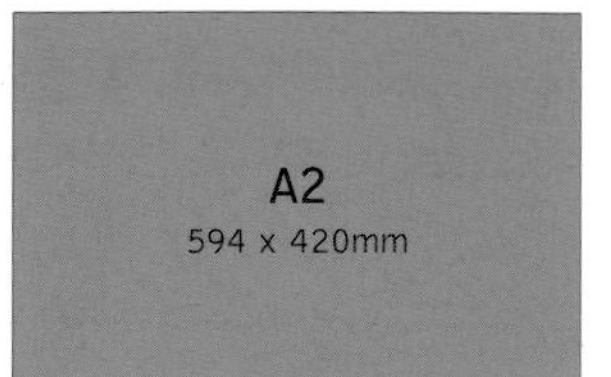

1

A0= 1188 x 840mm

A1= 840 x 594mm

A2= 594 x 420mm

A3= 420 x 297mm

A4= 297 x 210mm

A5= 210 x 148.5mm

A6= 148.5 x 105mm

The modern ISO (International Organization for Standardization) paper sizes system is based on an observation by German physics professor Georg Christoph Lichtenberg who in 1786 saw the advantages of paper sizes having a height-to-width ratio of the square root of two (1:1.4142). Paper with this Lichtenberg ratio will maintain its aspect ratio when cut in half.

France was the first country to adopt paper sizes equivalent to modern ISO sizes with a law issued in 1794. Today, Canada and USA are the only industrialised countries that do not use the ISO system.

The ISO sizes are based on the metric system using the square-root-of-two ratio with format A0 having an area of one square metre. As this does not allow the page height and width to be rounded metric lengths the area of the page has been defined to have a round metric value, which simplifies calculation of the weight of a document (format x number of pages) as paper is usually specified in g/m^2.

The A series comprises a range of paper sizes that differs from the next size by a factor of either 2 of $^1/_2$. B series sizes are intermediate sizes and C series sizes are for envelopes that can contain A size stationery. RA and SRA stock sizes are sheets of paper from which A sizes can be cut.

The theory that underpins this is derived from Fibonacci Numbers and the Golden Section, which are discussed in the Layout chapter.

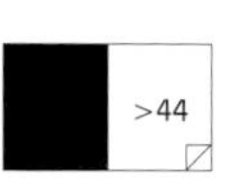

Below: Brochure for Merchant, a company specialising in annual report production. Standardisation is forsaken resulting in an unusual and engaging mixture of formats. Compartmentalised segments of information are allocated individual page sizes that become surprisingly easy to navigate. High gloss inner sections contrast with the cool hues of the introduction, bringing an element of surprise and a change of pace.

Design: NB: Studios

See Hue and Saturation

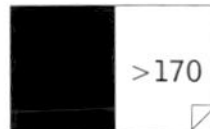

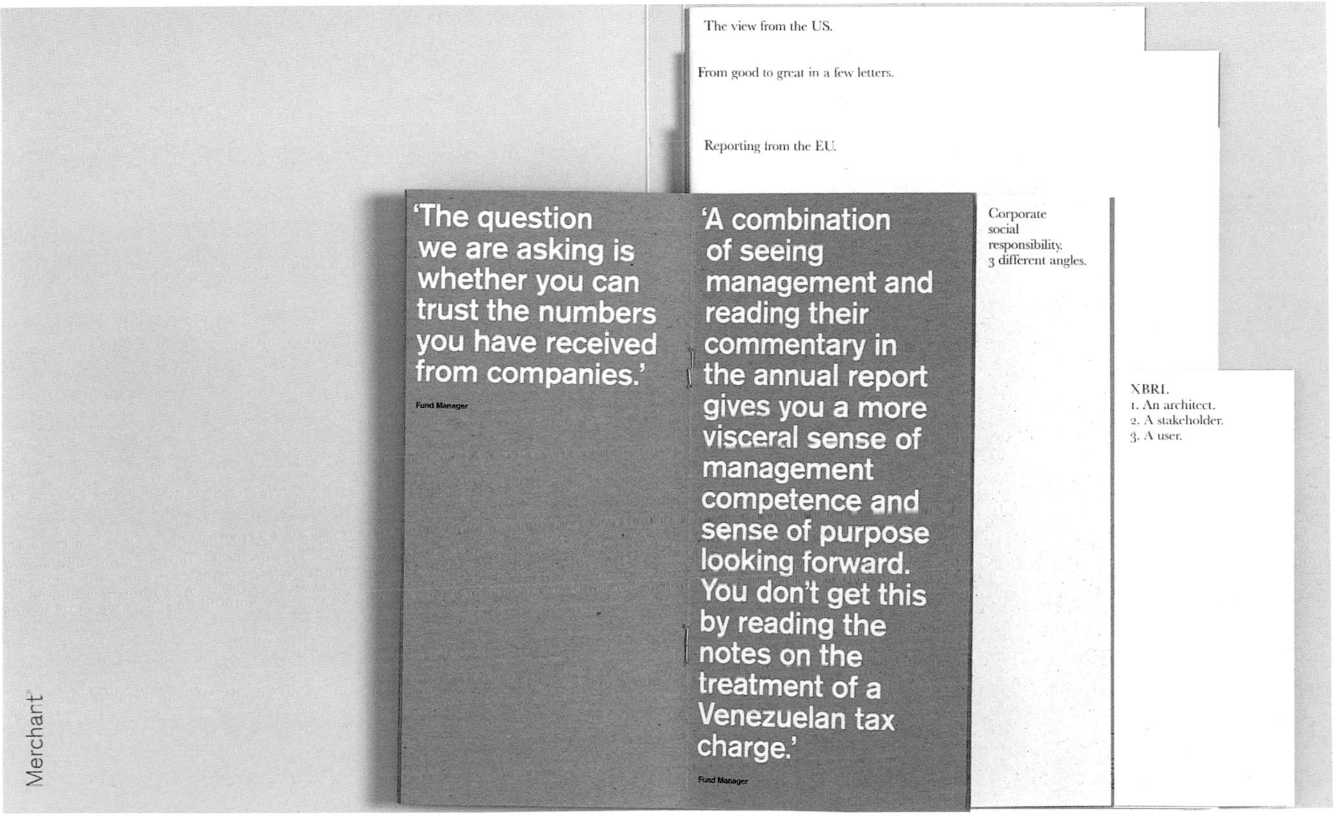

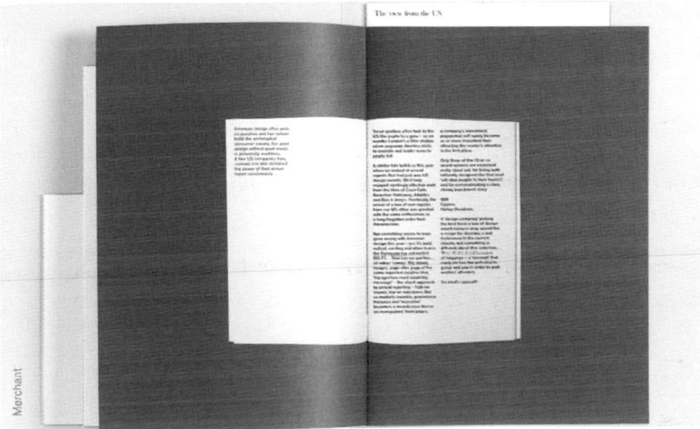

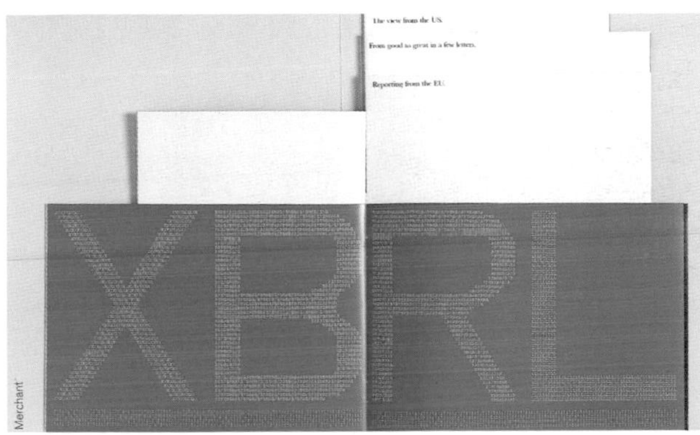

letterpress

Letterpress is a method of relief printing whereby an inked, raised surface is pressed against the paper. It was the first commercial printing method and is the source of many printing terms. The raised surface that makes the impression is typically made from pieces of type, but photoengraved plates can also be used. Letterpress printing can be identified by the sharp and precise edges to letters and their heavier ink border.

A defect of letterpress is appealing to modern designers. When improperly inked, patches appear in the letters giving them a uniqueness, where each impression is subtly different (see below).

This defect can be used to evoke nostalgia for a bygone era. The circus-inspired bill posters for the Royal Academy of Arts (top right) designed by Abbott Mead Vickers • BBDO were set and printed by Forme London using an eclectic mixture of original woodcut fonts.

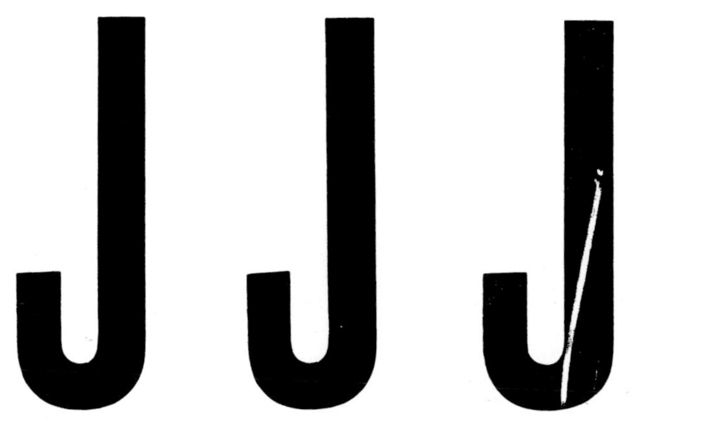

The President and Council
of the Royal Academy of Arts
invite you to the

Press View

1900: Art at the Crossroads
Wednesday 12 January 2000
10am to 2pm

Admit One

Tours of the exhibition will be given at 10.30am and 1pm

Royal Academy of Arts,
Piccadilly, London W1V ODS
Telephone 0171 300 5615
Fax 0171 300 5886

The exhibition is open to the public
from 16 January to 3 April 2000
Open daily from 10am to 6pm
Late Night Opening until
8.30pm every Friday

Sponsored by
CANTOR
Powered by eSpeed.

In association with
The Daily Telegraph

BEAUTY

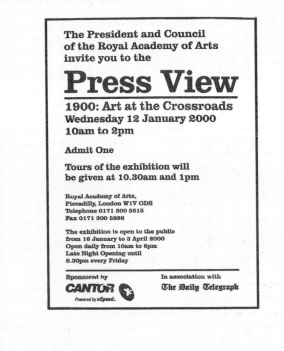

Above: The inherent uniqueness of the individual impressions can be used to produce simple, effective results as these cards by Forme London demonstrate.

Design: Abbott Mead Vickers • BBDO, printing by Forme London

A dramatic example of mixing type sizes and letterpress printing can be seen in this catalogue for Fourth Estate using a sans-serif font in majuscules. In addition to providing information, the sheer scale and clean lines of the sans-serif characters serve to divide and organise the page, acting like a baseline grid. This type is used as a graphic visual device in addition to performing a traditional textural role.

In the image bottom right, it is possible to read the text but this needs some persistence as words track, or read, in conflicting directions. This is a deliberately produced paradox because it is a contents page of a book. Making the information confusing and difficult to extract would seem to be contrary to the purpose of the page, providing information to guide the reader through the publication's contents.

Design: Frost Design

16

Timothy Taylor

THE PREHISTORY OF SEX

Four Million Years of Sexual Culture

One of the most illuminating, controversial books on human sexuality ever written

Drawing on recent archaeological discoveries such as skeletons of Amazon women, golden penis sheaths, the charred remains of aphrodisiac herbs, and a wealth of prehistoric erotic art, archaeologist Timothy Taylor traces practices such as contraception, homosexuality, transsexuality, prostitution, sadomasochism, and bestiality back to their ancient origins. And he links ancient sexuality with our own in a contemporary survey of artificial insemination, surrogate pregnancies, drag queens, brothels, pornography, and the spectre of racial dominance.

How has human sexuality changed – and how has it remained the same – over the span of millions of years? How did the ideas of eroticism, ecstasy, immortality, and beauty become linked to sex? Taylor explores these questions and sets out to prove that our sexual behaviour is and has always been a matter of choice rather than something genetically determined. He eloquently and accessibly explains how our sexual politics – issues of gender and power, control and exploitation – are not new but are deeply rooted in our prehistory, and provides an exhilarating sense of the myriad possibilities sexuality has offered men and women down the millennia, and could offer again.

Timothy Taylor is a lecturer in archaeology at the University of Bradford. He has presented his work on Down to Earth in an episode that won the British Archaeological Award for best popular archaeology on television in 1991-92. He has contributed numerous articles to *Scientific American*, *Antiquity* and *The Oxford Illustrated Prehistory of Europe*.

£18.99
September
Hardback
234 x 156mm 320pp
1 85702 352 8
Anthropology
UK & Comm. exc. Can.
Serial: Fourth Estate
Other rights: Brockman Inc.

Dava Sobel

LONGITUDE

An international bestseller which tells the dramatic human story of an epic scientific quest, and the unlikely triumph of an English genius.

Anyone alive in the eighteenth century would have known that 'the longitude problem' was the thorniest scientific dilemma of the day – and had been for centuries. Sailors throughout the great ages of exploration had been literally lost at sea as soon as they lost sight of land. Thousands of lives, and the increasing fortunes of nations, hung on a resolution. The quest for a solution to the problem of how to measure longitude while at sea had occupied scientists and their patrons for the better part of two centuries when, in 1714, Parliament upped the ante by offering a king's ransom (£20,000) to anyone whose method or device proved successful. Countless quacks weighed in with preposterous suggestions. The scientific establishment throughout Europe – from Galileo to Sir Isaac Newton – had mapped the heavens in both hemispheres in its certain pursuit of a celestial answer. In stark contrast, one man, John Harrison, dared to imagine a mechanical solution. Full of heroism and chicanery, brilliance and the absurd, *Longitude* is also a fascinating brief history of astronomy, navigation and clockmaking.

Dava Sobel is an award-winning former science reporter for the *New York Times*. She writes frequently about science for several magazines, including *Audubon*, *Discover*, *Life* and *Omni*.

'A wonderful story, beautifully told .... Sobel has done the impossible and made horology sexy.' *New Scientist*

'... an enthralling gem of a book. Sobel spins an amazing tale of political intrigue, foul play, scientific discovery and personal ambition.' *Publishers Weekly*

'An exquisitely told tale of perseverance, disappointment and vindication.' *Booklist*

£12.00
August
Hardback
187 x 111mm 192pp
1 85702 502 4
Popular Science/History
UK & Comm. exc. Can.
Serial: Fourth Estate
Other rights: Teresa Chris Agency

LONGIT

NEW BOOKS-96:97
FICTION 2
NON-FICTION 12
GUARDIAN BOOKS 38
PAPERBACKS 40
BACKLIST 41
SALES 43
INDEX 44

hot metal type

Hot metal, also known as hot type composition or cast metal refers to the process of casting the type in lines in molten metal. Text is typed into a machine to produce a punched paper tape that controls the characters cast by the casting machine. Hot metal type made it possible to create large quantities of type in a relatively inexpensive fashion.

Movable type

Movable type was the next leap from the earliest printing presses that used a wooden block carved with the text. This speeded up production of individual pages but meant a new block had to be carved for each page. Movable type is a typesetting method that uses single pieces of type that can be set in a block and printed. Each character is movable and can be used again.

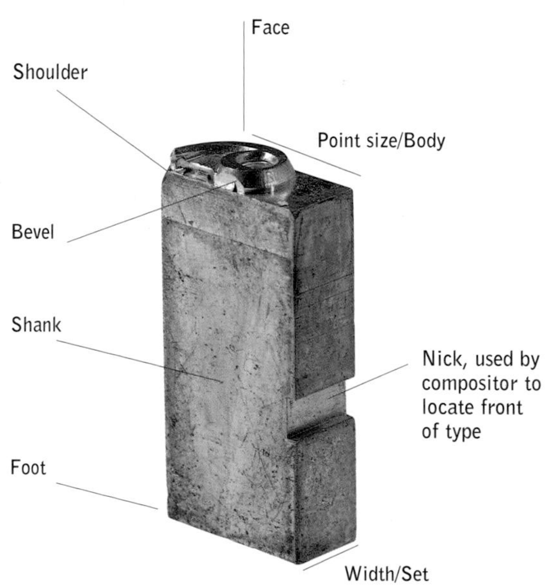

All work and no play makes Jack a dull boy. All work and no play makes Jack a dull boy. All work andno play makes Jack a dull boy. All work and no play mmakes Jack a dull boy. All v All work and no PLay makes Jack a dull boy. All work and no play makes Jack a dulllboy. All work and no play makes Jack a dyll boy. All work and no play makes Jack a dull boy.

All work and no play makes Jack a dull boy. All work and no play makes Jack a dullboy. All work and no Play m kes Jack a dull boy. All work and NO play makes Jack a dull boy. All work and no play makes Jack a dull boy. All work and no play Makes Jack a dull boy. All work and no play makes Jack a dull bog. All work and no play makes Jack a dull bot. All work and no play makes jack a dull boy. All workandno play makes Jack a dyll boy. All work and no play makes Jack Dull B oy. All work and no play makes Jack a dull boy.

All work and no play makes Jack a dull boy. All work and no play makes Jack a dull boy. All work and no play makes Jack a dull boy. All w+rk and n+ play makes Jack a dull boy. All work andnoplay makes Jack a dull boy. All work and no play makes Jack a dullboy. All workand no play makes Jack a dull boy. All work and no play makes Jack a dyll boy. All work and no play makes Jack a dull boy. All workand NO PLAY makes Jacj a dull boy.

All work and no play MAKES JACK a dull boy. All work and no play makes Jack a dull boy. All work and no play makes Jack a dull boy. All work and no play makes JACK a dulllboy. All work and no PLAY makes Jack a dull boy. All work and no play m kes Jack a dull boy. All work and no play makes Jack a dull boy. All work and no play makes Jack a Dull boy.All work and no Play makes Jack a dull boy. All w rk and no play m kes Jack a dull boy. All work and no play makes Jack a dyll boy. All work and no play makes Jack a dullboy. All work and no play makes Jack a dull boy. All work and no play makes Jack a Dull BOY. All work and no play makesJack adull boy. All work a no play makes Jack a dull boy. All work and no play makes Jack a dull boy. All work and no play makes Jack a dull boy. All work and no play makes Jack a dull boy.

Alexander McQueen The Overlook Autumn/Winter 1999/2000 Tuesday 23 February 1999 8.00pm. The Gatliff Road Warehouse, Gatliff Road, Victoria SW1.

Name . . . . Seat . . . . . .
Supported by American Express.

Press contact: Janet Fischgrund/Alexander McQueen. T 0171 729 0537, F 0171 256 1618. Buyers contact: Amanda Lewis/ Onward Kashiyama. T 0171 349 9926, F 0171 352 8294.

Alexander McQueen was inspired by Stanley Kubrick's film, *The Shining*, for a fashion show and created an invite to match. This was printed by letterpress in order to impart a heavy indent into the substrate to give the impression that each invite was individually typed on a typewriter. The invite mimics the 'All work and no play makes Jack a dull boy' scene.

Design: Studio Myerscough, printing by Forme London

And now for something completely different...

Funny thing, comedy. As soft as Charlie Chaplin fluttering his love-lorn lashes, as brutal as the Three Stooges poking each other's eyes out. As daft as Mr Bean, as deft as Groucho Marx's verbal napalming of the monumentally fireproof Margaret Dumont. A curious art indeed, to amplify and project images of our weakness and wonderfulness and have us love it. We laugh; and as Herman Melville's Billy Budd said, laughter is good.

Direct mail pieces for Morgan Stanley Dean Witter, using simple, pure type, proof that 'simple is better than complicated'.

Design: E–Fact , printing by Forme London

See Dieter Rams

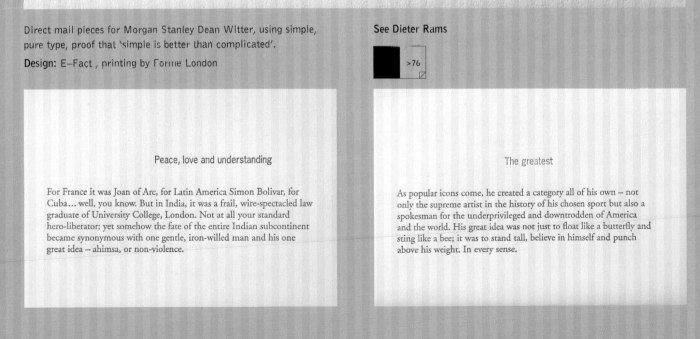

Peace, love and understanding

For France it was Joan of Arc, for Latin America Simon Bolivar, for Cuba… well, you know. But in India, it was a frail, wire-spectacled law graduate of University College, London. Not at all your standard hero-liberator; yet somehow the fate of the entire Indian subcontinent became synonymous with one gentle, iron-willed man and his one great idea – ahimsa, or non-violence.

The greatest

As popular icons come, he created a category all of his own – not only the supreme artist in the history of his chosen sport but also a spokesman for the underprivileged and downtrodden of America and the world. His great idea was not just to float like a butterfly and sting like a bee; it was to stand tall, believe in himself and punch above his weight. In every sense.

knoll

Left and opposite: The brief was further developed in the production of a calendar utilising line art profiles of various Knoll products that are used in place of the empty boxes typically found on a calendar. Titled 'Twenty-First Century Classics' the implication is that the designs are timeless and have a place in a new millennium.

Below: Thematic details are maintained in this series of four posters for Knoll, with simple designs against a bold, colourful background. Text is added discreetly to blend in with the design whether forming the warning sticker on an appliance plug or representing the lines on the palm of one's hand.

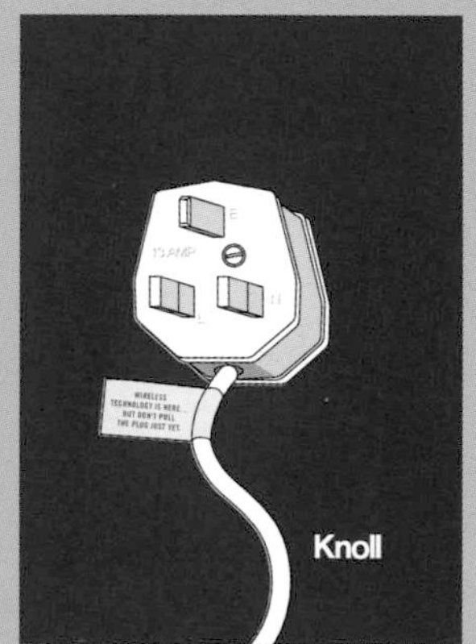

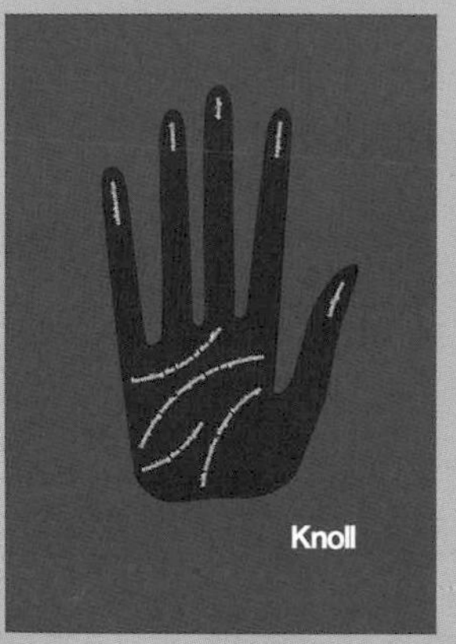

Brief

To create a series of full-page display advertisements to appear in the bi-monthly publication, *Blueprint*.

Process

NB: Studio chose to use line art for Knoll's 60th anniversary Classic posters (see opposite page) primarily due to financial constraints that meant there was no budget for photography. In an industry that promotes its products with photography, turning to an illustrative design was quite a departure but one that enabled the company to stand out from other producers of furniture. The line art set against a plain colour background focused the viewers' attention on the graceful lines of the furniture without the distraction of a room setting. The images are presented in a manner that reflects a quote from the designers who created the objects which gives a light-hearted effect.

Result

The success of the advertisements and the positive feelings they created led to them being silk-screened at A1 size and used as posters in Knoll outlets throughout Europe. Subsequently, they have been turned into postcards and reused as advertisements in Europe.

"The urge for good design is the same as the urge to go on living. The assumption is that somewhere, hidden, is a better way of doing things."
Harry Bertoia

Right and above right: Keeping it simple: four of the line art Classic series. Of particular interest is the Harry Bertoia Diamond Chair whose mesh seat intersections are represented by numbers that create a 'point cloud' (a rendering option in 3D design applications) that suggests something technically advanced, although they merely count the mesh intersections. Central to the Knoll brand is this juxtaposition of the practical and the graceful.

Design: NB: Studios

print finishing

4 colour photograph

4 colour photograph with online varnish

Monochrome image

Monochrome image with 60% shiner and online varnish

Embossing

Embossing produces an image in relief in the substrate using a metal die that strikes it from underneath. Reversing this process and striking the die from the front of the substrate results in a recessed image called debossing. Blind embossing is without colour and produces a subtle tone-on-tone look. (See front cover for example of embossing.)

Heat stamp, hot stamp, block print, foil emboss or foil stamp

This is a foil or coloured tape that is pressed on to a substrate using heat and pressure. If you take the dust jacket off most hardcover books, they have their title foil stamped into the cover.

Screen printing

A screen print is the direct imprinting of a design on to the surface of a substrate, usually using paint.

Die cut

A die is a piece of shaped metal used to cut or score irregular shapes in a substrate. This can be used to form the outline shape of the item or impart a design into its body. Scoring a substrate enables it to be easily folded at a precise position, or it can be used to create a portion that is to be torn off such as on a utility bill.

Spot varnish

Spot varnish is a liquid varnish that both serves as a protective coating to a printed substrate and enhances its appearance. It can be applied to the whole page or to specific parts of it via a separate printing plate.
See pages 17, 20, 21, 24, 25, 28, 29, 32

UV coating

A UV coating is a liquid applied to a printed substrate that is bonded and cured with ultraviolet light. It is applied in the same way as a spot varnish and creates a heavy, slightly raised reflective coating.

LOREM IPSUM DOLOR SIT AMET, CONSECTETUER ADIPISCING ELIT, SED DIAM NONUMMY NIBH EUISMOD TINCIDUNT UT LAOREET DOLORE MAGNA ALIQUAM ERAT VOLUTPAT. UT WISI ENIM AD MINIM VENIAM, QUIS NOSTRUD EXERCI TATION ULLAMCORPER SUSCIPIT LOBORTIS NISL UT ALIQUIP EX EA COMMODO CONSEQUAT. DUIS AUTEM VEL EUM IRIURE DOLOR IN HENDRERIT IN VULPUTATE VELIT ESSE MOLESTIE CONSEQUAT, VEL ILLUM DOLORE EU FEUGIAT NULLA FACILISIS AT VERO EROS ET ACCUMSAN ET IUSTO ODIO DIGNISSIM QUI BLANDIT PRAESENT LUPTATUM ZZRIL DELENIT AUGUE DUIS DOLORE TE FEUGAIT NULLA FACILISI.

Reverse of Studio AS's business card, showing the impression of a heavy deboss. Lorem Ipsum, the default dummy text often used when designing initial layouts becomes the final printed piece, with a highlighted A and S of the studio identity.

Design: Gavin Ambrose/Matt Lumby

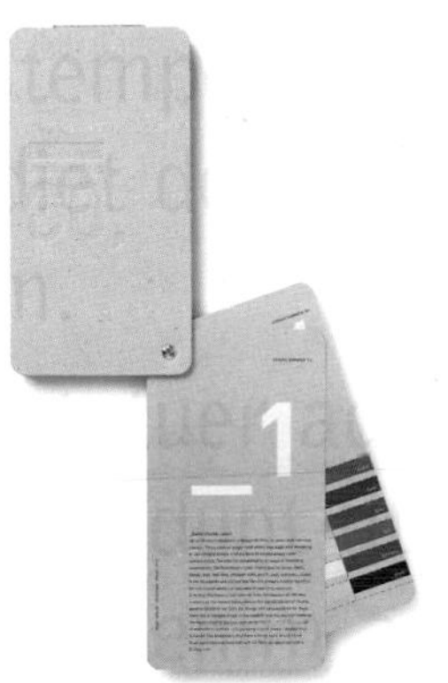

Barcelona-based Clase designed the catalogue for Pedro García's 2003 footwear collection. A thick greyboard cover is robust enough to accept the simple heavy deboss. The immediacy of the swatch-like package is enclosed using a simple bolt fixture, implying that the contents are both bespoke and recent.

Design: Clase

A fundraising mailer for Daniel Libeskind's proposed extension to the V&A takes on a three-dimensional structure. The outer packaging collapses to reveal a model of the complicated 24-plane continuous spiral construction: **'If the best way to understand the building was to look at a model, hey, let's send people a model,'** explains Johnson Banks.

Design: Johnson Banks

When we talk of print media we usually think of magazines and posters. These Tarot cards designed by Baba provide a unique means of packaging content. Instead of being bound in a book or magazine, the pages are kept in a box.

Design: Baba

Promotional brochure for a lighting company with a three-dimensional vacuum-formed outer. The cover has been photographed in different lighting conditions, clearly demonstrating the dramatic effect lighting can have.

Design: Sagmeister Inc.

image resolution

The spacing of the pixels in an image will determine the resolution of the image. This is measured in pixels per inch (ppi), also called dots per inch (dpi). The higher the resolution, the more pixels in the image. A higher resolution means an image can contain more information and so detail and colour transitions can be recorded in greater quantity. Conversely, at a low resolution, where insufficient information has been recorded, an image may appear pixelated. The number of pixels in an image is fixed, which is why resolution decreases as an image is enlarged. Monitors have a resolution of 72 dpi, which is why most Web graphics are produced at this resolution. Low-resolution images are also quicker to download. This is an inappropriate resolution for a printed image. Some magazines will print at a minimum of 300 dpi, but high-end imagesetters can print at 1,200 dpi, 2,400 dpi, or more.

Pixels

An image made of pixels will only reproduce correctly at a certain size. Any enlargement will cause a decrease in quality. The image below is at 300 dpi at 100%, and to the right is a lower resolution 72 dpi image enlarged to the same size showing the degradation in quality.

Vectors

As vectors are a mathematical process they can be enlarged infinitely without loss of quality or resolution. This 1000% enlargement of a section of the poster on page 19 demonstrates the clarity of type and line at such magnification.

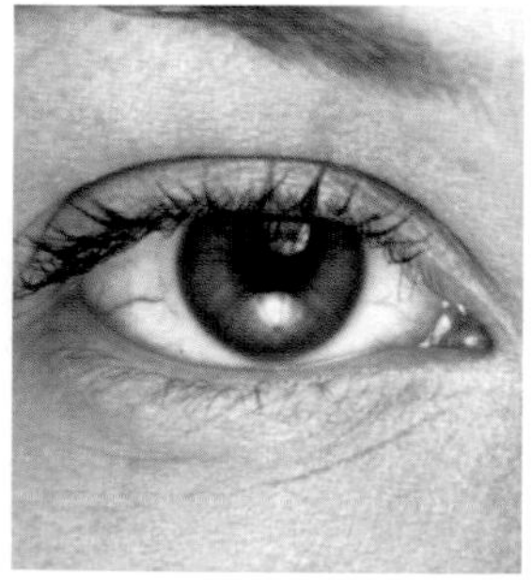

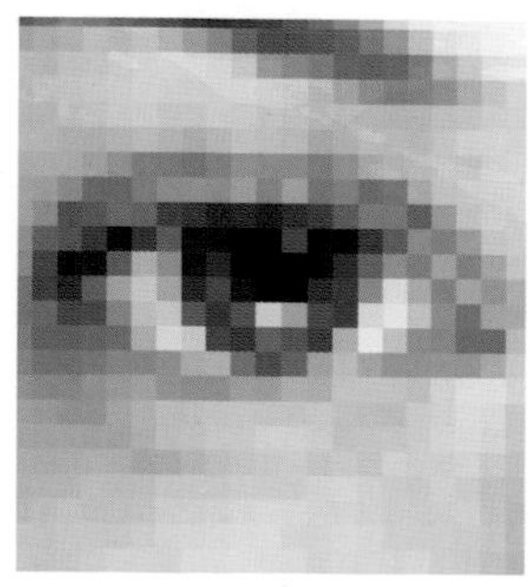

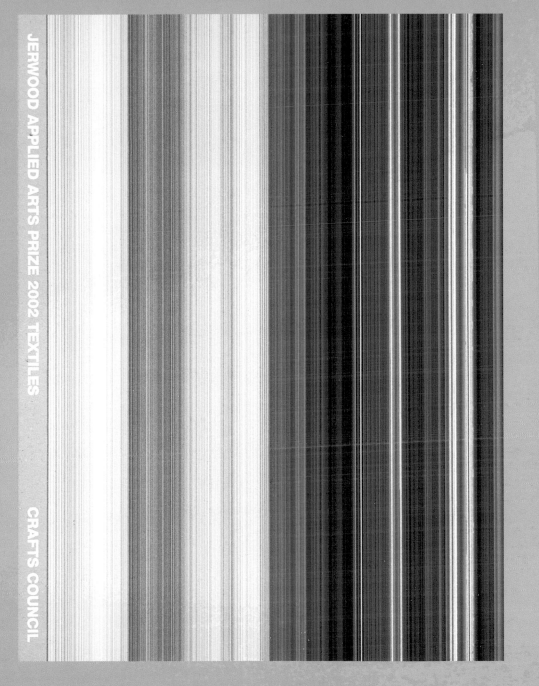

Outer cover for Jerwood Applied Arts Prize 2002 Textiles catalogue. A single row of pixels are elongated to create an abstract image. The ambiguity of the resulting graphic is used as an overall identity to the collection, rather than focusing on a single piece of work.

Design: NB: Studios

royal college of art

Brief

Redesign of the Critical & Historical Studies Lecture Series literature at the Royal College of Art, London.

Process

Each poster/brochure uses a different PMS colour to differentiate it from the others, as the titles are long-winded and confusing.

Result

A literature suite that utilises a simple, rationalised colour structure. The format is flexible enough to accommodate varying numbers of lectures – while formulaic enough to maintain consistency and facilitate familiarity.

Above: Clear hierarchy of text using the 3 numerals to depict the three steps students need to follow when writing their dissertation.

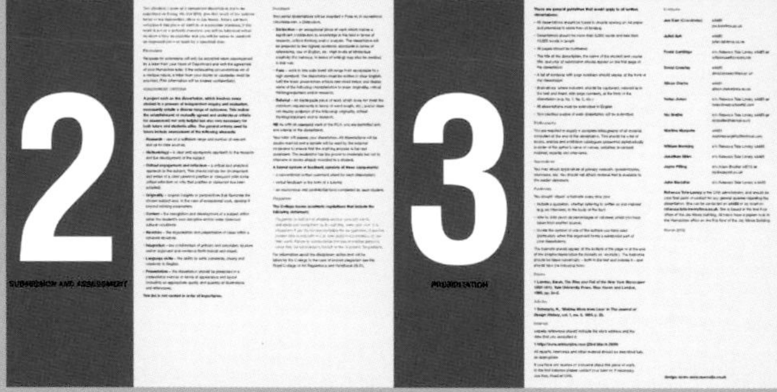

Below: The folds provide physical constraints on the design and the information to be presented. Here we see two ways of dealing with this. The dissertation guides were finished with five parallel accordion folds that make them easy to open. They use the physical constraints to format the page into smaller 'pages' upon which the various elements are positioned.

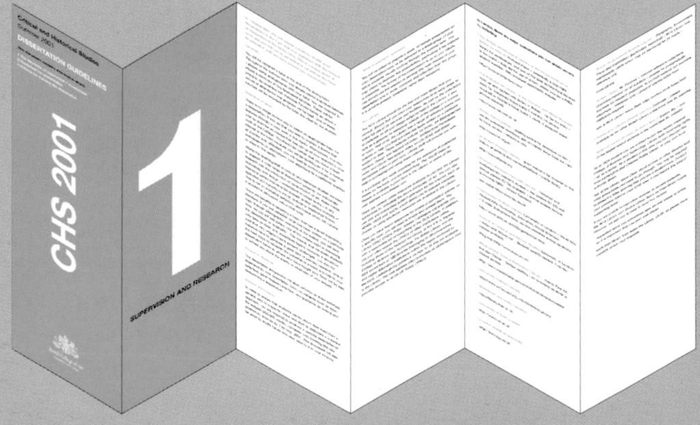

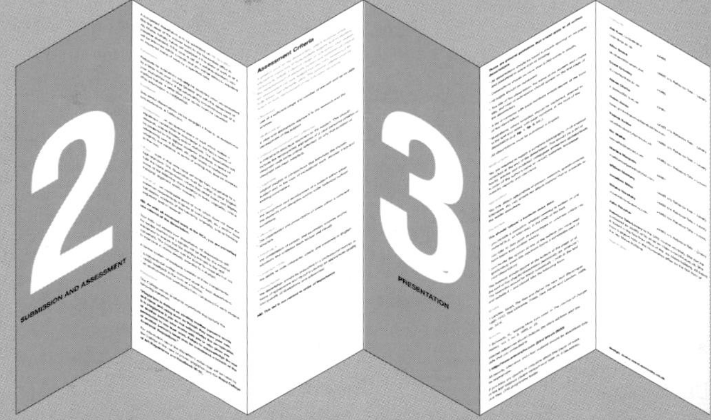

'A NEW LIFE ...'
FLOATING WORLDS
CULTURAL DESERTS FLOW
SPREAD!
REPETITION ... ONCE AGAIN
THIS POSTER PROVIDES DETAILS OF THE FORTHCOMING HUMANITIES CRITICAL AND HISTORICAL STUDIES COLLEGE-WIDE LECTURE PROGRAMME. THESE LECTURES REPRESENT THE SECOND TERM COMPONENT OF THE CHS PROGRAMME FOR FIRST YEAR MA STUDENTS, BUT THE LECTURES ARE ALSO OPEN TO ALL OTHER MEMBERS OF THE COLLEGE.
FIRST YEAR STUDENTS ARE REQUIRED TO SELECT AND ATTEND ALL THE LECTURES IN ONE OF THE SIX PROGRAMMES DETAILED HERE – ALTHOUGH YOU ARE WELCOME TO ATTEND AS MANY OTHERS AS YOU POSSIBLY CAN. YOU MUST REGISTER FOR YOUR CHOSEN OPTION IN THE FIRST WEEK OF THE SPRING TERM, USING THE REGISTERS SUPPLIED TO EACH STUDIO AREA. EACH SERIES WILL RUN FOR 7 WEEKS, AND THEY ARE EACH TIMETABLED FOR A DIFFERENT DAY, WITH THE EXCEPTION OF TWO SERIES ON TUESDAYS, TO ENCOURAGE AS WIDE A PARTICIPATION AS POSSIBLE. PLEASE NOTE THAT THE MAJORITY OF LECTURE PROGRAMMES START IN THE SECOND WEEK OF TERM, BUT PATRICK KEILLER'S SERIES 'A NEW LIFE ...' COMMENCES ON THE MONDAY OF THE FOLLOWING WEEK.
THE COLLEGE-WIDE LECTURE SERIES PERFORM A SPECIAL ROLE WITHIN THE CULTURAL LIFE OF THE COLLEGE, PROVIDING THE FORUM FOR STUDENTS FROM ACROSS ALL COURSES AND SCHOOLS TO MEET AND EXCHANGE IDEAS. THEY ARE DESIGNED TO EXPAND THE HUMANITIES PROGRAMME BEYOND THE BOUNDARIES OF THE DISCIPLINE-RELATED COURSES THAT RAN LAST TERM, BY DEALING WITH SUBJECTS THAT ARE INTENTIONALLY CROSS-DISCIPLINARY AND THAT WILL APPEAL TO STUDENTS FROM ANY PART OF THE COLLEGE. BY PRESENTING A BROAD SPECTRUM OF IDEAS, ISSUES AND APPROACHES, THEY HELP TO PREPARE STUDENTS FOR THE CHALLENGE OF SELECTING AND DEVELOPING THE SUBJECT FOR THEIR HUMANITIES DISSERTATION.
CHS HAS ALSO ORGANISED, IN COLLABORATION WITH THE CALOUSTE GULBENKIAN FOUNDATION, A SHORT SERIES OF PUBLIC EVENING LECTURES FOR THE SPRING TERM ENTITLED "STRANGE AND CHARMED". THE LECTURES ARE DESIGNED TO CREATE CONVERSATIONS BETWEEN ARTISTS AND SCIENTISTS, REFLECTING THE CURRENT EXCITEMENT ABOUT THE LINKS BETWEEN THESE DIFFERENT PRACTICES. THE SERIES WILL CONSIST OF SEVEN CHAIRED DEBATES BETWEEN PRACTITIONERS IN DIFFERENT FIELDS, WHOSE IDEAS AND WORK HAVE THE POTENTIAL TO SPARK OFF A PRODUCTIVE DIALOGUE ACROSS ART AND SCIENCE. THE THEMES THAT WE WILL INVESTIGATE INCLUDE: 'IMAGINING THE UNIMAGINABLE'; 'MAPPING AND COGNITION'; 'STRUCTURAL INTUITIONS – GUESSING AND CONNECTING'; 'DRAWING CONCLUSIONS', 'MAD SCIENTISTS', AND 'NEW NETWORKS'. THE FULL DETAILS OF THIS PROGRAMME WILL BE ADVERTISED EARLY IN THE SPRING TERM.

Left: Reverse of the poster/brochure opened out (showing fold lines) and its 'friendlier' size when folded.

Right: Inside of opened-out poster/brochure.

The poster/brochure uses the folds in a similar way for information printed on the outside. Essentially, both items use the folds to create a 'book' without using stitching or other binding methods. The reverse of the poster/brochure ignores the constraints of the folds and information is spread across the whole sheet. When folded, this information will not be visible but when unfolded it can fulfil its intended role as a poster.

The brochures were finished on a 16 page folder that gives one parallel fold and two right-angle folds. This is a format more commonly used for transportation schedules or maps, for example because it is simple to open view all the information presented, and it can be folded to a friendlier, more convenient, pocket size. In this instance, the item can be used as a wall poster when opened out, or a pocket guide, when folded.

Right: Reverse of poster/brochures in different specials.

See Specials

Design: Gavin Ambrose

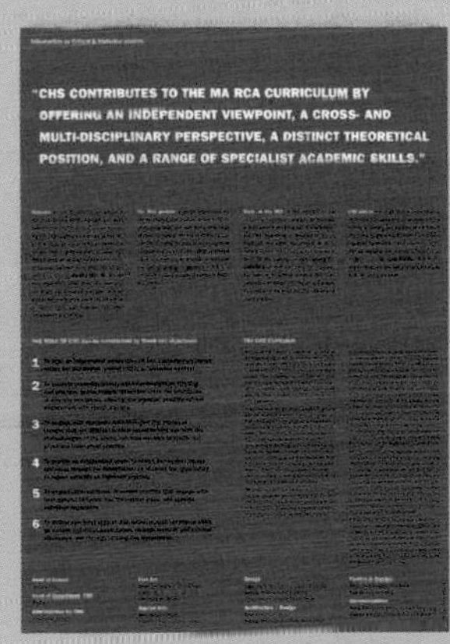

choosing a page size

Theoretically, a designer can use whatever size page he or she likes although the visual impact may be questionable. A body of theory has developed that divides and defines the space on a page that is logical, easy to work with, and more importantly, gives proportions that are easy on the eye. For the designer, having a variety of page sizes at his or her disposal with appealing proportions saves time and provides a sound starting point for any design.

Page size

Although a designer is free to choose any page size there are practical and economic considerations that will influence that choice, such as paper wastage and the cost of cutting non-standard sizes. The existence of ISO (International Organization for Standardization) paper sizes provides a range of paper sizes that while it may be unadventurous, nevertheless works and is freely available.

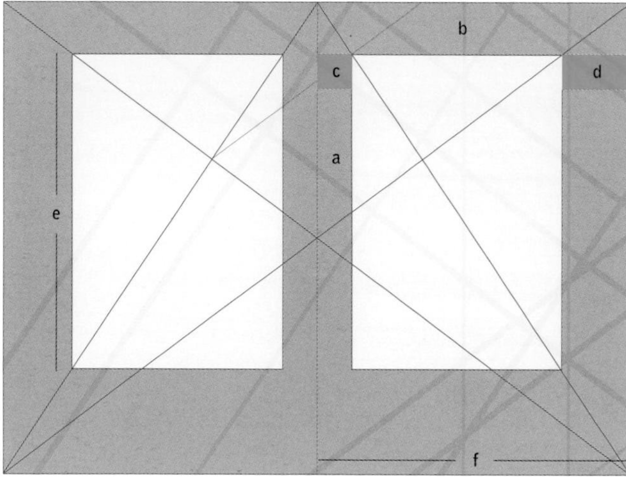

Left: Classic layout pioneered by German typographer Jan Tschichold (1902–1974) based on a page size with proportions of 2:3. The spine (a) and head (b) margins are positioned as a ninth of the page. The simplicity of this page is created by the spatial relationships that 'contain' the text block.

The grid creates harmonious proportions: the inner margin (c) is half the size of the outer margin (d), while the height of the text block (e) is equal to the width of the page (f).

See ISO

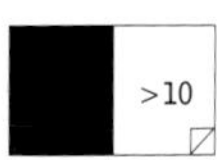

Layout developments

For over a thousand years page sizes have been constructed using pentagons, hexagons, octagons, circles, squares and triangles. Early scribes and typographers, influenced by organic phenomena such as the hexagonal construction of honeycomb to the pentagonal structures found in the growth of flowers, used these shapes as the basis of page sizes. In turn, they were the basis of determining the active area on the page within which the text and graphics will be positioned.

Jan Tschichold left Germany in 1933 and worked in Switzerland as a typographer until 1946. Between 1946 and 1949 he lived and worked in England overseeing the typographic redesign of the fast expanding publisher, Penguin Books.

Page size generation

1 – Tall Pentagon Layout

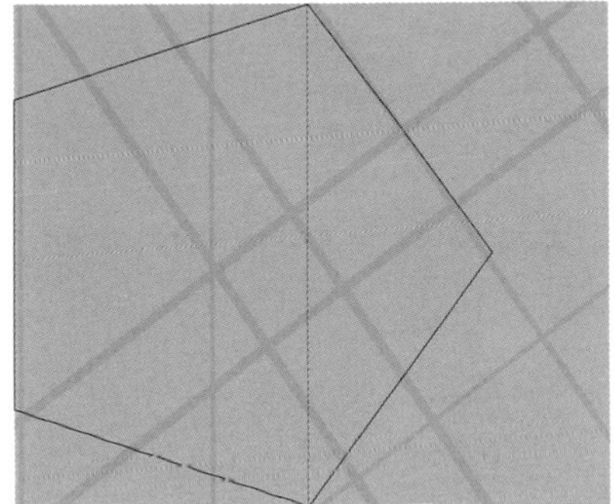

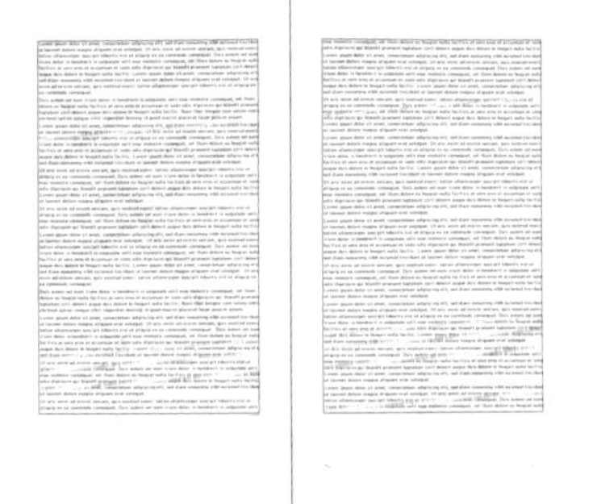

Above: The Tall Pentagon page is constructed by vertically dissecting a rotated pentagon. This gives a page size that when doubled creates a double-page spread.

Above: The double-page spread is then dissected from bottom left to top right, bottom right to top left, bottom left to top centre and bottom right to top centre. The header and spine widths are then inserted to complete the necessary anchor points for the text block. These are usually based on a division of the height i.e. a twelfth.

Above: The resulting layout gives a basic indication of the position for the main body copy or text block.

This process can be repeated to create different page formats using different areas of the same pentagon (see below).

2 – Truncated Pentagon Layout

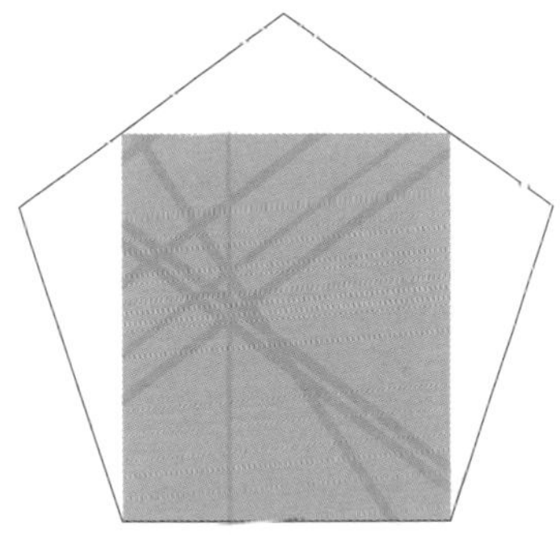

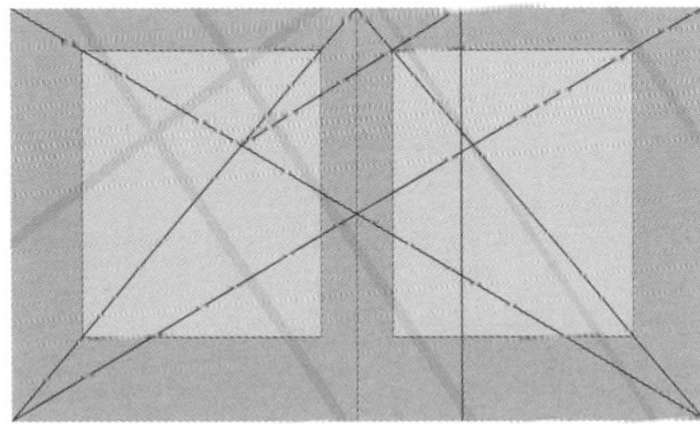

3 – Short Pentagon Layout

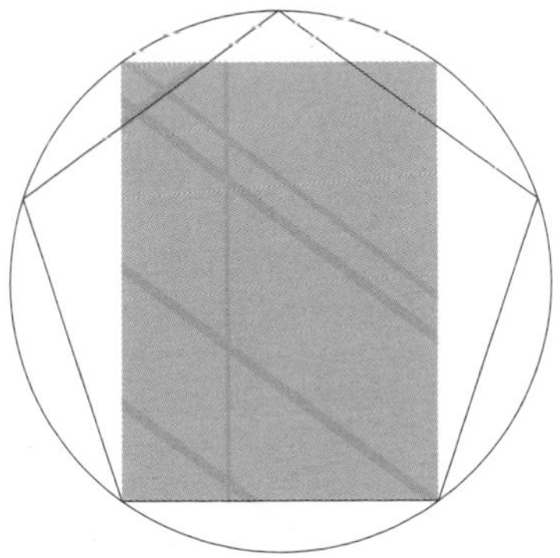

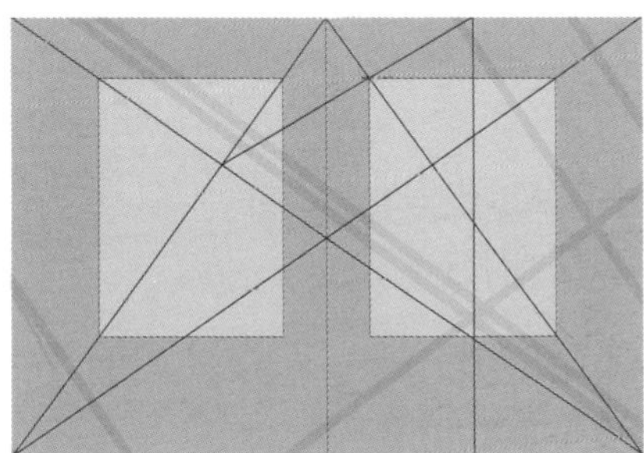

Layout is the arrangement of the elements of the design in relation to the space that it occupies according to an overall design scheme. This could also be called the management of form and space. The objective of layout is to present the visual and textural elements that are to be communicated in a manner that enables the reader to receive it with the minimum of effort. With good layout, a reader can be navigated through quite complex information in both print and electronic media.

Layout addresses the practical and aesthetic considerations of the job in hand such as where and how the content will be viewed, regardless of whether the final format is a magazine, website, television graphic or bottle of bubble bath. Positioning of the various elements in the layout is guided by use of a grid, a series of reference lines that allows quick and accurate placement of items that ensures a consistent visual identity from page to page, or item to item across a range of products.

Layout, guided by a grid, can produce exciting and dramatic designs but monomaniacal adherence to it can act as a straightjacket that throttles the design and obstructs the passing of information to the reader. It is important to achieve a balanced look or feel to a page, which means there will be occasions when you have to break with the confines of the grid. This section will explain the fundamentals of grid usage and explore how various grid patterns can be used to present different types of information.

layout

Layout is the positioning of elements on a page. How this is done has a dramatic influence on visual impact and how effectively information is communicated to the reader. Layout is influenced by the material that is to be presented, the wishes of who it is being produced for, and of course, the creativity of the designer. Most designers use a baseline grid of varying degrees of complexity to assist in the placement of the elements and provide some kind of order.

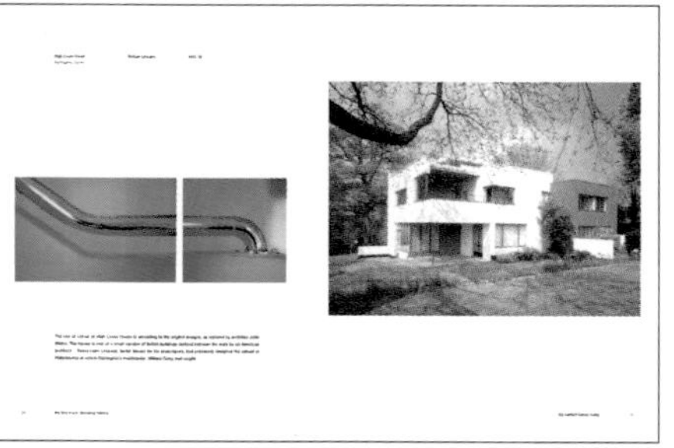

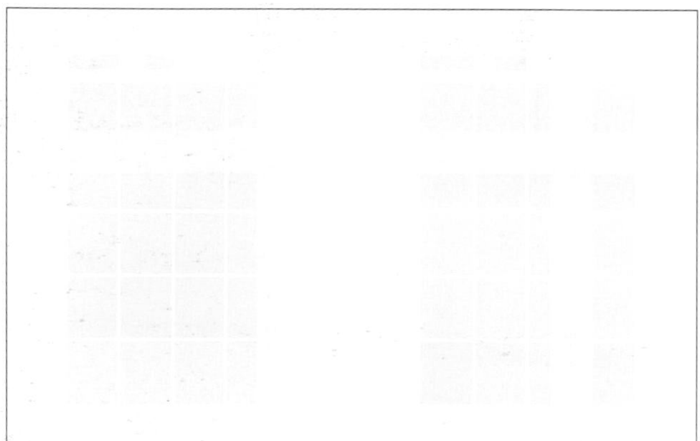

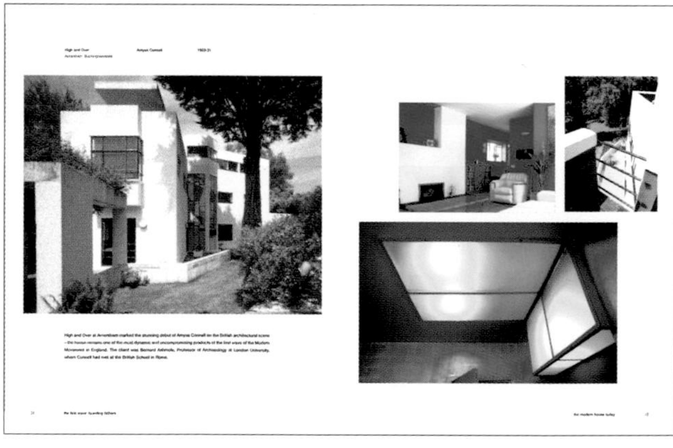

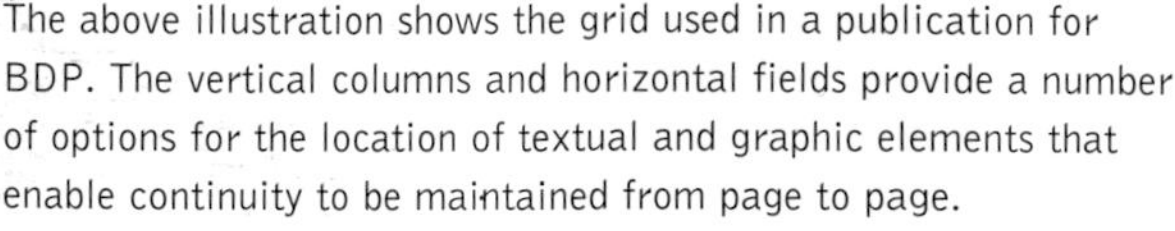

The above illustration shows the grid used in a publication for BDP. The vertical columns and horizontal fields provide a number of options for the location of textual and graphic elements that enable continuity to be maintained from page to page.

Design: Gavin Ambrose for BDP

Fallout from Chernobyl

The Second World War dispersed populations across Europe and the Americas; Gec's father was a tiny particle of the human fallout. Similarly, many Albanians and Slavs in Britain today arrived in the 1990s following the violent reopening up of ethnic divisions which had festered beneath arbitrary nationalities imposed on them throughout this century. In this context we can appreciate the emotional as well as poetic impact on Gec when, at 1.24 am on Saturday 26 April 1986, the Chernobyl nuclear plant in the Ukraine exploded following an error in the shutdown procedure in Block 4.

It is clear from the brief diaries Gec wrote when he visited the site in 1995, that he sensed Chernobyl and nearby Pripyat were still locked in time by the events of 1986:

The van passed through the city centre of Pripyat. Rows upon rows of high rise flats, shops, a large hotel, a ferris wheel in the distance. We climbed out of the van into the silent city. Thousands of empty windows looked down at us. Telephone boxes sat on the street corners. We gathered under a sign over a government building doorway which read INTO LIFE. In 1986 President Gorbachev used this as part of his perestroika speeches in the historic resolutions of the XXVII Party Congress. Chernobyl is trapped in time. A truck rumbled in the distance.

Gec is clearly responding here to the 30 km exclusion zone around Chernobyl, the equivalent of an 'airlock' beyond which no one could go. The themes of dislocation, entrapment, and the transformation of geographical space were key to the artist. He is often interested in subjects where it is possible for physical space to be torn from its moorings and deposited elsewhere. What one might term the 'psycho-geographics' of Chernobyl was to spur Gec on to many major works.

Taking a Geiger Counter reading outside Chernobyl's Fire Station

Above Opposite: Cots inside an abandoned nursery, Pripyat

Below Opposite: Fire engine and memorial, Chernobyl (the mark, top left, was made by a radioactive particle coming into contact with the negative)

Following pages: Derelict nursery, Pripyat

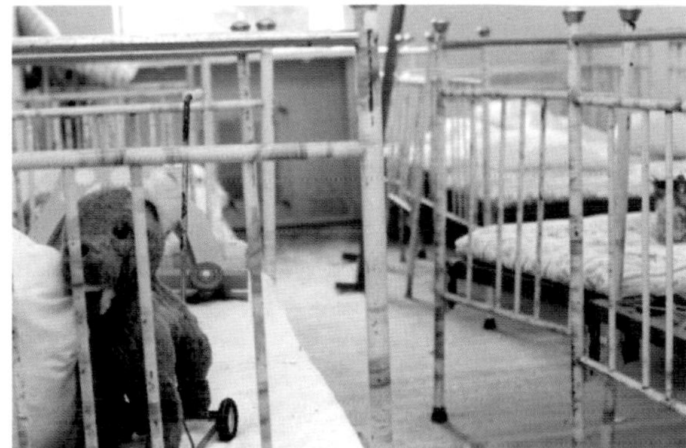

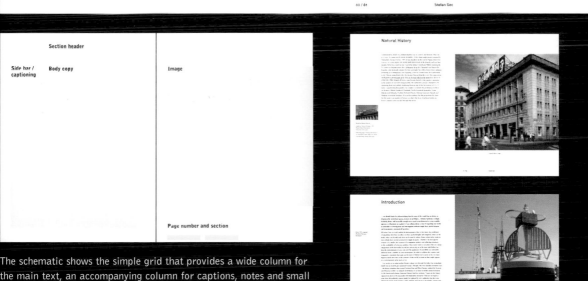

Section header

Side bar / captioning

Body copy

Image

Page number and section

The schematic shows the simple grid that provides a wide column for the main text, an accompanying column for captions, notes and small graphic elements, and a large area for the main visual elements.

Design: Gavin Ambrose for BDP

virtue
ngs May 21-July 1 1997
an unlikely
ment signified the

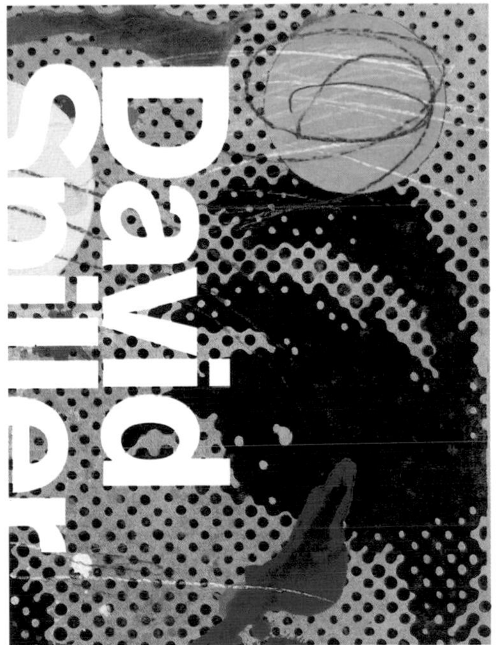

Above and below: Catalogues using gatefolds; the colourful surprise of David Spiller's imagery hidden under bold typographic sections, while the scale of Elisabeth Frink's sculptures are revealed through a dual fold out.

Left: A 16-page concertina-fold exhibition catalogue for John Virtue, with paintings reproduced in proportion allowing the reader to construct a miniature gallery.

Design: Studio AS

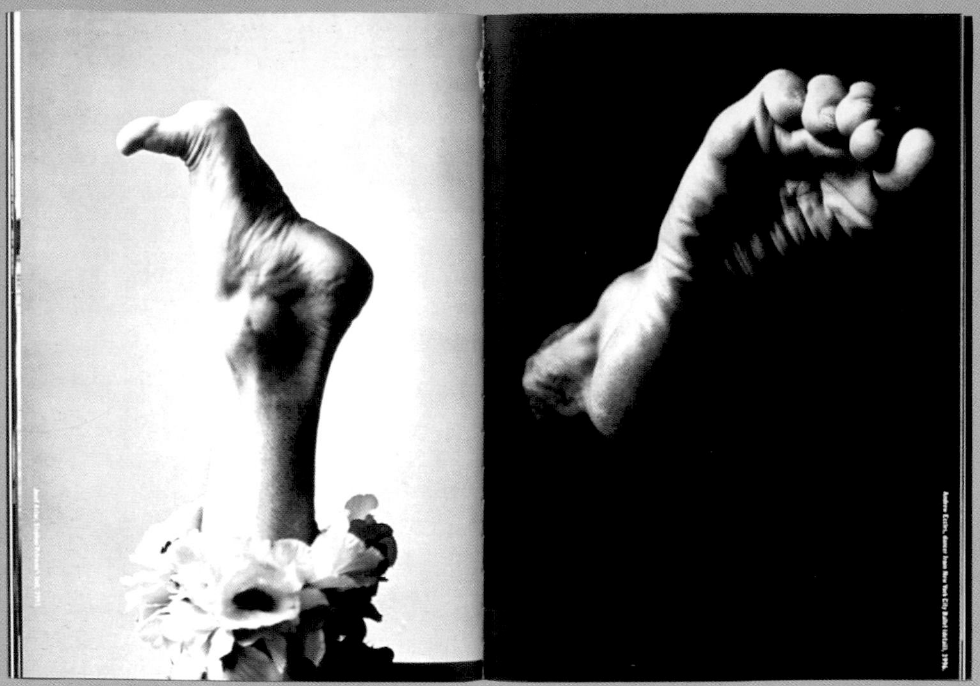

Typographic conventions are often broken in the name of creativity or when they can enhance the message being delivered. *2wice* magazine mixed letters and numbers in its title, by using a '2' rather than a capital 'T' to give it added visual emphasis.

Design: Pentagram

The cover of *architecture* magazine is not large enough to contain its masthead, which literally flows into the contents pages. This wraparound method is a bold approach for a masthead, which is traditionally an undisturbed visual signature for a publication.

Design: Pentagram

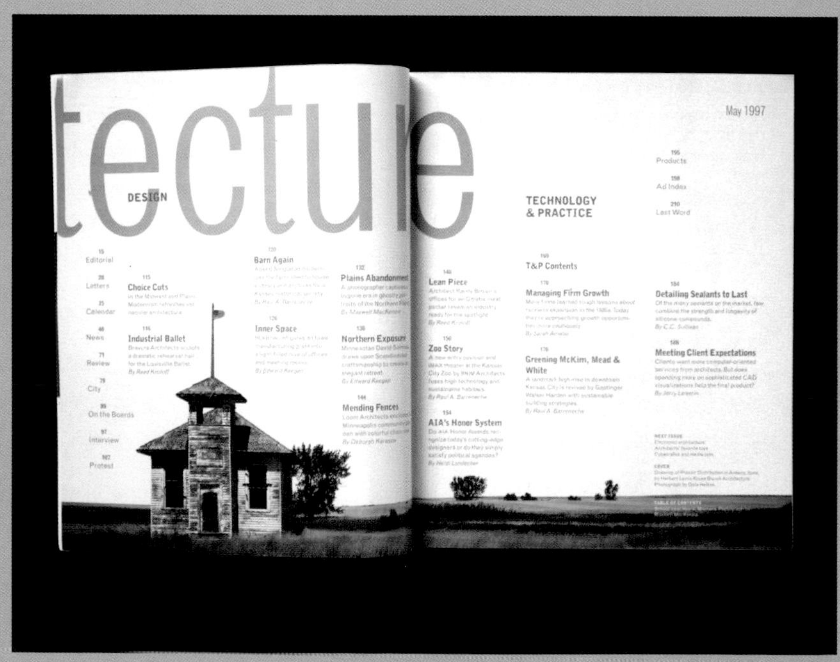

Post-Cubist

How a hip, young, Turkish designer is breaking down the square American office system.

By Matt Steinglass
Photography by François Robert

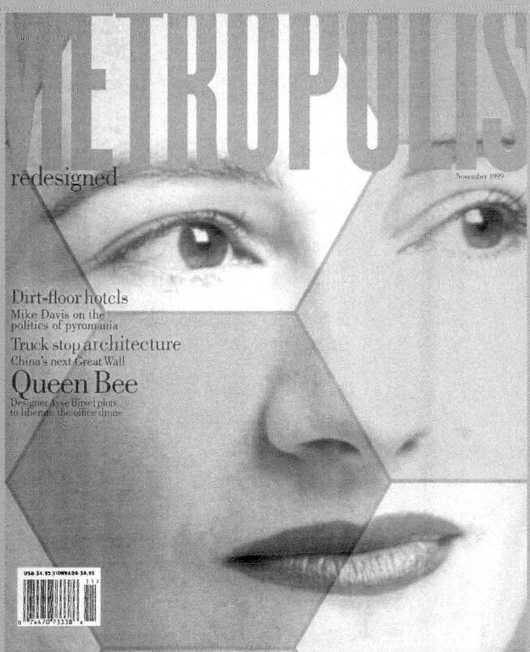

The above spread is a wonderful example of the layout being influenced by the subject matter. In this instance the use of an angled grid mirrors the coverage of office design in an article in *Metropolis,* influencing all elements including how the main image is cropped, headers, standfirst and body text. The unusual angle leaves large areas of white space that contrast with the cluttered office photograph and reinforces the message in the article; that abstract design ideas can improve the world around us. The angles of the grid are taken from a hexagon, which conveniently allows a hexagon to be used to frame a head shot of the designer being written about.

The hexagon is also used on the *Metropolis* cover, being turned into a honeycomb that dissects the close up of a face. The use of shading in some of the honeycomb segments visually drops those segments into the background and dramatically emphasises the eye.

Design: Pentagram

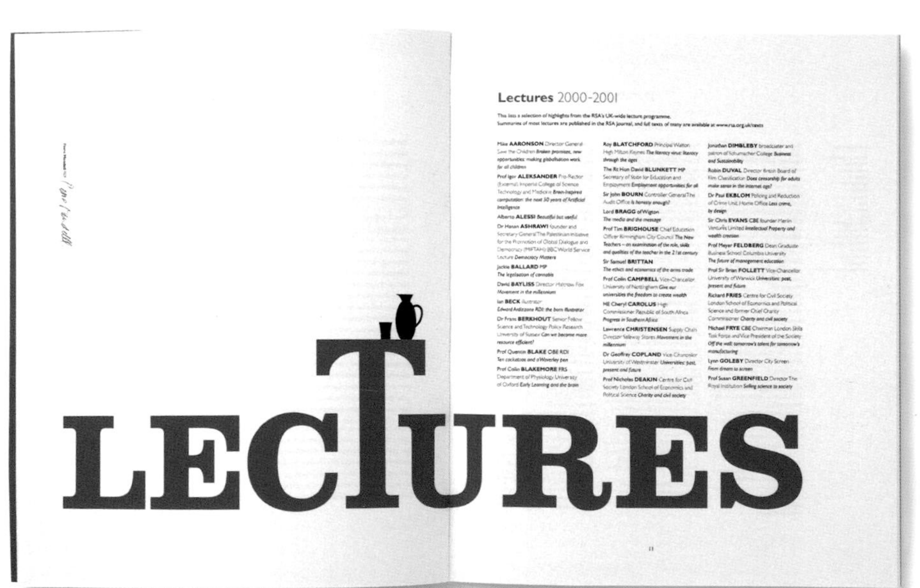

Lectures 2000-2001

This lists a selection of highlights from the RSA's UK-wide lecture programme.
Summaries of most lectures are published in the RSA Journal, and full texts of many are available at www.rsa.org.uk/texts

Mike **AARONSON** Director General Save the Children *Broken promises, new opportunities: making globalisation work for all children*

Prof Igor **ALEKSANDER** Pro-Rector (External) Imperial College of Science Technology and Medicine *Brain-inspired computation: the next 50 years of Artificial Intelligence*

Alberto **ALESSI** *Beautiful but useful*

Dr Hanan **ASHRAWI** founder and Secretary General The Palestinian Initiative for the Promotion of Global Dialogue and Democracy (MIFTAH) BBC World Service Lecture *Democracy Matters*

Jackie **BALLARD** MP *The legalisation of cannabis*

David **BAYLISS** Director Halcrow Fox *Movement in the millennium*

Ian **BECK** Illustrator *Edward Ardizzone RDI: the born illustrator*

Dr Frans **BERKHOUT** Senior Fellow Science and Technology Policy Research University of Sussex *Can we become more resource efficient?*

Prof Quentin **BLAKE** OBE RDI *Ten cockatoos and a Waverley pen*

Prof Colin **BLAKEMORE** FRS Department of Physiology University of Oxford *Early Learning and the brain*

Roy **BLATCHFORD** Principal Walton High Milton Keynes *The literacy virus: literacy through the ages*

The Rt Hon David **BLUNKETT** MP Secretary of State for Education and Employment *Employment opportunities for all*

Sir John **BOURN** Controller General The Audit Office *Is honesty enough?*

Lord **BRAGG** of Wigton *The media and the message*

Prof Tim **BRIGHOUSE** Chief Education Officer Birmingham City Council *The New Teachers – an examination of the role, skills and qualities of the teacher in the 21st century*

Sir Samuel **BRITTAN** *The ethics and economics of the arms trade*

Prof Colin **CAMPBELL** Vice-Chancellor University of Nottingham *Give our universities the freedom to create wealth*

HE Cheryl **CAROLUS** High Commissioner Republic of South Africa *Progress in Southern Africa*

Lawrence **CHRISTENSEN** Supply Chain Director Safeway Stores *Movement in the millennium*

Dr Geoffrey **COPLAND** Vice-Chancellor University of Westminster *Universities: past, present and future*

Prof Nicholas **DEAKIN** Centre for Civil Society London School of Economics and Political Science *Charity and civil society*

Jonathan **DIMBLEBY** broadcaster and patron of Schumacher College *Business and Sustainability*

Robin **DUVAL** Director British Board of Film Classification *Does censorship for adults make sense in the internet age?*

Dr Paul **EKBLOM** Policing and Reduction of Crime Unit, Home Office *Less crime, by design*

Sir Chris **EVANS** CBE founder Merlin Ventures Limited *Intellectual Property and wealth creation*

Prof Meyer **FELDBERG** Dean Graduate Business School Columbia University *The future of management education*

Prof Sir Brian **FOLLETT** Vice-Chancellor University of Warwick *Universities: past, present and future*

Richard **FRIES** Centre for Civil Society London School of Economics and Political Science and former Chief Charity Commissioner *Charity and civil society*

Michael **FRYE** CBE Chairman London Skills Task Force and Vice President of the Society *Off the wall: tomorrow's talent for tomorrow's manufacturing*

Lynn **GOLEBY** Director City Screen *From dream to screen*

Prof Susan **GREENFIELD** Director The Royal Institution *Selling science to society*

The layout for the Royal Society of Arts (RSA) annual report is deliberately kept simple as its target audience – the high-powered opinion formers that are the RSA's sponsors and fellows – often doesn't have time to read. RSA is a charity and so it was important that its report did not look too corporate nor that the organisation was in need of sponsorship. The result is short, uncluttered and discursive.

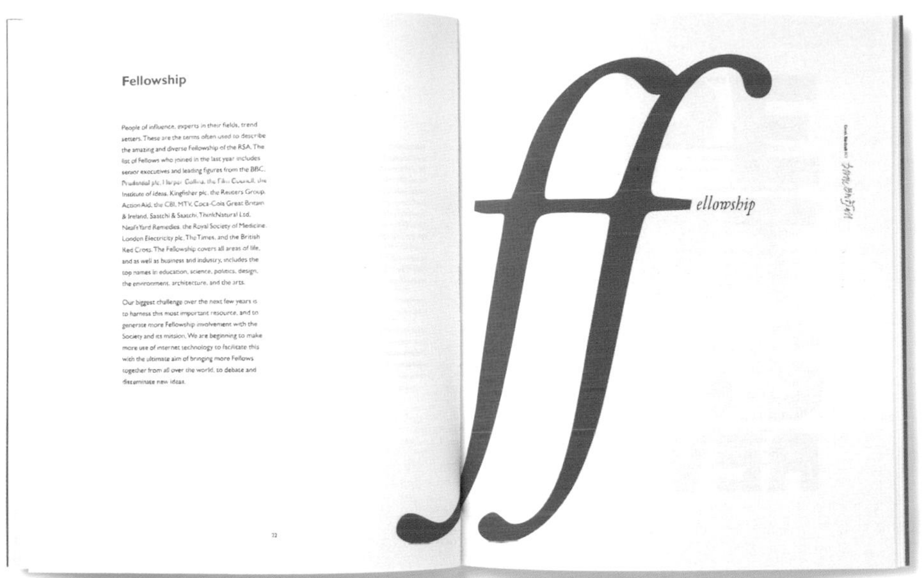

Fellowship

People of influence, experts in their fields, trend setters. These are the terms often used to describe the amazing and diverse Fellowship of the RSA. The list of Fellows who joined in the last year includes senior executives and leading figures from the BBC, Prudential plc, Harper Collins, the Film Council, the Institute of Ideas, Kingfisher plc, the Reuters Group, Action Aid, the CBI, MTV, Coca-Cola Great Britain & Ireland, Saatchi & Saatchi, ThinkNatural Ltd, Neal's Yard Remedies, the Royal Society of Medicine, London Electricity plc, The Times, and the British Red Cross. The Fellowship covers all areas of life, and as well as business and industry, includes the top names in education, science, politics, design, the environment, architecture, and the arts.

Our biggest challenge over the next few years is to harness this most important resource, and to generate more Fellowship involvement with the Society and its mission. We are beginning to make more use of internet technology to facilitate this with the ultimate aim of bringing more Fellows together from all over the world, to debate and disseminate new ideas.

Atelier Works used the idea of multiplicity and expressed it through typefaces, formats, sub-identities and paper stocks to create a low-key, elegant and worldly design. It is enriched with a variety of typographic illustrations from RSA's own Royal Designers for Industry.

Design: Atelier Works

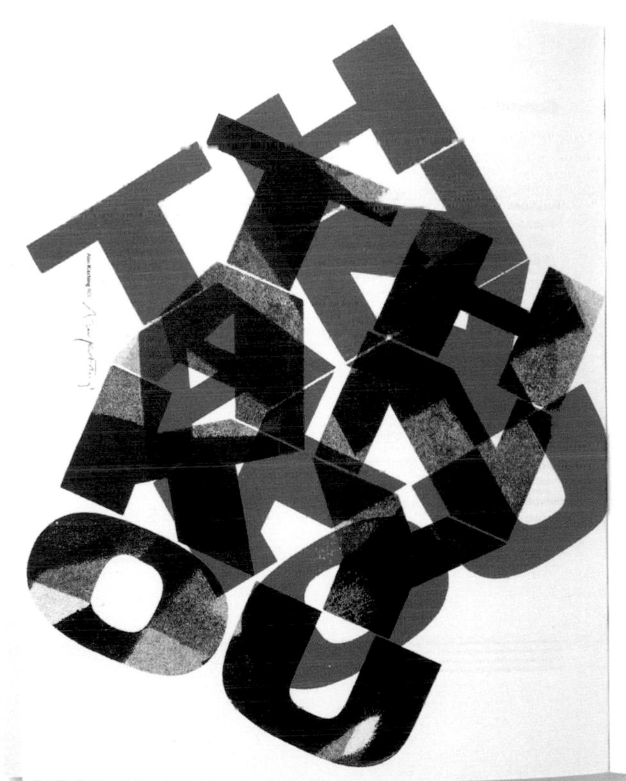

Development

The RSA's raises funds for the Society's programmes from individuals, companies and charitable trusts.

Fellowship subscriptions provide about one-third of the RSA's annual budget. Another third is earned through our commercial activities, and the final one-third has to be sourced from donations and grants. Fundraising is therefore an integral part of the work of the RSA. Without a dynamic fundraising department, the Society's activity would be severely limited.

Telephone campaign

Over winter 2000/01 the RSA ran a telephone campaign to 5,000 Fellows in order to raise funds for the Society, and to engage in a more active dialogue with the Fellowship.

The Campaign has been very successful, with over £140,000 pledged towards the work of the Society. The Campaign will run again in January and February 2002 contacting an additional 5,000 Fellows. The telephone campaign is designed to create opportunities for Fellows to air their views about the RSA and to feedback comments about the Society's work, its programmes and publications. We are extremely grateful to all Fellows who took part in the campaign, the names of those who donated are listed on the following pages.

House restoration

Also this year, a campaign was launched to conserve and restore the original Adam ceilings on the first floor of the House, including the elegant Angelica Kauffman panels. As well as approaching charitable trusts, we received a number of generous gifts from our US Fellows, and are very grateful for their response.

Next year the campaign will seek funds for Phases II and III of the campaign, enabling us to create a new home for the Library and Research Room on level -2, including the Gallery and adjacent undercroft. We plan to create a determinedly modern series of rooms using natural oak, stainless steel and glass, to accommodate a fully modern library, computer-based information service and reference materials.

The Development Office is pleased to receive donations for its ongoing work and for specific projects. We are also available to discuss making a bequest to the RSA. For further information on making a gift of cash or shares, or leaving a legacy, please visit our website or contact, in confidence:

Wilder **Gutterson**
020 7451 6960
wilder.gutterson@rsa.org.uk

33

CARDIO
LIFECIRC
LIFESTRE
FREE WEIG
STRETCH

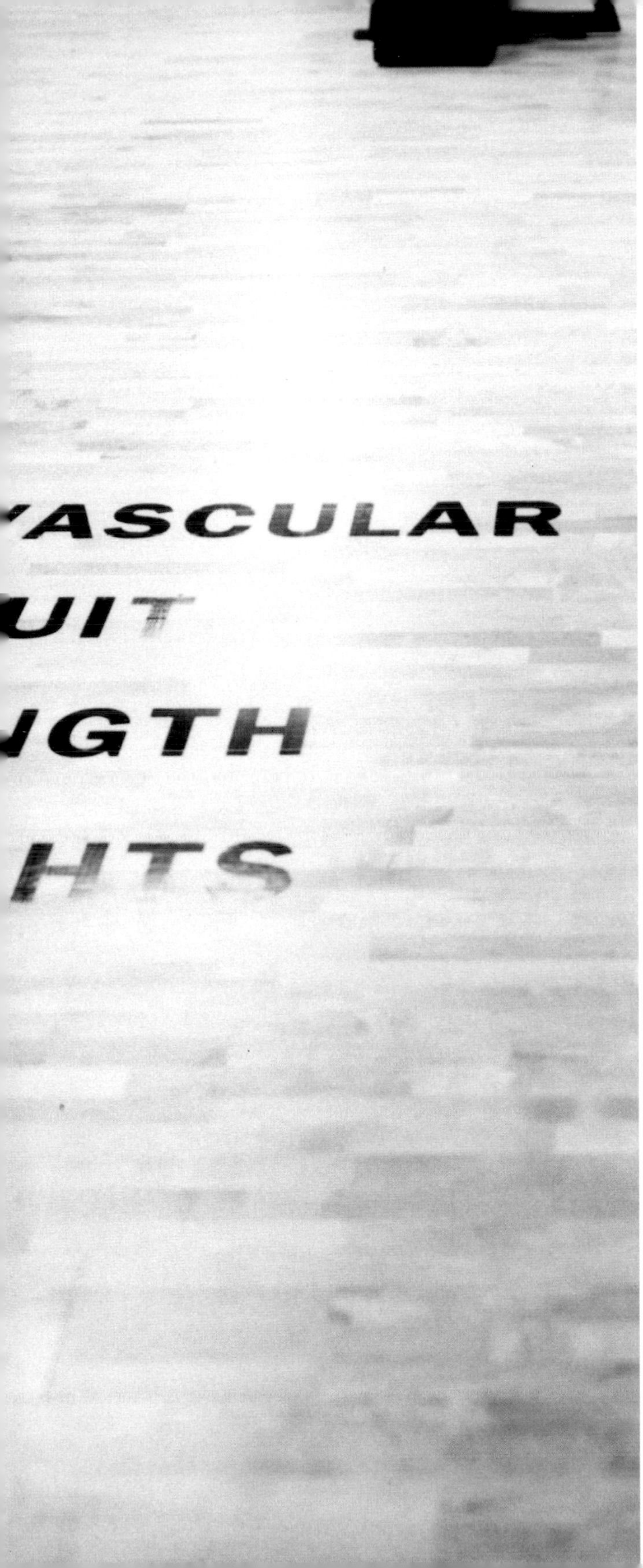

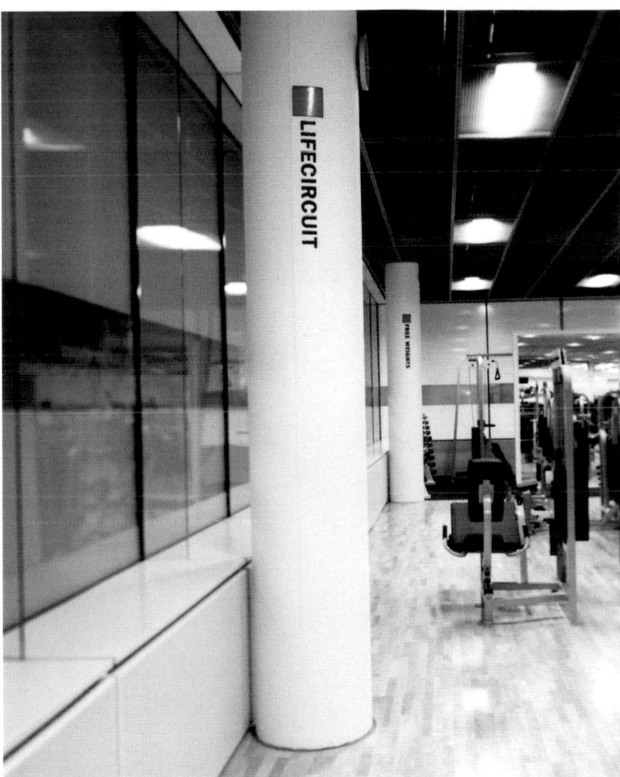

Environmental and literature graphics for a city centre leisure complex. The strong typography of the brochure (see following pages) is echoed in the signage, printed directly on to columns and floors. The simple colour scheme, typographic style and bold confident use of imagery creates a seamless identity.

Design: Studio Myerscough

I LOVE THE REST OF MY LIFE
THOUGH IT IS TRANSITORY
LIKE A LIGHT AZURE MORNING GLORY.

A series of Haiku poems, consisting of 17 syllables, punctuate the aspirational imagery of the brochure. Heavy type is carefully justified and softened through the use of flat colour.

Design: Studio Myerscough

See Justification

HAIKU

A JAPANESE HAIKU IS A TRADITIONAL FORM OF CALM AND CONTEMPLATIVE POETRY WHICH REMAINS VERY POPULAR EVEN IN THE FRANTIC, MATERIALISTIC WORLD THAT IS JAPAN TODAY. ITS DISTINCTIVE CHARACTER STEMS FROM THE UNIQUE METHOD OF COMPOSING FROM ONLY SEVENTEEN SYLLABLES, BUT THE IDEAL OF THE HAIKU IS TO CAPTURE SOMETHING OF THE VERY ESSENCE OF EXISTENCE WITHIN THIS HIGHLY CONDENSED FORM; TO ILLUMINATE THE WIDER WORLD THROUGH THE MICROCOSM OF A SINGLE EVENT. A DROP OF WATER, OR THE PLAY OF MORNING LIGHT ON AUTUMN FROST. DISTILLING THOUGHT AND OBSERVATION INTO THIS TINY PARCEL OF WORDS EVOKES PURE EMOTION. THE PAIN OF REALISING PASSING TIME PERHAPS, OR THE TRANQUILLITY OF EXPERIENCING NATURE. THE HAIKU POEMS SELECTED FOR THE BROADGATE CLUB WEST REFLECT A MIX OF ANCIENT AND MODERN VERSES, AND ARE INTENDED TO PROVOKE A MOMENT OF CAREFUL THOUGHT WITH WHICH TO PUNCTUATE THE RELENTLESS PACE OF MODERN LIFE.

golden section & fibonacci numbers

The Golden Section was thought by the ancients to represent infallibly beautiful proportions. Dividing a line by the approximate ratio of 8:13 means that the relationship of the longer part to the shorter is the same as that of the longer part to the whole. Objects that have this ratio are pleasing to the eye and can be found in a series of numbers called Fibonacci numbers. This ratio can be seen in nature in the growth patterns of plants and the shells of certain animals. Perhaps it is because of its presence in nature that these proportions are so pleasing to the eye. In the field of graphic arts, the Golden Section is the basis for paper sizes and its principles can be used as a means of achieving balanced designs.

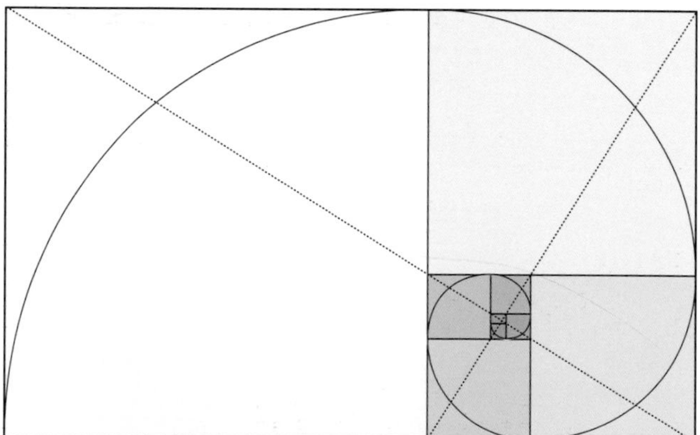

A set of Fibonacci rectangles and a Fibonacci spiral.

If you draw two small squares together, then draw another square using the combined lengths of the two squares as one side and carry on repeating this process you create a set of Fibonacci rectangles. This is a set of rectangles whose sides are two successive Fibonacci numbers in length, composed of squares with sides that are Fibonacci numbers, or in other words, the ratio of the sides of these rectangles equals that of the Golden Section.

A Fibonacci spiral can be created by drawing quarter circles through each square that together form the spiral. A similar curve occurs in nature in the shape of a snail's shell.

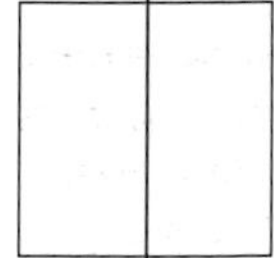

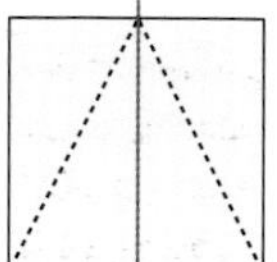

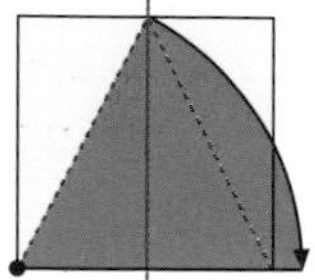

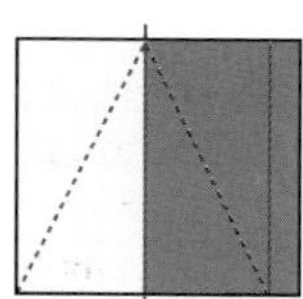

To form a Golden Section; take a square, dissect it, form an isosceles triangle, extend the arc, form a Golden Section.

5 8 13 21 34 55 89 144

6 **10** **16** **26** 42 68 110 178

7 **11** **18** **29** 47 76 123 199

Fibonacci, or Leonardo of Pisa, born in Pisa, Italy about 1175, has been called the greatest European mathematician of the Middle Ages because of a discovery he made that has excited natural biologists and mathematicians for hundreds of years. The series of numbers that bear his name, Fibonacci numbers, are also a cornerstone of design practice.

Fibonacci numbers are a series of numbers where each number is the sum of the preceding two. The series starting from zero can be seen across this spread. Why is this important? Fibonacci numbers are important because of their link to the 8:13 ratio also known as the Golden Section.

If you take two successive numbers in Fibonacci's series and divide the higher value by the one before it you get a number close to 1.6. For example 13/8 = 1.625. If you continued doing this through the series the outcome hones in on a value that is approximately 1.61804, called the Golden Ratio, Golden Number or Golden Section.

0 1 1 2 3 5 8 13 21 34 55 89 144 233 377 610 987 1597 2484 4181 6765, 10,946 17,711

The Modulor

A harmonic measure to the human scale, universally applicable to architecture and mechanics, which has since been adopted by designers of all disciplines.

In 1947 Le Corbusier's Modulor system, protected by patent, was made public, and the following year appeared in his seminal book *Le Modulor*.

'A range of dimensions which make the good easy and the bad hard.'

10 ten point type
11 on eleven point leading

16 sixteen point type
18 on eighteen point leading

26 twenty-six point type
29 on twenty-nine point leading

The modulor system is essentially a slide rule, with measurements derived from human proportions that can be used in design and construction. The relationship of human form to measurement creates an harmonious balance, be it in architecture, page sizes or even type. Often more than one set of integers are used, as with the three examples of type and leading (above), which have been set to the values of two consecutive Fibonacci number systems.

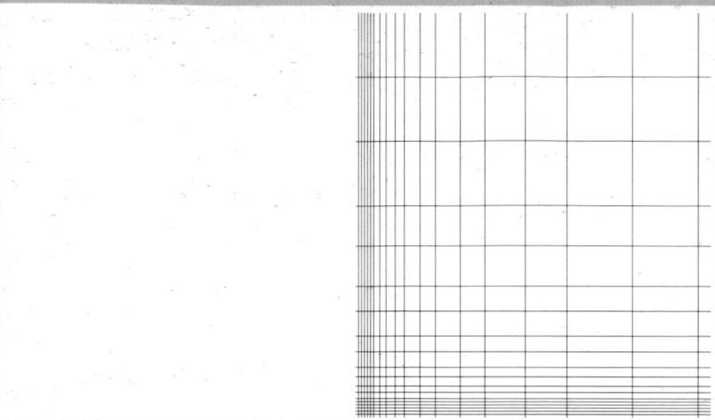

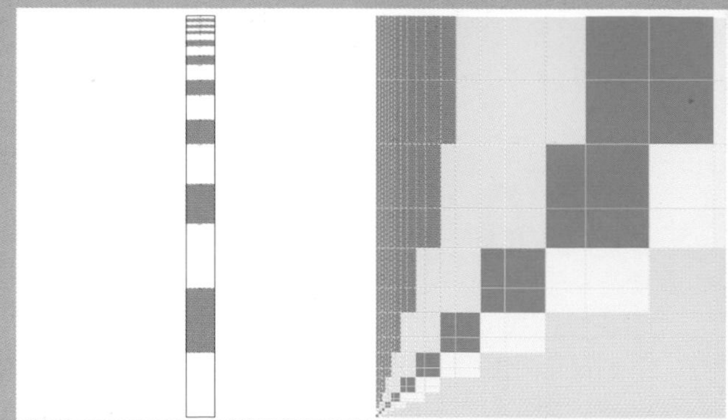

The illustration above shows the complex grid system utilised by Studio AS for the Robyn Denny project. From the spine, the interval between succeeding grid lines increases exponentially towards both the vertical and horizontal edges of the page. This results in a remarkable assortment of different sized boxes to position elements, with no two boxes having the same dimensions that provides unlimited scope for creative positioning, while maintaining some semblance of order and structure.

Design: Studio AS

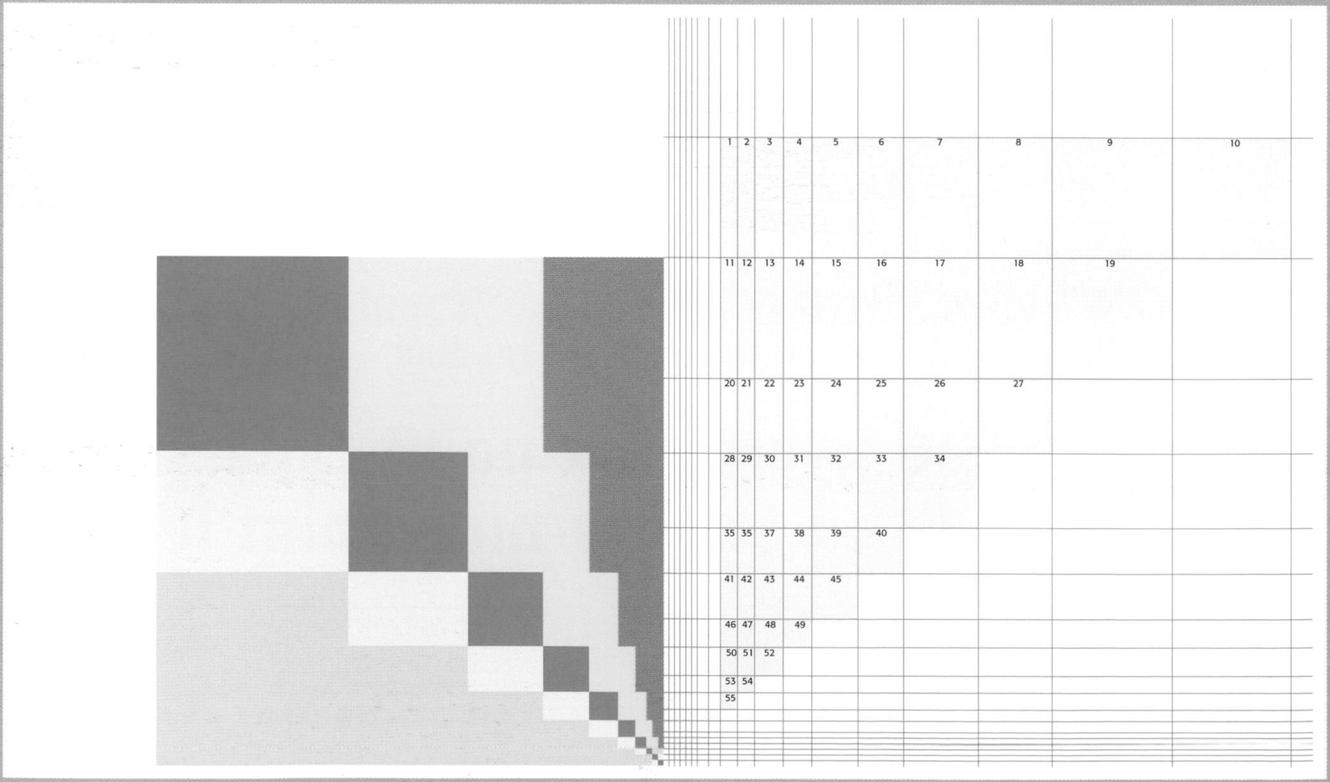

Early development spreads demonstrating how text boxes, images, titles, footers, captions and folios are positioned on the page using the complex grid system.

Secrets, Remember, Forever, Together, One Day, A Time, And Then, A Sense Of Occasion, Slow Hand, Between Ourselves, Seeing Things, Thinking of England, Sweet O'Zeeta, Windward Steam And Angel Dust, Gothic-A-Go-Go, Razzle Dazzle, Oh! Quel Culture, Passion Spent, Pepsi Tokyo, Aeria P., Purple Passage, Honey Trap, Misc. Cyn., Kiss Kiss, Love Wall, Low Life, Songs, Shadows, Ghosts, & Glory In The Air,
David Alan Mellor
The colour blue begins to predominate in these paintings of the later 70s – celestial, as in Moonshine, and mechanically spiritualised in Standing Still. He was trying to affirm a monumentality which was slipping or strolling away, attempting the "... re-introduction of the 'slab'" with the play of illusory presences which he had vapourised into ineffable colour-perfumes after the barbicans and trellis' of the later 60s.' (Koudielka refers to the unearthly condition of winter light in Minnesota in 1966/67, when Denny was teaching there). About 1980 he paints another restoration of slab reliefs, Out of the Blue. It was the potential kinesis of blue as a colour which interested him and which drew him to California in 1982, pursuing a blue which would unfix him and his career: "... blue has the most extraordinary property of moving which I found in California... it was having an exhibition in LA... because I was stuck as an artist in London, [I had] a past but no future... I was in LA for four weeks and I liked it, staying on and off for six or seven years."

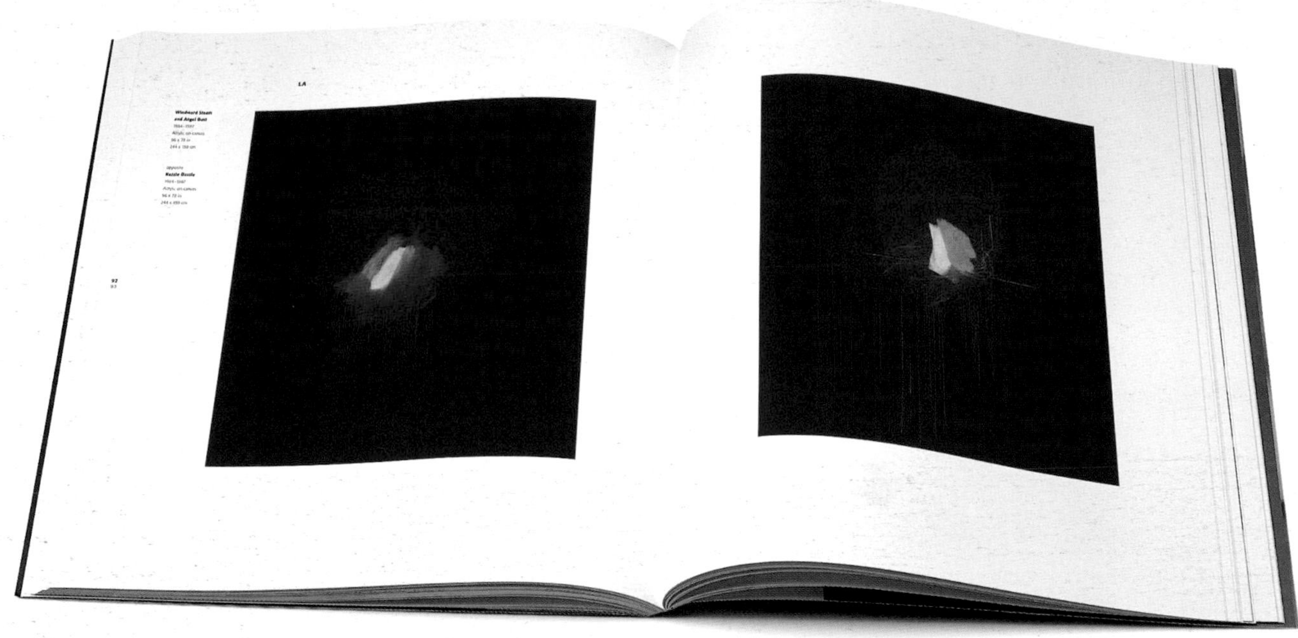

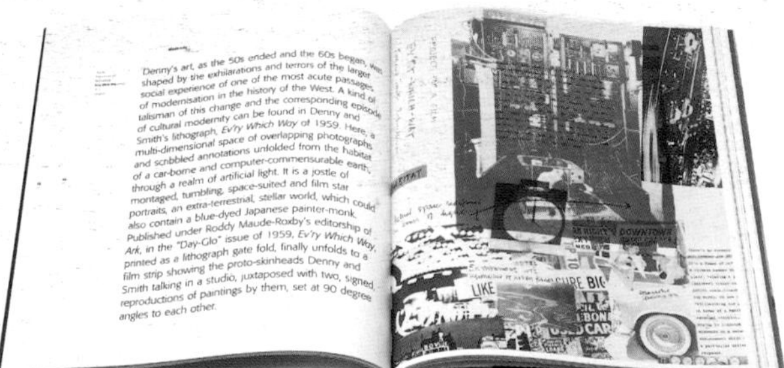

Denny's art, as the 50s ended and the 60s began, was shaped by the exhilarations and terrors of the larger social experience of one of the most acute passages of modernisation in the history of the West. A kind of talisman of this change and the corresponding episode of cultural modernity can be found in Denny and Smith's lithograph, *Ev'ry Which Way* of 1959. Here, a multi-dimensional space of overlapping photographs and scribbled annotations unfolded from the habitat of a car-borne and computer-commensurable earth, through a realm of artificial light. It is a jostle of montaged, tumbling, space-suited and film star portraits, an extra-terrestrial, stellar world, which could also contain a blue-dyed Japanese painter-monk. Published under Roddy Maude-Roxby's editorship of Ark, in the "Day-Glo" issue of 1959, *Ev'ry Which Way*, printed as a lithograph gate fold, finally unfolds to a film strip showing the proto-skinheads Denny and Smith talking in a studio, juxtaposed with two, signed, reproductions of paintings by them, set at 90 degree angles to each other.

The final book is deceptively simple. Works of varying configurations and sizes are accommodated with ease through the use of the grid system. Rather than introducing restrictions the grid system offers liberation.

Design: Studio AS

a

to construct the argument objectively with the means of visual communication

b

to construct the text and illustrative material systematically and logically

c

to organise the text and illustrations in a compact arrangement with its own rhythm

d

to put together the visual material so that it is readily intelligible and structured with a high degree of tension

Josef Müller-Brockman

Josef Müller-Brockman established his own design practice in 1936 having been an apprentice in Zürich. He is often cited as an influence on modern design and in particular grid systems.

baseline grid

The baseline grid is the graphic foundation on which a design is constructed. It serves a similar purpose to the scaffolding used in building construction, providing a means of support and a guide to positioning elements on the page with an accuracy that is difficult to achieve by eye alone.

Designing each page separately is time consuming and indulgent though sometimes necessary. The grid helps proportion a page in both the vertical and horizontal planes, making the design process quicker and easier while helping to ensure a visual consistency and explaining how the design works. The grid will often vary throughout a publication to present different information in different ways.

The baseline grid has important relationships with many key elements of the design such as the baseline-to-baseline distance, and by implication, the typeface size and leading. Another consideration is whether the grid is positioned to the x-height or cap height.

See X-height

>121

Grids are as much of a tool as a designer chooses them to be. Some feel the grid is their best friend while others find it restrictive. Flexibility is important to make designs interesting and accessible and is made possible by the complexity of the grid. We are familiar with a page divided into columns but adding a horizontal grid provides zones where text and images start. Complexity and freedom can be increased by overlaying two or more grids that create odd spaces for elements to be positioned.

Simple grid structure showing:

1. Columns of type with lines depicted running top to bottom and bottom to top
2. Position of captions
3. Margin
4. Gutter
5. Position of running heads and chapter headers
6. Bleed
7. Position of folio
8. Baseline of text area
9. Trim size

the guardian

Brief

When Pentagram was asked to redesign *The Guardian* daily newspaper in 1988 it was given quite a challenge. The studio had to create a design with a contemporary style that applied the benefits of new technology that was radically changing the newspaper industry. The caveat was that David Hillman, a partner at Pentagram, had to retain the traditions of the newspaper for its long established readership.

Process

The design also had to be robust enough and straightforward to use in order to meet the needs of the newspaper's editorial team that compiles pages in haste to meet an endless stream of deadlines, many of which have little design experience.

Result

The relaunched newspaper, complete with a strikingly modern masthead was a great success and went on to garner a number of prestigious awards. The masthead is unique as it mixes both serif and sans-serif typefaces. The layout simultaneously offers flexibility and standardisation. The traditional 8 column grid of British broadsheets is standardised to advertising sales space, where uniformity is necessary. Internally, flexibility is introduced through the use of a 24-column grid that can accommodate columns of different measures.

Design: Pentagram

See Baseline Grid

Computer Guardian

27 Computer Guardian Jack Schofield on ten years of a pillar of computer publishing

34 Movie Guardian Derek Malcolm reports from the Berlin Film Festival

36 Grapevine Geoffrey Beattie in a home for psychoanalytics

37 Law Report The foreign student caught in a visa wrangle

Systems on the up

Education Guardian

Who needs sociologists?

Media Guardian

Risk-risk at the tip-top

Review Guardian

Guardian Tomorrows

Flying saucers are not a mug's game

Life or death?

Choices Guardian

Review, page 25
Paul Kennedy: Yale's favourite Geordie history man

People, page 2
Marion Serravalli's prison wedding

Opinion, page 23
John Biffen looks in vain for the opposition

Arts, page 28
Clint Eastwood conducts Charlie 'Bird' Parker

25p
Friday
12 February
1988
Published in London and Manchester

The Guardian

Alliance woe

Ian Katz on the world's raciest publisher

Big Random, Little Random

Guardian 2: with today's television

Martin Walker on the new Republicans

Mean old man or bland blancmange?

Profile G2 pages 4/5

The selling of Nick Leeson

Media

With 21 pages of jobs

45p
Monday
February 19
1996
Published in London
and Manchester

*The*Guardian

Eight injured as bus ripped apart ☐ IRA 'own goal' theory ☐ Police say no warning was given

Bomb blasts West End

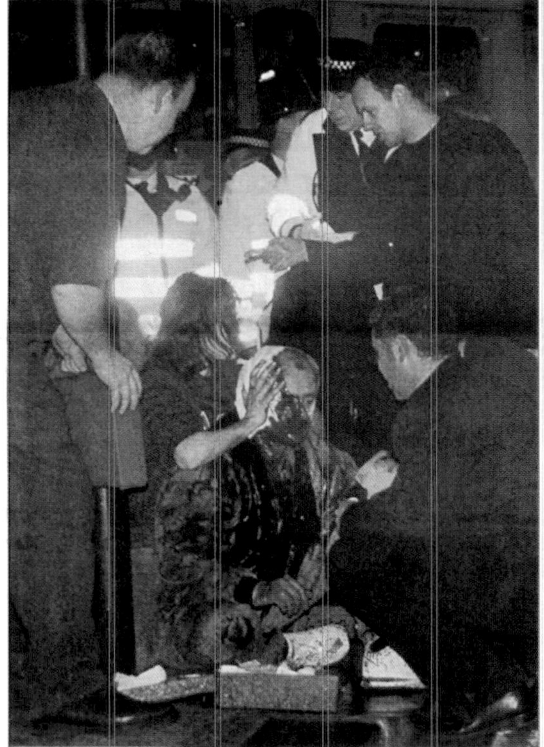

An injured man is tended by emergency services at the scene of the blast near the Aldwych in central London last night

Sally Weale, John Mullin, David Sharrock, Barbie Dutter and Paul Myers

A N EXPLOSION ripped through a double decker bus in the heart of London's West End last night injuring eight people.

EXPLOSION ROCKS CENTRAL LONDON

One mile

Aldwych:
Blasts hits bus

Full details, page 3

Attack 'shows IRA not interested in peace'

David Sharrock

THE third bomb in London in just over a week prompted a swift and angry response last night from Unionist politicians in Northern Ireland.

Inside	News 2	**G2**	Pass Notes 3	Media 13
	International news 9		Profile 4	Crossword 38
	Comment, letters 12		Women 6	Weather 38
	Obituaries 14		Arts 8	Radio 39
	Financial news 16		Reviews 10	Television 40

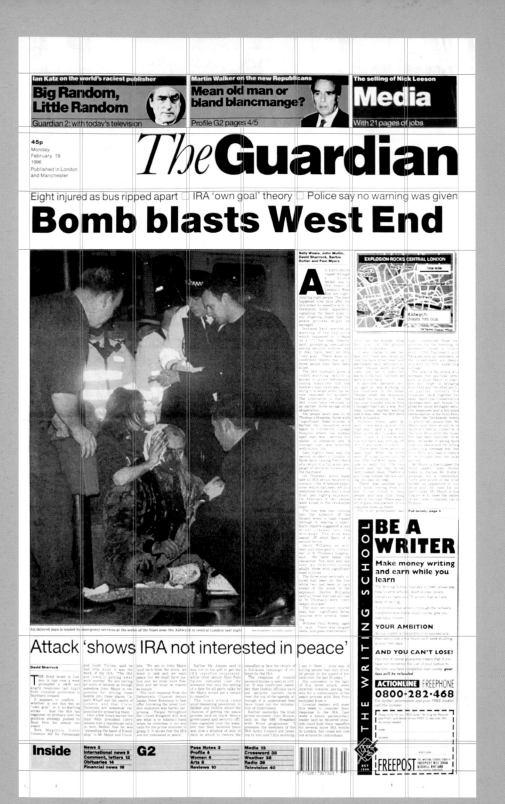

An additional masthead makeover brought a welcome dash of colour to the front page and gave greater prominence to the photo leader, both taking advantage in developments in four-colour printing technology.

Design: Pentagram

The Guardian Weekend

Hostage: Brian Keenan's own story

In April 1986, four months into his job as a lecturer at Beirut's American University, Brian Keenan was kidnapped by Islamic Jihad. He, like at least 87 other westerners, had fallen foul of the savage chaos at the heart of Middle Eastern politics. A handful of those abducted were murdered. Many were held for a matter of hours. Keenan's ordeal continued for four and a half years. In his new book, An Evil Cradling, he describes his life as a prisoner in the Lebanon. Today, and for the next two weeks, we publish exclusive extracts from his story. As our narrative begins, Keenan has been alone in captivity for several weeks

Hostage

The redesign of the *Weekend* colour magazine created a bold look with strong typographic style to make it significantly different from its rivals, while retaining the newspaper's identity. As these spreads show, the magazine has a different pace to the main newspaper, using large-scale photography to give a more relaxed, leisurely feel to the content. The content comprises feature length articles with no-nonsense typography and a clean and simple layout, dramatically illustrated with large-scale photographs. This tone is established from the outset by the text-barren cover.

Design: Pentagram

CENTREPIECE

JUST DOO IT

For generations men have coveted their birds in bitumen black lofts in the shadows of Glasgow's Celtic Park. But they are not tending homing pigeons. For these are the doo-men and their story is one of love and passion for the doos, who come before everyone else – including family. STUART COSGROVE reports

Typography is the means by which a written idea is given a visual form. The selection of the visual form can dramatically affect the readability of the written idea and a reader's feelings towards it due to the hundreds, if not thousands of typefaces available. Typography can produce a neutral effect or rouse the passions, symbolise artistic, political or philosophical movements, or express the personality of a person or organisation. Typefaces vary from clear and distinguishable letterforms that flow easily before the eye and are suitable for extended blocks of text, to more dramatic and eye-catching typefaces that grab attention and are used in newspaper headlines and advertisements.

Typography is anything but static and continues to evolve. Many typefaces in use today are based upon designs created during earlier historic epochs. The fledgling printing industry established Roman capitals and Carolingian minuscules from the reign of Charlemagne as standard forms in the 15th century, which are still widely used today.

Typography sets the tone of a piece of text and a typeface should be chosen that is appropriate and sympathetic to the message being presented and the audience being presented to. While there are no hard and fast rules, there are technical aspects to bear in mind that will help with typeface selection. This section will dissect the anatomy of a typeface, provide examples of typefaces from the main classification categories and comment on their usability. As with many other elements of design, typeface selection is heavily influenced by the taste, style and personal preferences of the designer, together with current fashions, and is thus open to a great deal of experimentation.

type

Type size is the vertical size of the body of a character including the space above and below its strokes. Type size is commonly thought of as the size of the typeface, but it historically refers to the size of the body that holds the printing face of a character in the days of letterpress. A character will always be slightly smaller than its given type size because of this. Normal reading type sizes are usually 8pt to 14pt and the use of different type sizes in the same text indicates a hierarchy of importance as size influences what is read first.

6 7 8 9 10 11 12 14 16 18 21 24 36 48 60 72

Point system

The point system is used to specify the typographical dimensions of a page. This is represented in points and picas. The British and American system is based on a metric point with dimensions as follows: the point is 1/72 of an inch. All type is designed in points. Points are always used to specify type size.

12 points = 1 pica
1 point = 0.35mm
1 pica = 4.22mm

The European didot system is slightly different but provides similar values:

12 Didot = 1 Cicero
1 Didot = 0.38mm
1 Cicero = 4.56mm

There are 12 points to a pica, about 6 picas to an inch. The pica is used for linear measurement of type. The length of a line is specified in picas.

Em

An em is a basic unit of measurement for a given typeface derived from the width of its lower case 'm' i.e. 1 em = the point size of the typeface. The letter 'm' was originally as wide as the type size. The em is actually a square with sides equal to the point size of the typeface. This is used as a constant against which to base other measurements for the typeface such as the set width, which determines how much horizontal space a given amount of copy will occupy in a given type size. The em is also used for paragraph indents and fixed spacing. An em dash is a dash one em in length; an en dash is half the length of an em dash.

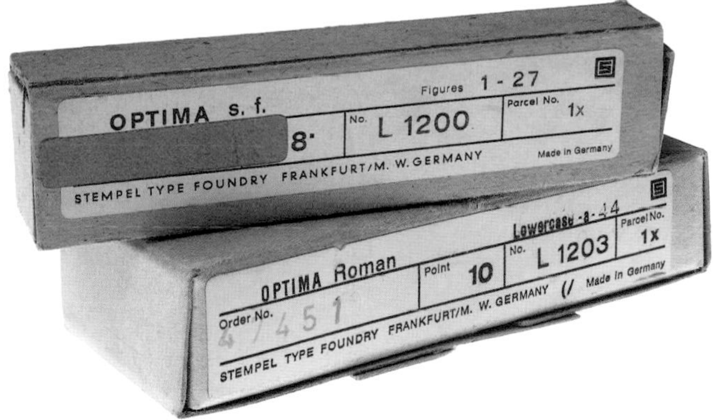

Towards the end of the 16th century a standard set of type sizes was developed, and has remained in use since. This made the standard production of metal type possible.

During the early part of the 20th century many foundries reissued older typefaces in metal. Many of these had subtle differences, accounting for the variations in modern digital fonts.

Right, top to bottom: Akzidenz Grotesk BE, BQ and Buch, all at medium weight have evident differences in counter size and stroke width.

g6

g6

g6

legibility of typefaces

Cheltenham 1896 Morris Fuller Benton/Bertram G Goodhue

Designed with exaggerated ascenders and descenders following studies of legibility of typefaces that found readers scanned using the tops of letters

Type sizes

Modern typesetting technology allows for fonts to be set in any combination of sizes. Early Renaissance typographers, however, tended to compose using a single typeface, in a single weight and a single size. Giving the impression of even text block coverage, this pattern was punctuated only by the insertion of drop caps in the chapter openers.

Upper case and lower case

Derived from the trays that type used to be stored in, the upper case containing 'Capitals' and the lower case containing 'Roman'. Later, type was stored in a Double Case, which, as the name suggests, contains all the characters, punctuation and spacing necessary for typesetting (see below).

— [] æ œ () j
& b c d e
ffl
ffi l m n h
thin
z v u t mid
x

thick ' ? ! ; fl
i s f g ff
k fi
o y p , w en em
a r q : quads
. –

1	2	3	4	5	6	7
8	9	0	£	$		/
A	B	C	D	E	F	G
H	I	K	L	M	N	O
P	Q	R	S	T	V	W
X	Y	Z	Æ	Œ	U	J

Typography was a cornerstone of the Yellow Pages redesign by Johnson Banks. The old typeface was difficult to read, especially at small point sizes. An entirely new typeface was commissioned to cope with the constraints of huge volume printing. This had characters that were carefully created to be more legible at small sizes and to allow more information to go on a line. Special features included a condensed basic form of type with ascenders and descenders at 75% of normal height and junctions chiselled away to allow for ink fill at very small type sizes.

Design: Johnson Banks

See Anatomy of a typeface

Yellow regular

ABCDEFGHIJKLMNOPQRSTUVWXYZ
abcdefghijklmnopqrstuvwxyz
0123456789!?,"£$&%@*

Yellow bold

ABCDEFGHIJKLMNOPQRSTUVWXYZ
abcdefghijklmnopqrstuvwxyz
0123456789!?,"£$&%@*

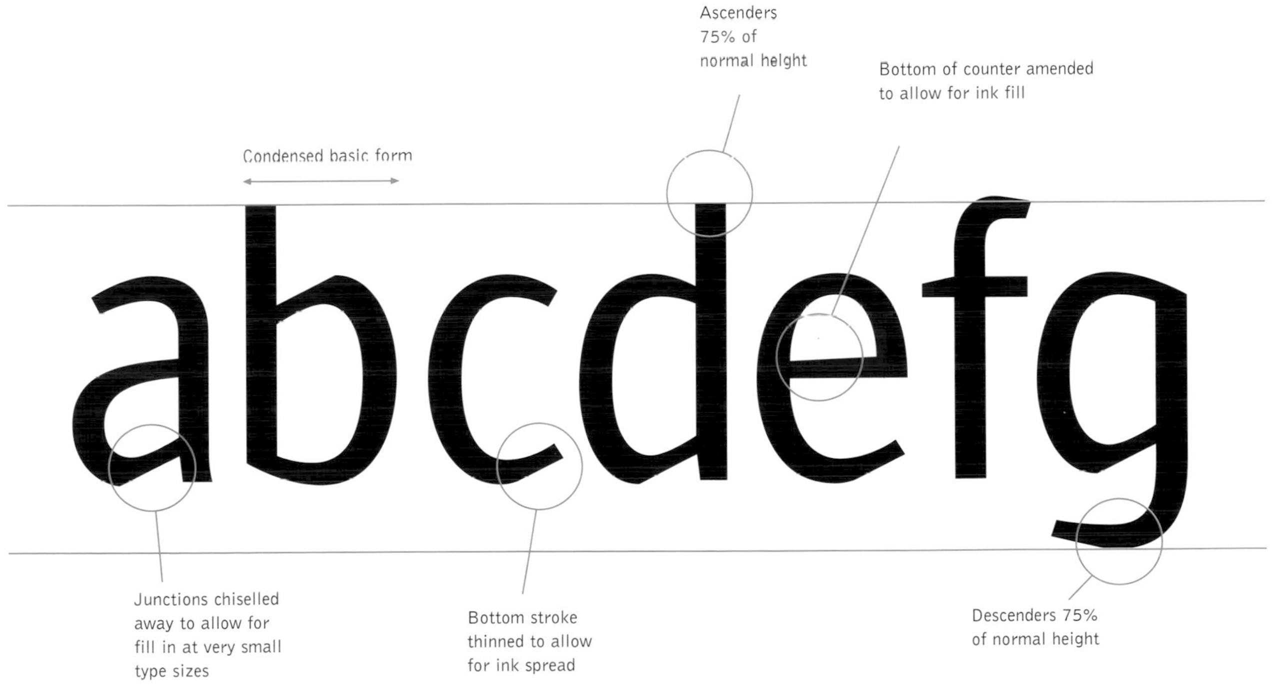

kerning & ligatures

Kerning concerns the space between two letters. Certain combinations have too much space between them, which may make some words difficult to read. This excess is reduced by kerning, the removal of unwanted space between letters. Some letter combinations frequently need to be kerned and are known as kerning pairs. The practice of kerning is particularly common to achieve a balanced look for display type.

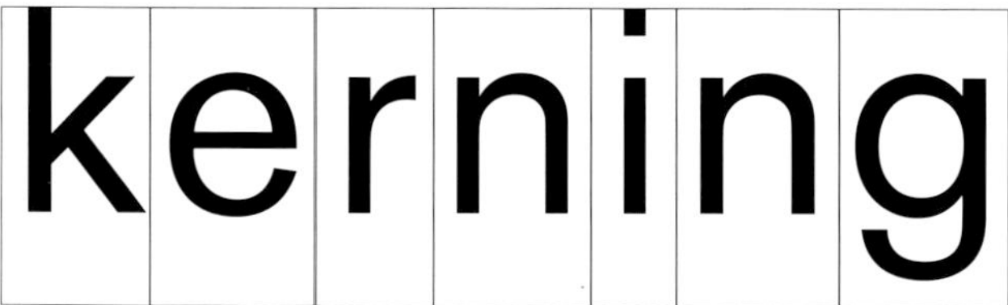

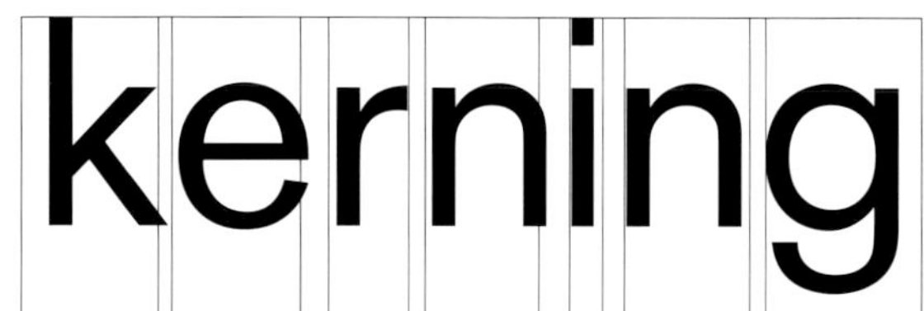

With too much space between them, the letters of the word on the left (above) seem awkward and appear to be floating away from each other. By reducing this space – known as kerning back – the word is visually tighter and looks more natural as shown on the right.

Latin combinations

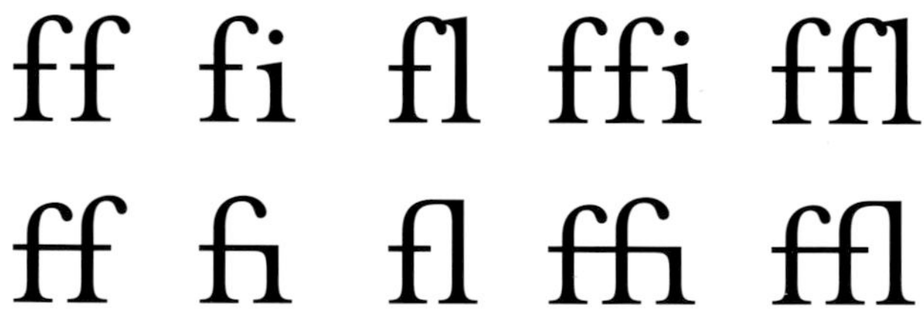

Text set with and without ligatures.

Non-Latin combinations

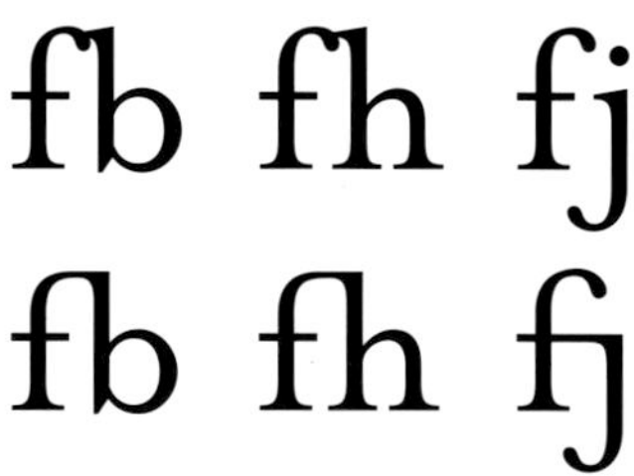

Text set with and without ligatures.

The 'f' ascender and the serif of the ascender of a following letter sometimes look like they are interfering with each other. Rather than trying to separate them they are often joined by a ligature as shown above. Similarly, where the dot of the 'i' or 'j' looks messy following the 'f'. This ligature joins at the crossbar and the dot is removed.

AT AT AY AY AV AV AW AW

Ay Ay Av Av Aw Aw FA FA

TO TO TA TA Ta Ta Te Te

To To Ti Ti Tr Tr Tu Tu

Ty Ty Tw Tw Ts Ts Tc Tc

LT LT LY LY LW LW Ly Ly

PA PA VA VA Va Va Ve Ve

Vo Vo Vi Vi Vr Vr Vu Vu

Vy Vy RT RT RV RV RW RW

RY RY Ry Ry WA WA Wa Wa

We We Wo Wo Wi Wi Wr Wr

WU WU WY WY YA YA Ya Ya

Ye Ye Yo Yo Yi Yi Yp Yp

Yq Yq Yu Yu Yv Yv

leading

If type is set solid (without additional spaces) there is a certain amount of white space above and below the text because some is incorporated as part of each typeface to accommodate ascenders and descenders, and to prevent different lines being too jammed together. Leading is used to add extra space on the bottom of each line of type, typically to make it easier to read. Leading is named after the strips of lead that performed this function on a letterpress, it is expressed in points, and its effect is also called line feed or interlinear spacing. Type size and leading may be annotated as 10/12 Garamond, meaning the Garamond type size is 10 point, the distance between the baselines is 12 point, so the leading is therefore 2 point. 10/10 Garamond signifies no leading. Differences in typefaces mean the effect of leading will depend on its point size and x-height.

Leading and measure
Leading works in conjunction with the measure of the column being set. That is to say that two identically set texts (same leading, typeface and type size) will appear differently over different measures. The measure is the width of the column.

Characters per line
As a general rule, type on a wider measure will appear heavier and will benefit from additional leading. Notice how the column below right looks greyer than the column below left.

12 pica column

If type is set solid (without additional spaces) there is a certain amount of white space above and below the text because some is incorporated as part of each typeface to accommodate ascenders and descenders, and to prevent different lines being too jammed together. Leading is used to add extra space on the bottom of each line of type, typically to make it easier to read.

10pt type on 11pt leading

24 pica column

If type is set solid (without additional spaces) there is a certain amount of white space above and below the text because some is incorporated as part of each typeface to accommodate ascenders and descenders, and to prevent different lines being too jammed together. Leading is used to add extra space on the bottom of each line of type, typically to make it easier to read. Leading is named after the strips of lead that performed this function on a letterpress, it is expressed in points, and its effect is also called line feed or interlinear spacing. Type size and leading may be annotated as 10/12 Garamond, meaning the Garamond type size is 10 point, the distance between the baselines is 12 point, so the leading is therefore 2 point. 10/10 Garamond signifies no leading. Differences in typefaces mean the effect of leading will depend on its point size and x-height.

10pt type on 11pt leading

18 pica column

If type is set solid (without additional spaces) there is a certain amount of white space above and below the text because some is incorporated as part of each typeface to accommodate ascenders and descenders, and to prevent different lines being too jammed together. Leading is used to add extra space on the bottom of each line of type, typically to make it easier to read.

10pt type on 11pt leading

If type is set solid (without additional spaces) there is a certain amount of white space above and below the text because some is incorporated as part of each typeface to accommodate ascenders and descenders, and to prevent different lines being too jammed together. Leading is used to add extra space on the bottom of each line of type, typically to make it easier to read.

10pt type on 12pt leading

If type is set solid (without additional spaces) there is a certain amount of white space above and below the text because some is incorporated as part of each typeface to accommodate ascenders and descenders, and to prevent different lines being too jammed together. Leading is used to add extra space on the bottom of each line of type, typically to make it easier to read.

10pt type on 13pt leading

If type is set solid (without additional spaces) there is a certain amount of white space above and below the text because some is incorporated as part of each typeface to accommodate ascenders and descenders, and to prevent different lines being too jammed together. Leading is used to add extra space on the bottom of each line of type, typically to make it easier to read.

10pt type on 14pt leading

As point size and measure are linked you can calculate using the following methods in any given font.

The optimum line length is around 9 words (based on the average word being 5 characters in length).

Lorem ipsum dolor sit amet, autem zzril elit, sed

The optimum line length is around one and a half times the length of the lower case alphabet.

abcdefghijklmnopqrstuvwxyzabcdefghijklm

Around 26 characters is considered minimum, 38 optimum, and 68 maximum.

abcdefghijklmnopqrstuvwxyz
abcdefghijklmnopqrstuvwxyzabcdefghijklm
abcdefghijklmnopqrstuvwxyzabcdefghijklmnopqrstuvwxyzabcdefghijklmnop

hyphenation, justification & tracking

If the text in a column is ranged left or ranged right there is a fixed space between each word and one end of the column of text will appear ragged. Fully justified text has both sides of the text body neatly aligned as the space between words is varied to achieve balance. Justified text with many long words and many large spaces can result in a visual fault where there are literally rivers of white space flowing down the text block.

This type is set loose
This type is set normal
This type is set tight
This type is set very tight
This type is set overlapping

Tracking

Tracking refers to the amount of space between all letters, which can be adjusted to make the characters distinguishable. Reducing tracking reduces the space between letters, condenses the text, and may allow more text to be fitted into a given area, but if tracking is reduced too much the letters begin to hit each other. Space should not be added to the extent that letters become separated from the words they are part of.

Text justification

Special attention needs to be paid to justification of type, particularly on a narrow measure. Consecutive hyphenation, widows, irregular spacing (white acne) and rivers (vertical shapes formed by adjacent gaps), are all commonplace to automatically set text (right).

**Lorem ipsum dolor sit amet, con-
sectetuer adipiscing elit, sed diam nonummy nibh euismod tincidunt ut laoreet
dolore magna aliquam erat volutpat. Ut
wisi enim ad minim veniam, quis nostrud exerci tation ullamcorper suscipit
lobortis nisl ut aliquip ex ea commodo
consequat. Duis autem vel eum iriure
dolor in hendrerit in vulputate velit esse
molestie consequat, vel illum dolore eu
feugiat nulla facilisi at vero eros et
accumsan et iusto odio dignissim qui
blandit praesent luptatum zzril delenit
augue duis dolore te feugait nulla facilisi. Lorem ipsum dolor sit amet, consectetuer adipiscing elit, sed diam nonummy nibh euismod tincidunt ut laoreet
dolore magna aliquam erat volutpat. Ut
wisi enim ad minim veniam, quis nostrud exerci tation ullamcorper suscipit
lobortis nisl ut aliquip ex ea commodo
consequat.**

Anything between 40–76 characters per line (CPL) (this includes spaces and punctuation) is considered satisfactory, while 66 CPL is generally cited as the optimum for readability. Typographers try to avoid more than two consecutive hyphenations, but hyphenations are considered preferable to 'loose' setting, and Flush Left or Right better still.

Flush Left (FL), by default is Ragged Right (RR), and can be described as FL/RR. Conversely, Flush Right (FR), by default is Ragged Left (RL), and can be described as FR/RL.

A common problem with justified type is 'white acne' or 'pig bristles'; the sporadic appearance of white spaces that occur in the 'gaps' between words. 'Rivers', or lines formed through connecting white gaps are also to be avoided. A valuable tip for identifying problems is to look at text with squinted eyes, so you *see* only shapes and don't *read* the words, turning your text upside down also works.

Minimum: 50 Optimum: 80 Maximum: 120

Anything between 40–76 characters per line (CPL) (this includes spaces and punctuation) is considered satisfactory, while 66 CPL is generally cited as the optimum for readability. Typographers try to avoid more than two consecutive hyphenations, but hyphenations are considered preferable to 'loose' setting, and Flush Left or Right better still.

Flush Left (FL), by default is Ragged Right (RR), and can be described as FL/RR. Conversely, Flush Right (FR), by default is Ragged Left (RL), and can be described as FR/RL.

A common problem with justified type is 'white acne' or 'pig bristles'; the sporadic appearance of white spaces that occur in the 'gaps' between words. 'Rivers', or lines formed through connecting white gaps are also to be avoided. A valuable tip for identifying problems is to look at text with squinted eyes, so you *see* only shapes and don't *read* the words, turning your text upside down also works.

Minimum: 80 Optimum: 100 Maximum: 150

Anything between 40–76 characters per line (CPL) (this includes spaces and punctuation) is considered satisfactory, while 66 CPL is generally cited as the optimum for readability. Typographers try to avoid more than two consecutive hyphenations, but hyphenations are considered preferable to 'loose' setting, and Flush Left or Right better still.

Flush Left (FL), by default is Ragged Right (RR), and can be described as FL/RR. Conversely, Flush Right (FR), by default is Ragged Left (RL), and can be described as FR/RL.

A common problem with justified type is 'white acne' or 'pig bristles'; the sporadic appearance of white spaces that occur in the 'gaps' between words. 'Rivers', or lines formed through connecting white gaps are also to be avoided. A valuable tip for identifying problems is to look at text with squinted eyes, so you *see* only shapes and don't *read* the words, turning your text upside down also works.

Minimum: 100 Optimum: 140 Maximum: 200

Anything between 40–76 characters per line (CPL) (this includes spaces and punctuation) is considered satisfactory, while 66 CPL is generally cited as the optimum for readability. Typographers try to avoid more than two consecutive hyphenations, but hyphenations are considered preferable to 'loose' setting, and Flush Left or Right better still.

Flush Left (FL), by default is Ragged Right (RR), and can be described as FL/RR. Conversely, Flush Right (FR), by default is Ragged Left (RL), and can be described as FR/RL.

A common problem with justified type is 'white acne' or 'pig bristles'; the sporadic appearance of white spaces that occur in the 'gaps' between words. 'Rivers', or lines formed through connecting white gaps are also to be avoided. A valuable tip for identifying problems is to look at text with squinted eyes, so you *see* only shapes and don't *read* the words, turning your text upside down also works.

Minimum: 140 Optimum: 170 Maximum: 250

Anything between 40–76 characters per line (CPL) (this includes spaces and punctuation) is considered satisfactory, while 66 CPL is generally cited as the optimum for readability. Typographers try to avoid more than two consecutive hyphenations, but hyphenations are considered preferable to 'loose' setting, and Flush Left or Right better still.

Flush Left (FL), by default is Ragged Right (RR), and can be described as FL/RR. Conversely, Flush Right (FR), by default is Ragged Left (RL), and can be described as FR/RL.

A common problem with justified type is 'white acne' or 'pig bristles'; the sporadic appearance of white spaces that occur in the 'gaps' between words. 'Rivers', or lines formed through connecting white gaps are also to be avoided. A valuable tip for identifying problems is to look at text with squinted eyes, so you *see* only shapes and don't *read* the words, turning your text upside down also works.

Minimum: 170 Optimum: 200 Maximum: 300

Anything between 40–76 characters per line (CPL) (this includes spaces and punctuation) is considered satisfactory, while 66 CPL is generally cited as the optimum for readability. Typographers try to avoid more than two consecutive hyphenations, but hyphenations are considered preferable to 'loose' setting, and Flush Left or Right better still.

Flush Left (FL), by default is Ragged Right (RR), and can be described as FL/RR. Conversely, Flush Right (FR), by default is Ragged Left (RL), and can be described as FR/RL.

A common problem with justified type is 'white acne' or 'pig bristles'; the sporadic appearance of white spaces that occur in the 'gaps' between words. 'Rivers', or lines formed through connecting white gaps are also to be avoided. A valuable tip for identifying problems is to look at text with squinted eyes, so you *see* only shapes and don't *read* the words, turning your text upside down also works.

Minimum: 200 Optimum: 250 Maximum: 350

COMMUNITY ARCHITECTURE

ROD HACKNEY

INAUGURAL SPEECH AS RIBA PRESIDENT, 3 JULY 1987

OUR ENVIRONMENT IS A BATTLEGROUND BETWEEN THE VARIOUS FORCES THAT THREATEN TO DISTORT, END AND OVERWHELM SOCIETY. PRESSURE, CONFLICT, STRESS AND APPREHENSION IS THE NORMAL EXPERIENCE OF MILLIONS OF US LIVING IN THESE AREAS. THE INNER CORE OF OUR CITIES BEAR THOSE DEEP SCARS THAT SHOULD HAVE BEEN REMOVED LONG AGO. SCARS OF DECAY IN HOUSING, INDUSTRIAL DERELICTION, ENTRENCHED UNEMPLOYMENT, LACK OF INVESTMENT OPPORTUNITIES, PESSIMISM AND POVERTY.

ENSURE THAT BUILDINGS WE PRODUCE ARE FIT FOR THEIR PURPOSE

URBAN REGENERATION HAS TO BE A PRIORITY IF WE ARE TO RETAIN OUR CIVIL PEACE AND OUR LIBERTIES – BUT IT IS NOT A SOLUTION THAT SHOULD BE IMPOSED ENTIRELY FROM ABOVE.

What is most at risk in the city and the countryside alike is the sense and reality of community. We must rebuild these communities to give them a means of survival. We must prevent communities being dispersed or obliterated. This profession must lead – architects must lead because it is about architecture. The influx of new population into decaying inner cities can be as damaging as it is in the rural villages. The process of bringing new service employment to these areas can be as devastating in its way than the Industrial Revolution was two centuries ago.

We can make our society far more democratic by creating new forms of public service – in the early post-war years Britain built a huge public sector industry – a machine – to deliver the sort of infrastructure we had to have as a modern state. Its main spring was a concept of dedicated common purpose, not least among the architects who served in it.

The machinery is now reduced to virtual impotence, but needs to remain – and we must take a pro-active role in bringing about new forms of public service appropriate to the 1990s. Battles between central and local government tend to leave as debris the very communities they profess to serve. Putting architects in these places to live and work has to be a major way forward, where they can achieve the most good. It is very much a role for our regional structure – and a network of architecture centres.

There are a number of key issues which the professional must attack from a central base – with renewed vigour and as a united front. As an institute we must play a part in the new and potentially dynamic alliance with government.

We must never yield on our concern to produce high quality – architecture is about quality – when a building becomes a place that raises the spirits it becomes architecture. We must never yield that responsibility – it is our responsibility to ensure that buildings we produce are fit for their purpose – well-designed and built. Good architecture, as opposed to competent building – must by its very definition be a building that raises spirits.

As a profession, we can admit to being far too elitist in the past – and this has diminished our capacity to contribute to and communicate with the communities that most needed our skills. But to abandon all standards and present ourselves as 'no-nothings' who slavishly produce instant solutions would be an inverted elitism as absurd and alienating as professional arrogance.

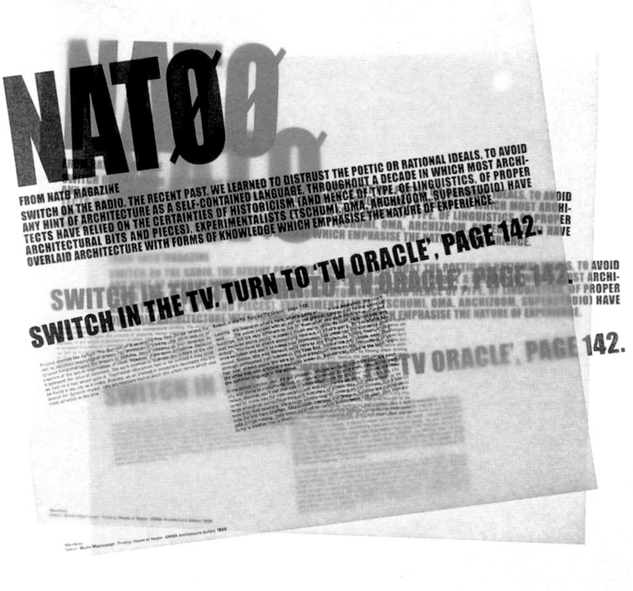

Radical Architecture
Exhibition graphics and catalogue design for the RIBA (Royal Institute of British Architects). A strong constructivist colour scheme and manifesto style catalogue combine to create an impactful exhibition. The catalogue, printed on wafer-thin Bible stock, is printed as a series of individual pads, allowing visitors to take selected pages. The typography is intentionally small, with long line lengths, necessitating visitors to retain the manifesto sections for later reading.

Design: Studio Myerscough

See Hyphenation, Justification & Tracking

8vo used an intriguing array of typeface styles over an amorphous yellow shape for this poster for the seventh anniversary of Manchester's legendary Haçienda nightclub. The Haçienda brand was so well known that little information needed to be given other than the date. The brand itself, reduced to its highly identifiable first three letters 'Haç' stretches across the poster over Fac 51, an equally familiar brand mark of the club. Several special inks including a luminescent are used to create a poster that functions effectively in the early hours – the time the intended audience see it!

Design: 8vo

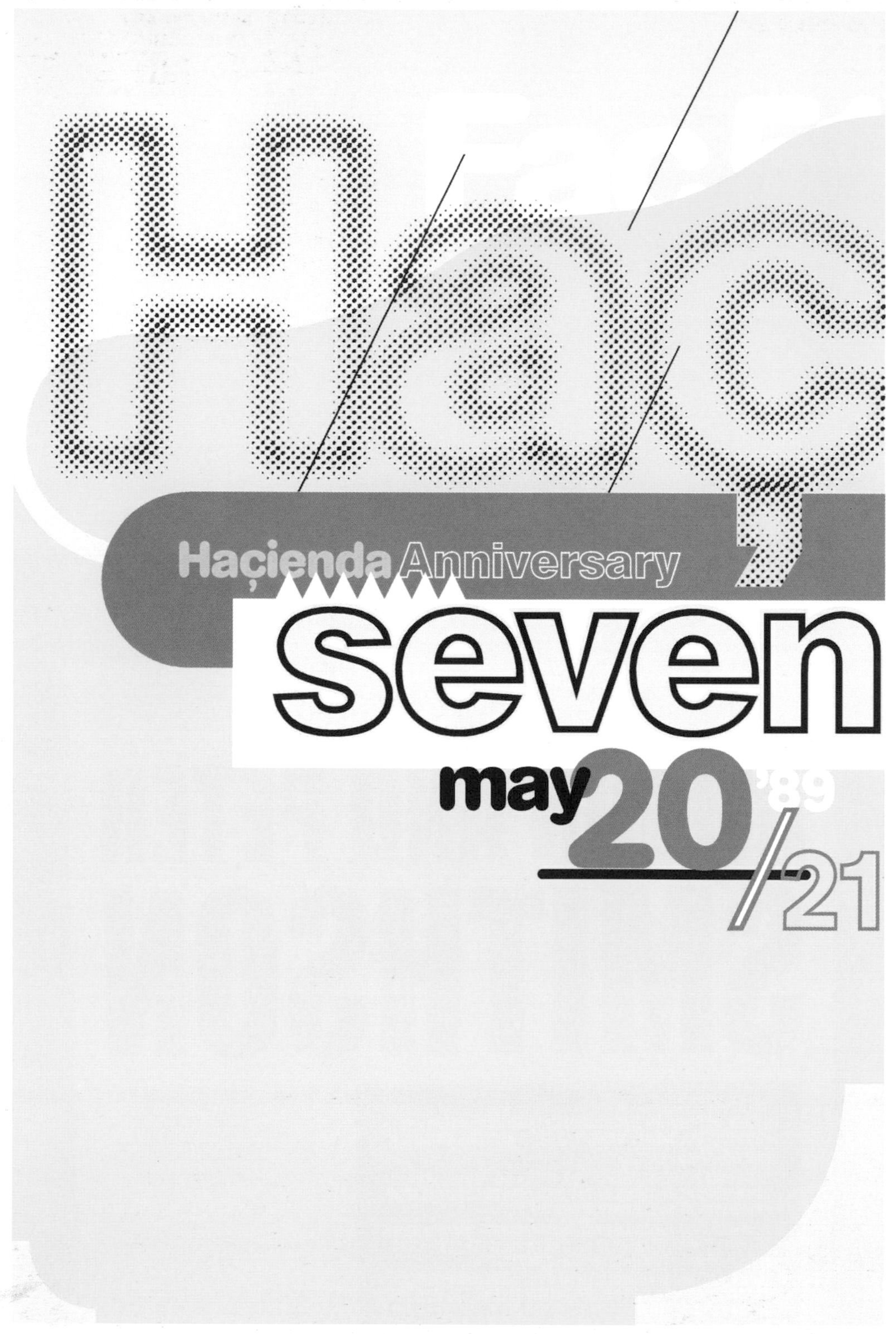

MODERN ART

MODERN ART
73 REDCHURCH STREET LONDON E2 7DJ
TEL +44 (0)20 7739 2081 FAX +44 (0)20 7729 2017
MODERNARTINC.COM INFO@MODERNARTINC.COM

73 REDCHURCH STREET LONDON E2 7DJ
TEL +44 (0)20 7739 2081 FAX +44 (0)20 7729 2017
MODERNARTINC.COM INFO@MODERNARTINC.COM

CHRISTIAN MOONEY

MODERN ART

Simon Earith of Blue Source. designed a bespoke typeface, *Standard Modern,* as an integral part of an identity for Modern Art, a contemporary art gallery in London's East End. Resulting in the creation of elements including business cards, letterhead, continuation sheet, comp slips, signage and regular preview cards.

An identity needn't be a logo, a shape, or colour, a united communication can be built around a single element, a typeface.

All elements were printed using a letterpress.

Design: Blue Source.

See Letterpress

>12

design reflects prevailing thoughts and ideas. during the last century the prevalent schools of thought have been modernism and post-modernism.

from the end of the 19th century, modernism was shaped by the industrialisation and urbanisation of western society. it marked a departure from the rural and provincial towards cosmopolitanism, rejecting or overthrowing traditional values and styles as functionality and progress became key concerns as part of an attempt to move beyond the external physical representation of reality as depicted by cubism and the bauhaus.

the bauhaus

the bauhaus opened in 1919 under the direction of the renowned architect walter gropius, and was intended to be a fresh approach to design after the first world war.

de stiyl

an art and design movement founded around the magazine of the same name. founded by theo van doesburg, de stiyl used strong rectangular forms, employed primary colours and celebrated asymmetrical compositions.

constructivism

russian constructivism was influential to modernism through its use of black and red sans-serif typography, arranged in asymmetrical blocks.

■●

in 1923 kandinsky proposed that there was a universal relationship between the three basic shapes and the three primary colours. with the yellow triangle being the most active and dynamic, through to the passive cold blue circle.

Universal 1925 Herbert Bayer

Bayer's Universal typeface was developed at the Bauhaus and is a reduction of Roman forms to simple geometric shapes. The circular form features heavily, and you can see how each character is closely based on the others.

ABCDEFGHIJKLMNOPQRSTUVWXYZ
abcdefghijklmnopqrstuvwxyz 1234567890

Kabel 1927–29 Rudolf Koch
Uniform nature of the characters.

ABCDEFGHIJKLMNOPQRSTUVWXYZ
abcdefghijklmnopqrstuvwxyz 1234567890

Eurostyle 1962 A Novarese
Letterforms are square shaped.

ABCDEFGHIJKLMNOPQRSTUVWXYZ
abcdefghijklmnopqrstuvwxyz 1234567890

Frutiger 1974 Adrian Frutiger
Uniform nature of the characters.

ABCDEFGHIJKLMNOPQRSTUVWXYZ
abcdefghijklmnopqrstuvwxyz 1234567890

Futura 1927–30 Paul Renner
Note the straight tail of the Q and the geometric form of the G.

ABCDEFGHIJKLMNOPQRSTUVWXYZ
abcdefghijklmnopqrstuvwxyz 1234567890

Pump 1970 Estelle Letraset Ltd.
Inspired by the simple geometric shapes of early Bauhaus fonts.

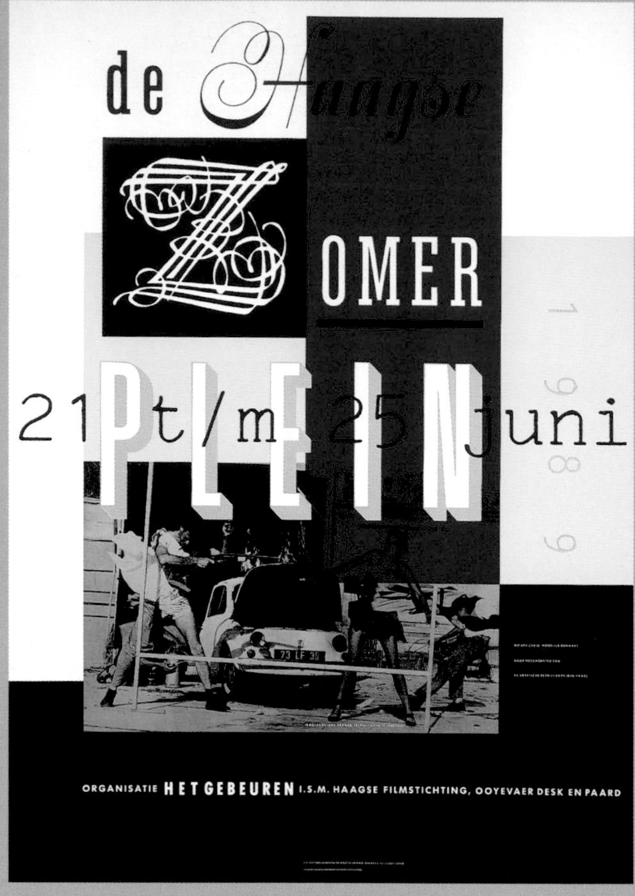

Faydherbe/De Vringer created strong images for the De Haagse Zomer (The Hague Summer Festival) to stand out from other posters that are displayed in a city. Bright colours and images from old magazines were cut and pasted together by hand with typography taken from old typeface manuals and inspired by pioneers such as Piet Zwart en Schuitema in Holland and Russian constructivists like El Lissitzky and Rodchenko, but with the studio's own twist.
Design: Faydherbe/De Vringer

de Haagse
ZOMER
VAN MUZIEKTHEATER TOT KURHAUS
DE
ndergang
4 JULI 1987
EEN COMPOSITIE VAN GILIUS VAN BERGEIJK
DE PROCESSIE LOOPT VAN 18 UUR TOT 24 UUR

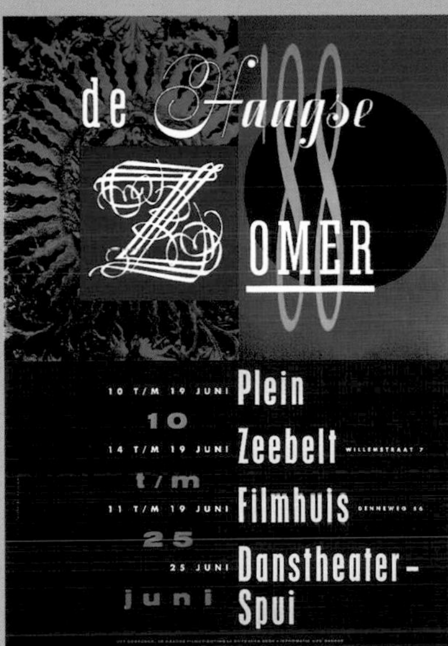
de Haagse
ZOMER
10 T/M 19 JUNI Plein
10
14 T/M 19 JUNI Zeebelt
t/m
11 T/M 19 JUNI Filmhuis
25
25 JUNI Danstheater-
juni Spui

plein
de haagse
zomer
92
THEATER AAN DE HAAG
VRAAG NAAR DE GRATIS FESTIVALKRANT

PLEIN
de haagse
ZOMER
26 T/M 30 Juni
1991
het Gebeuren
VRAAG NAAR DE GRATIS FESTIVALKRANT:

26 3
HAAGS FILMHUIS
FILM AND NEW MEDIA
IMAGE + SOUND
PARKEERTERREIN NIEUWE SCHOOLSTRAAT
EXTRA HAAGS ZOMERPODIUM
FILM, PERFORMANCES EN MUZIEK
123
juli
de Haagse
ZOMER

To me good design means as little design as possible.

Simple is better than complicated.

Quiet is better than loud.

Unobtrusive is better than exciting.

Small is better than large.

Light is better than heavy.

Plain is better than coloured.

Harmony is better than divergency.

Being well balanced is better than being exalted.

Continuity is better than change.

Sparse is better than profuse.

Neutral is better than aggressive.

The obvious is better than that which must be sought.

Few elements are better than many.

A system is better than single elements.

Dieter Rams, 1987

Dieter Rams, the German industrial designer, who worked for Braun electrical company, was a pioneer of the modernist movement. His work later became synonymous with 'quiet simplicity'.

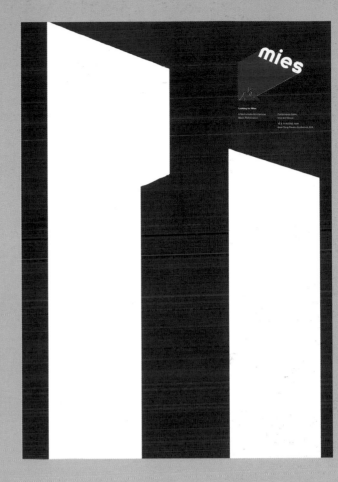

London design studio Mono was asked to art direct printed matter for a performance on the life and works of architect Ludwig Mies van der Rohe at the Kwai Fong Auditorium in Hong Kong. The performance used various media including typography and installation to explore architectural concepts.

Following van der Rohe's maxims such as 'Less is more', and 'God is in the details', Mono used three-dimensional letters with a white face against a white background, picked out only by the colour of their exaggerated depth. This extreme depth represents the Chicago skyscrapers that van der Rohe was famous for, an association further strengthened by the huge billboard size that the posters were produced at.

Design: Mono

* the differences between regions' or countries' speech

'Vernacular design' used to describe 'finding' reference in the differences. An example of which is Barry Deck's Template Gothic font based on Americana signage. 'The sign was done with lettering templates and it was exquisite. It had obviously been done by someone who was totally naive,' explained Deck.

Arcadia 1990 Neville Brody

Brody based Arcadia on a banner he designed for *Arena* magazine that was itself inspired by the characters from an IBM golf-ball typewriter.

Industria 1989 Neville Brody

Industria was designed for *The Face* magazine.

Often utilising vernacular* and undesigned artifacts, post-modernism was pioneered by the Basle School in Switzerland and later Cranbrook Academy of Art in the United States.

Post-modernism Post-modernism developed following the Second World War and questions the very notion that there is a reliable reality through deconstructing authority and the established order of things by engaging in the idea of fragmentation, incoherence and the plain ridiculous. **Post-modernism** returned to earlier ideas of adornment and decoration, celebrating expression and personal intuition in favour of formula and structure.

Mrs Eaves 1996 Zuzana Licko

A revival of Baskerville. Named after Sarah Eaves, John Baskerville's housekeeper.

ABCDEFGHIJKLMNOPQRSTUVWXYZ
abcdefghijklmnopqrstuvwxyz 1234567890

Blur 1992 Neville Brody
The traditional letterforms are 'blurred' to create a new font.

ABCDEFGHIJKLMNOPQRSTUVWXYZ
abcdefghijklmnopqrstuvwxyz 1234567890

Template Gothic 1990 Barry Deck
Inspired by stencilled lettering.

ABCDEFGHIJKLMNOPQRSTUVWXYZ
abcdefghijklmnopqrstuvwxyz 1234567890

Trixie 1991 Erik van Blokland
Distressed lettering informed by the manual nature of the typewriter.

ABCDEFGHIJKLMNOPQRSTUVWXYZ
abcdefghijklmnopqrstuvwxyz 1234567890

Dot Matrix 1994 Cornel Windlin
Electronic data-signage influenced font.

ABCDEFGHIJKLMNOPQRSTUVWXYZ
abcdefghijklmnopqrstuvwxyz 1234567890

Keedy Sans 1989 Jeffery Keedy
Eclectic sans-serif font with irregular bar widths.

fuse

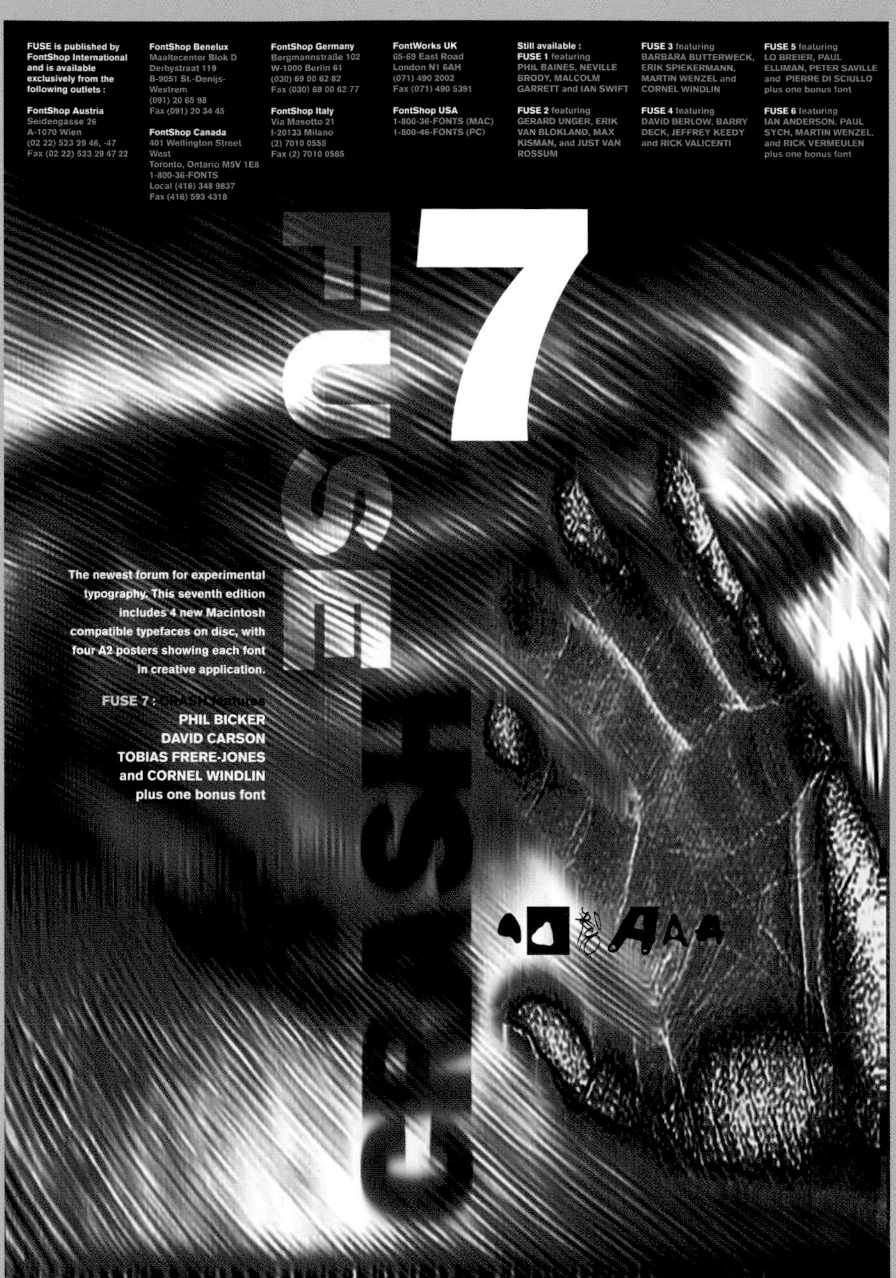

Fuse 7, Crash: Edition Poster design by Neville Brody, 1993

Through *Fuse* magazine – founded by Neville Brody and John Wozencroft – typography exploded into uncharted realms as type designers grabbed hold of the 'free reins' that computer technology put in their hands and indulged their imaginations to the full. The symbolism of type stepped to the fore and gained the upper hand over mere functionality, such as readability, by addressing societal issues through the shapes and style of the letters, as in the example, right, about pornography. Each issue of *Fuse* came with a disk of new typefaces.

Design: Research Studios London

PORNO-GRAPHY NEEDS YOU

Fuse 11, Pornography: Tape Type Poster by Fuel, 1994

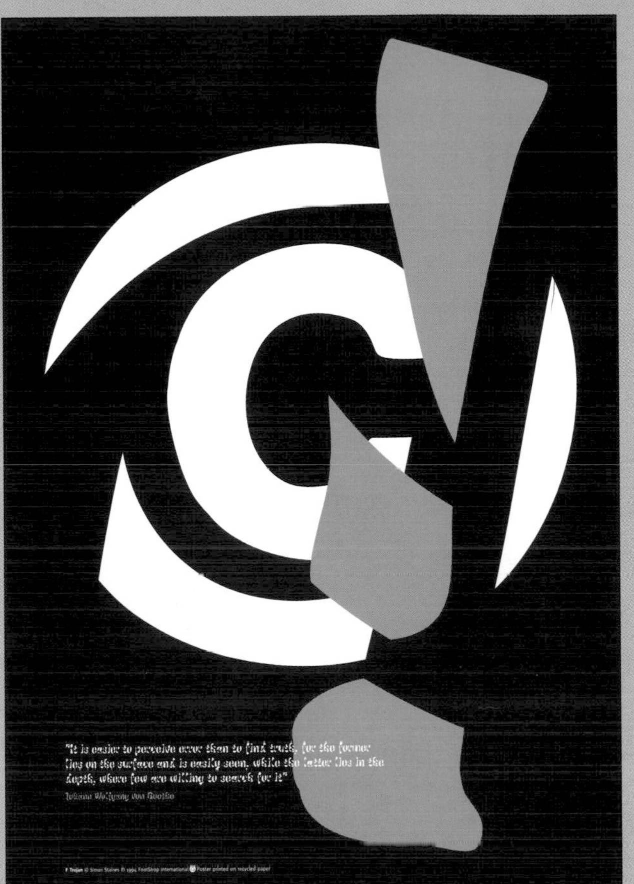

Fuse 12, Propaganda: Trojan Poster by Simon Staines, 1994

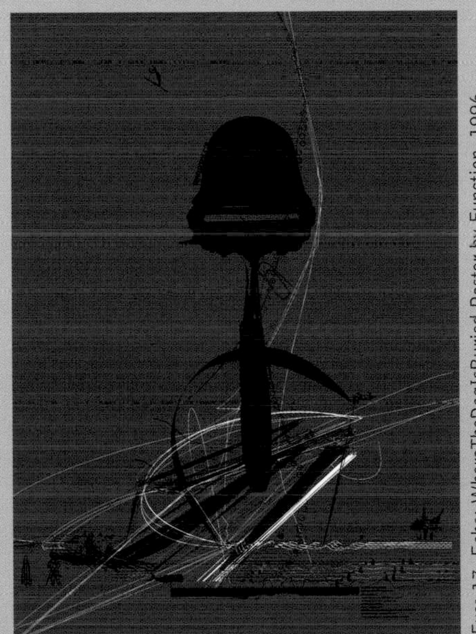

Fuse 17, Echo: WhereTheDogIsBuried Poster by Function, 1996

Fuse 2, Runes: Edition Poster design by Neville Brody, 1991

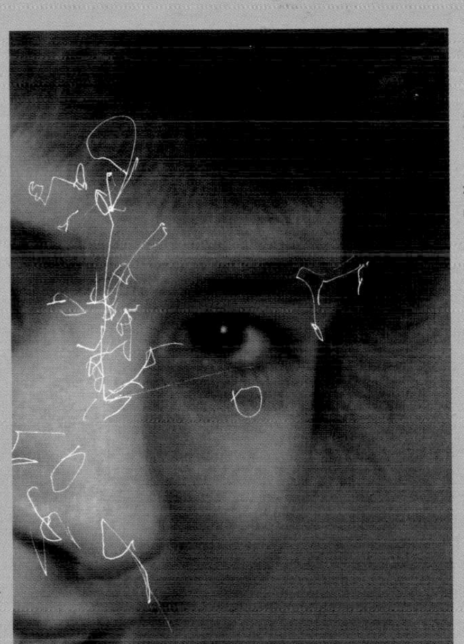

Fuse 18, Secrets: Sclerosis Script Poster By Jason Bailey, 2000

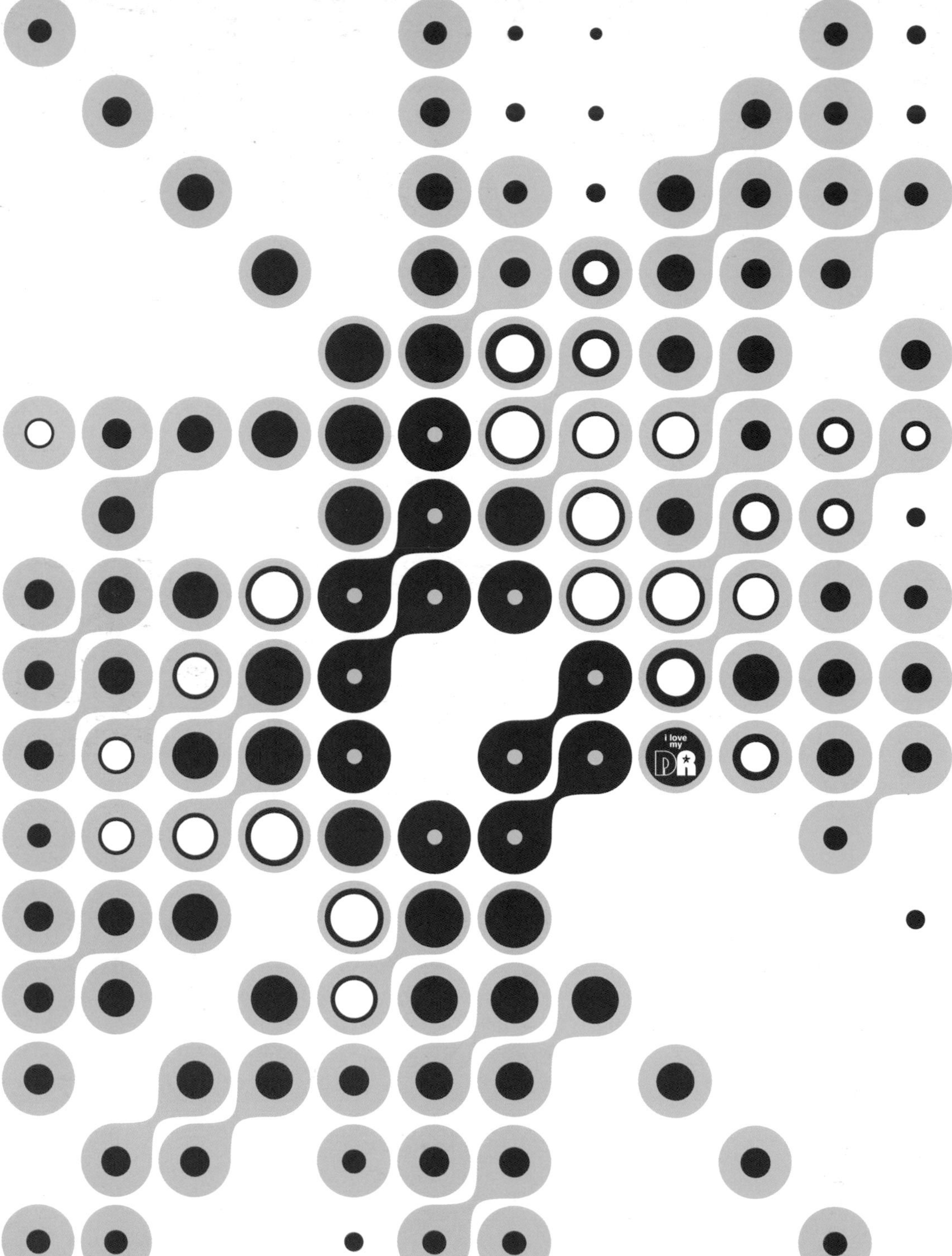

Fuse 6, Codes: Dr Nob Poster by Ian Anderson for The Designers Republic, 1992

∀ A

Right & above: The Western alphabet was derived from hieroglyphs, or picture writing. The letter 'A' for example can trace its origins back past the Greeks and the Phoenicians to a picture of the head of an ox. The Greeks, when developing their alphabet borrowed symbols including the Semitic name for Alef, later to be known as Alpha. At some stage the symbol became inverted to resemble our modern drawing of the letter A.

Images and symbols continue to play a role in typography as this example of an experimental typeface – that is based on the theme of superstition – by F Santo Domingo shows.

Design: Research Studios London

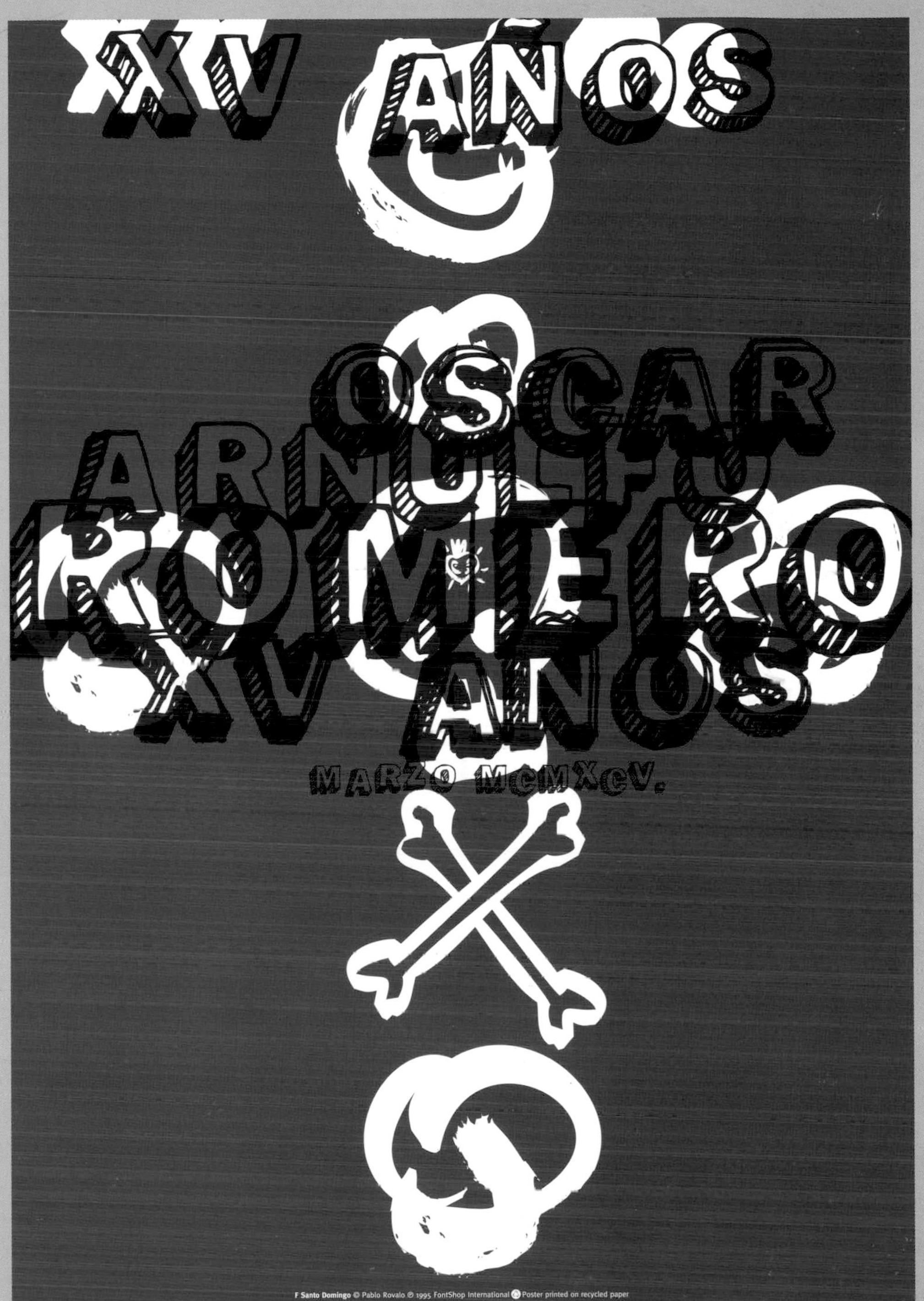

Fuse 13, Superstition: Santo Domingo Poster by Pablo Rovalo, 1995

anatomy of a typeface

Typefaces and type families can be classified according to their inherent characteristics. To understand the classification system and the means by which a typeface is classified one must be familiar with the terminology used to describe the elements that form a character. Many typefaces originate in designs from the past 500 years that would have originally been cast in metal. Other typefaces have a lineage that goes back to the work of stonemasons. Though now in digital format, such typefaces still contain distinct elements associated with the physical necessities of the times in which they were created. The digital age has led to an explosion of the number of typefaces available to the designer, and has made it simpler to design a new typeface or alter an existing one.

Roman

The basic letterform. So called as the origins of the letter are in the inscriptions found on Roman monuments. Some typefaces also carry a slightly lighter version called 'Book'.

Light

A lighter version of the Roman cut.

Boldface

Using a wider stroke than the Roman, Boldface, also called Medium, Semibold, Black, Super (as in the case with Akzidenz Grotesk) and Poster (as found with Bodoni, see page 110).

Italic

Italic is a version of the Roman cut that slopes to the right. Most typefaces have an Italic family member.

Condensed

Condensed is a narrower version of the Roman cut.

Extended

Extended type is a wider version of the Roman cut.

Grotesque 1926 Monotype Corporation

Popular with Swiss designers in the 1950s Akzidenz Grotesk was the inspiration for modern sans-serifs such as Univers and Helvetica.

Bembo 1929 Monotype

The original 'Old Face' first used in Cardinal Bembo's *De Aetna*, 1495, inspired many faces over the following two centuries including Garamond (also known as Garamont). Note the divergent serifs on the capital T.

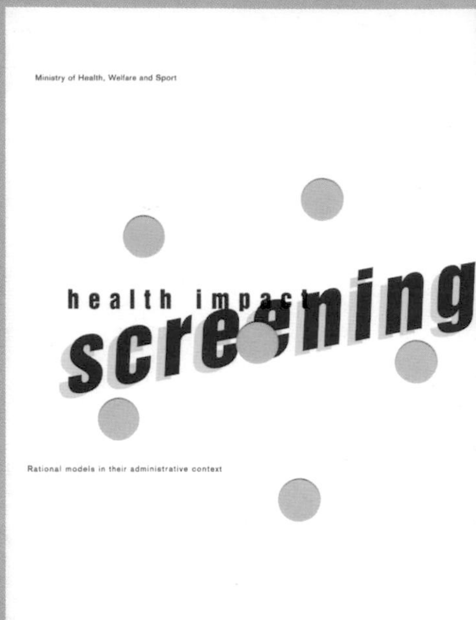

Ministry of Health, Welfare and Sport
health impact
screening
Rational models in their administrative context

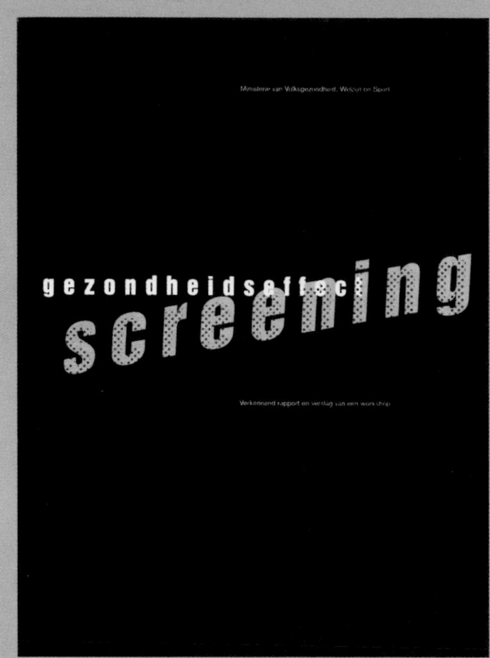

gezondheidseffect
screening

Uitgave
Centrum
Gezondheidszorg
Vluchtelingen
'S LANDS wijs ?
VROUWENBESNIJDENIS EN SOMALISCHE VROUWEN IN NEDERLAND
'S LANDS eer

MEDISCH
WETENSCHAP
PELIJK ONDER
ZOEK MET WILS
ONBEKWA
MEN
Advies inzake regeling van medisch-wetenschappelijk onderzoek met minderjarigen en meerderjarige wilsonbekwamen

Left: In this series of report covers for Ministerie van VWS (Ministry of Health), Faydherbe/De Vringer used typography as a means to portray the subject of the report beyond the words. Photography is often used for this purpose but the studio believes it can be too explicit at times, and is often used as a collage to explain the subject matter rather than simply as a pleasing background image. The typography was styled to enhance the titles of the reports and convey a feeling of the subject matter, with a clean and simple design.

Design: Faydherbe/De Vringer

Right: These posters utilise the characteristically bold and inventive typography favoured by the Faydherbe/De Vringer studio.

Design: Faydherbe/De Vringer

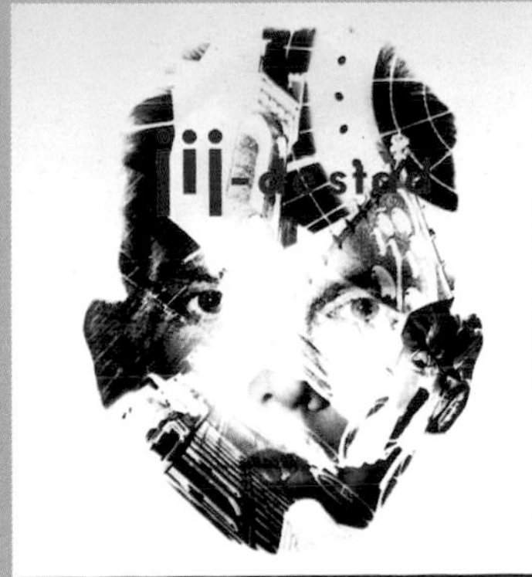
5/6 T/M 22/6'90
RESERVEREN 070-3543202

HET GEBEUREN
19 87/88
VEROLME

BIZARRE
symfonie

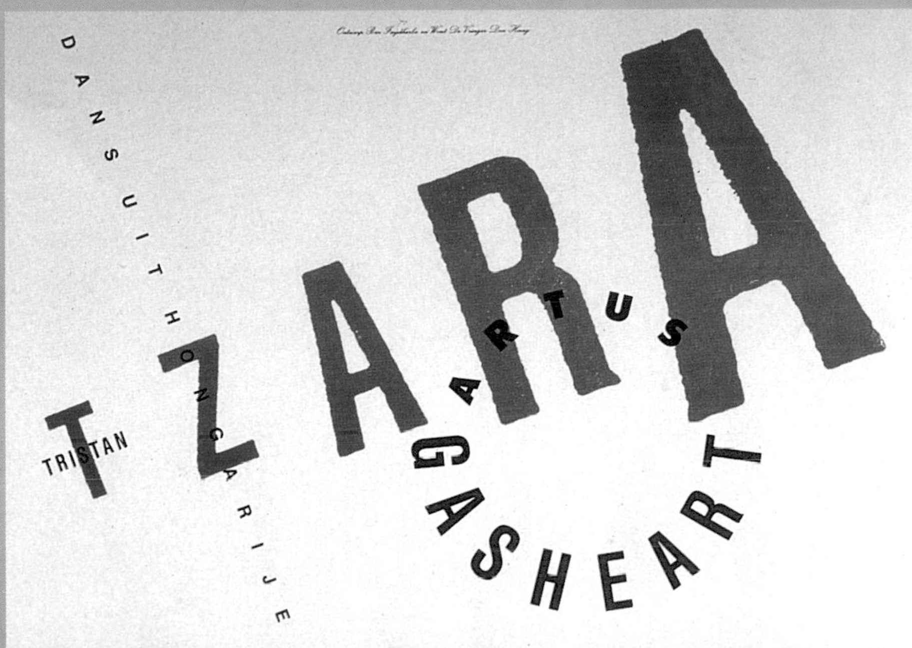
DANS UIT HONGARIJE
TRISTAN TZARA
ARTUS
GASHEART

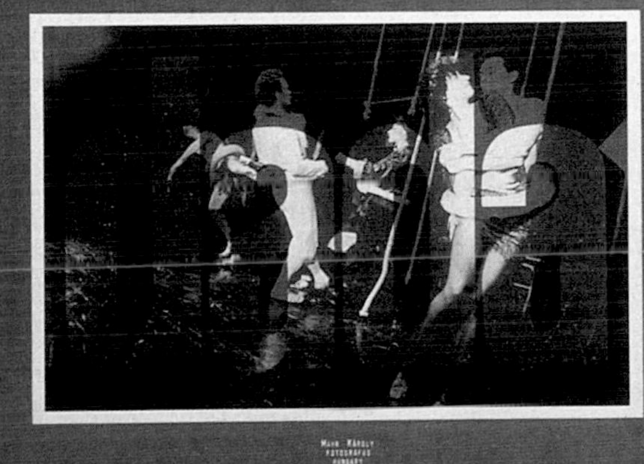
AMSTERDAM
SHAFFY
13 T/M 21 MEI
BEHALVE 15 MEI
AANVANG ALLE DAGEN 21.00 UUR
BEHALVE ZONDAG 17.00 UUR
[020] 231311
GRONINGEN
KRUITHUIS
23 EN 24 MEI
AANVANG 20.30 UUR
ROTTERDAM
LANTAREN
26 EN 27 MEI
AANVANG 21.00 UUR
[010] 4364998
GENT
VOORUIT
30 MEI
AANVANG 20.30 UUR
[091] 238201
DEN HAAG
HET GEBEUREN
THEATER AAN DE HAVEN
1 EN 2 JUNI
AANVANG 20.30 UUR
[070] 543202

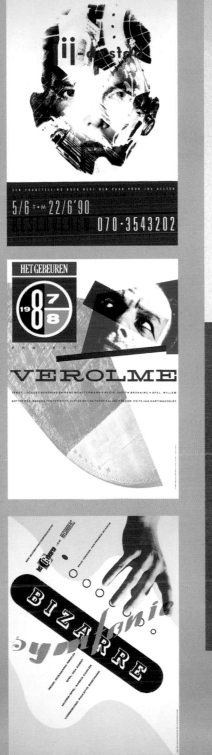

type personality

The variety of typeface designs makes different connections in our minds. We automatically associate personality characteristics to a typeface; for example, we say some fonts are authoritative while others are playful. The personalities we find in typography extend to our interpretation of the message a piece of text conveys. It also reflects the values of the person or organisation that has produced it. If the atmosphere value of a font has a consistent meaning with what the words actually say it is said to have congeniality. With poor congeniality, or inconsistency, a reader will respond slower to the text and may not accept the message. What is your reaction to the words below? Too much personality can be a bad thing and reduce legibility.

The personality of a typeface can add to the overall design effect, detract from it or have a neutral effect. To use fonts to their full advantage an awareness of typeface personality is therefore important.

CONTEMPORARY?

Monotype Gallia

A Monotype Classic Font with no accompanying lower case.

SERIOUS?

Playbill 1938 Robert Harling

Extra heavy slab serif typeface.

TRADITIONAL?

(above) Pop 1992 Neville Brody

A modern typeface referencing bitmap technology – anything but traditional.

(opposite) Trade Gothic 1948 J Burke

A very 19th-century design – apart from the lower case 'g', which isn't the single bowl variety you would expect.

T IS HARDLY POSSIBLE TO CREATE A GOOD TYPEFACE THAT WILL DIFFER RADICALLY FROM THE ESTABLISHED FORMS OF THE PAST

T IS STILL POSSIBLE TO SECURE NEW EXPRESSIONS OF LIFE AND VIGOUR

GOUDY

THE ONLY ART WHICH RECALLS ALL OTHERS

LEMOINE

THE MORE UNINTERESTING A LETTER, THE MORE USEFUL IT IS TO THE TYPOGRAPHER

ZWART

TYPE IS A UNIQUELY RICH SET OF MARKS BECAUSE IT MAKES LANGUAGE VISIBLE

KANE

LETTERS ARE THINGS, NOT PICTURES OF THINGS

GILL

TYPOGRAPHY IS NOT SELF-EXPRESSION

BAYER

A LOVE OF LETTERS IS THE BEGINNING OF TYPOGRAPHICAL WISDOM. THAT IS, THE LOVE OF LETTERS AS LITERATURE AND THE LOVE OF LETTERS AS PHYSICAL ENTITIES, HAVING ABSTRACT BEAUTY OF THEIR OWN, APART FROM THE IDEAS THEY MAY EXPRESS OR THE EMOTIONS THEY MAY EVOKE

BIGGS

USING THE WRONG FONT MAY GIVE PEOPLE THE WRONG IMPRESSION ABOUT YOU AND COULD AFFECT DECISIONS THAT WILL SHAPE YOUR FUTURE

DR SIGMAN

WE SHOULD WELCOME TYPOGRAPHIC VARIETY AS THE NATURAL CONSEQUENCE OF HUMAN CREATIVITY

CARTER

TYPOGRAPHY IS AN ART

FRUTIGER

A 10-LETTER WORD, PERFECTLY SPACED, PREFERABLY RANGED LEFT

PLACE

PEOPLE CHANGE SLOWLY

NIELSEN

CREATIVITY INVOLVES BREAKING OUT OF ESTABLISHED PATTERNS IN ORDER TO LOOK AT THINGS IN A DIFFERENT WAY

DE BONO

GRAPHIC DESIGN WILL SAVE THE WORLD RIGHT AFTER ROCK AND ROLL DOES

CARSON

I FIRST EXPERIENCED THE POWER OF TYPE TO MAKE THE WHOLE INTELLECTUAL WORLD READABLE WITH THE SAME LETTERS IN THE DAYS OF METAL. THIS AWAKENED IN ME THE URGE TO DEVELOP THE BEST POSSIBLE LEGIBILITY

FRUTIGER

SIMPLICITY, WHEN CARRIED TO AN EXTREME, BECOMES ELEGANCE

FRANKLIN

I AM SURE IN SOME YEARS FROM NOW YOU WILL SEE NEW POSTERS WITH JUST WHITE SPACE AND FOUR LINES IN GARAMOND

FRUTIGER

A PRINTED WORK WHICH CANNOT BE READ BECOMES A PRODUCT WITHOUT A PURPOSE

RUDER

O OTHER ART IS MORE JUSTIFIED HAN TYPOGRAPHY IN LOOKING HEAD TO FUTURE CENTURIES; OR THE CREATIONS OF YPOGRAPHY BENEFIT COMING ENERATIONS AS MUCH AS RESENT ONES

ODONI

LETTERING IN ITS WIDEST SENSE IS NOT MERELY ARTISTIC EXPRESSION WITH LETTERFORMS OR AN INSTRUMENT OF AESTHETIC VALUES; IT IS FIRST OF ALL A COMMUNICATION TOOL FOR THE EASIEST TRANSMISSION OF INFORMATION

ZAPF

UNIVERSAL

KELLY

TYPOGRAPHY IS THE ART OF ENDOWING HUMAN LANGUAGE WITH A DURABLE VISUAL FORM

BRINGHURST

GENIUS CULTIVATES FIELDS IN NEW WAYS

GOUDY

YOU CANNOT NOT COMMUNICATE

WATZLAWICK

CLEAR AND PRECISE SEEING BECOMES AS ONE WITH CLEAR AND PRECISE THINKING

TUFTE

TYPE, AFTER ALL, IS MERELY HANDWRITING DIVESTED OF THE EXIGENCIES AND ACCIDENTS OF THE SCRIBES

GOUDY

PICK GOOD ONES AND STICK TO THEM

DWIGGINS

WITH OVER 4000 TYPEFACES READILY AVAILABLE FOR THE COMPUTER WE SEEM TO BE SPOILT FOR CHOICE, BUT MOST OF THESE TYPEFACES WERE CREATED FOR A DIFFERENT SOCIETY WITH DIFFERENT THOUGHTS, WHICH IT NEEDED TO COMMUNICATE IN DIFFERENT WAYS TO OURSELVES

WOZENCROFT

SIMPLICITY IS GOOD, BUT SO IS PLURALITY

BRINGHURST

MADE THE THOUGHTS OF THE SOUL VISIBLE TO ALL

GOUDY

'GOOD DESIGN' TO A TYPOGRAPHER, MEANS A TYPEFACE DEVELOPED FROM AND BASED ON THE PRINCIPLES OF THE CLASSICAL ORIGINALS

FRUTIGER

PERSONAL TYPOGRAPHY IS DEFECTIVE TYPOGRAPHY. ONLY BEGINNERS AND FOOLS WILL INSIST ON USING IT

TSCHICHOLD

TYPE WHICH, THROUGH ANY ARBITRARY WARPING OF DESIGN OR EXCESS OF 'COLOUR' GETS IN THE WAY OF THE MENTAL PICTURE TO BE CONVEYED, IS BAD TYPE

WARDE

ANYONE WHO WOULD LETTERSPACE LOWER CASE WOULD STEAL SHEEP

GOUDY

IF A BOOK APPEARS TO BE ONLY A PAPER MACHINE, PRODUCED AT THEIR OWN CONVENIENCE BY OTHER MACHINES, ONLY MACHINES WILL WANT TO READ IT

BRINGHURST

g

AS I WRITE A GALLEY OF TYPE IS ON MY LEFT, A DRAWING BOARD AND ENGRAVING TOOLS ARE ON MY RIGHT, AND IT BECOMES IMPOSSIBLE TO THINK OF ONE WITHOUT THE OTHER

GIBBINGS

WEAR THE OLD COAT AND BUY THE NEW BOOK

PHELPS

INFORMATION PRESENTED WITH CLEAR AND LOGICALLY SET OUT TITLES, SUBTITLES, TEXTS AND ILLUSTRATIONS AND CAPTIONS WILL NOT ONLY BE READ MORE QUICKLY AND EASILY BUT THE INFORMATION WILL ALSO BE BETTER UNDERSTOOD AND RETAINED IN THE MEMORY

MÜLLER-BROCKMANN

NON-PRESENCE IS JUST AS IMPORTANT AS PRESENCE

FRUTIGER

TO WRITE/PRINT USING STANDARD ELEMENTS

FROSHAUG

THE MOST IMPORTANT THING I HAVE LEARNED IS THAT LEGIBILITY AND BEAUTY STAND CLOSE TOGETHER AND THAT TYPE DESIGN, IN ITS RESTRAINT, SHOULD BE ONLY FELT, BUT NOT PERCEIVED, BY THE READER

FRUTIGER

type as image

So far, we have addressed type primarily in relation to its principle function: using letters to communicate words. Type is also used as a symbol or icon that speaks more through its visual representation than the meanings of the constituent letters, although, of course, the fact that the letters may mean something gives an added significance to such an image. Logos are a common example of this. How do we associate a logo with a company? Is it through its visual statement or the letters that comprise it?

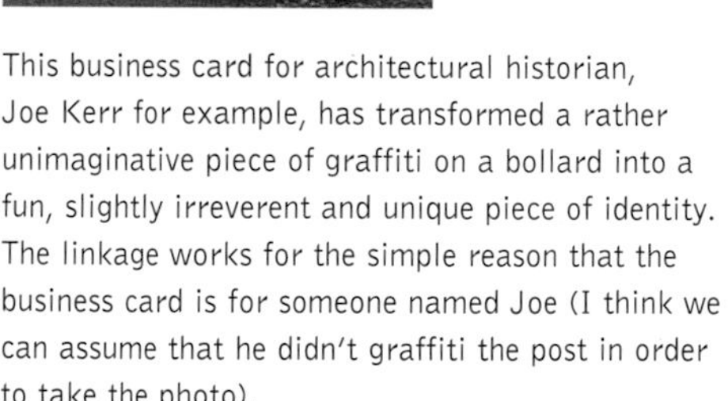

This business card for architectural historian, Joe Kerr for example, has transformed a rather unimaginative piece of graffiti on a bollard into a fun, slightly irreverent and unique piece of identity. The linkage works for the simple reason that the business card is for someone named Joe (I think we can assume that he didn't graffiti the post in order to take the photo).

Design: Studio Myerscough

For Portuguese wine, Herdade Do Peso, Lewis Moberly specifically cut into the typography to convey an authentic feel that is abetted by colour-coded full-length neck labels. These incorporate photos depicting the region's landscape in different seasons to differentiate the varieties.

Design: Lewis Moberly

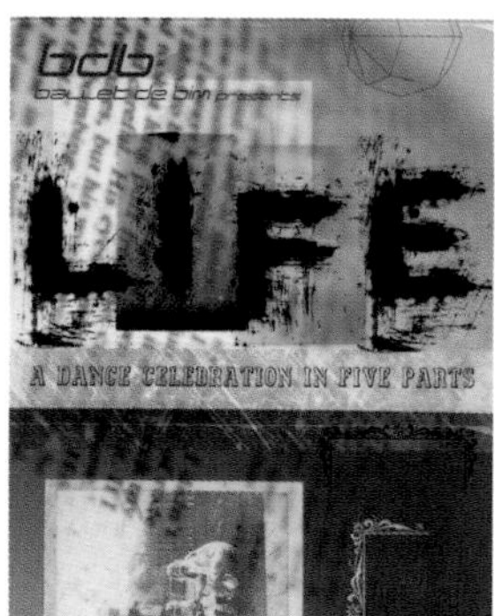

Craig Yamey chose an alphabet of rudimentary letters in this poster advertising a dance celebration event entitled Life. The slapdash urgency of the letters gives a sense of energy and vitality that perfectly matches the event's title.

Design: Craig Yamey

Type as image is powerful because it harnesses the emotion, energy and meaning that we associate with a given style or graphic with the extra element of communication of what the type says or represents. Our interpretation and translation of the type is moulded by the media in which it is made.

This is a poster designed by New York studio Sagmeister Inc. for AIGA Detroit. Richie Manic, of the Manic Street Preachers, famously cut the words 'for real' into his arm with a razorblade in answer to a journalist's question, 'Are you for real?', and Stefan Sagmeister chose to do likewise, asking an intern to cut the design into his skin to convey the pain that seems to accompany design projects. This is perhaps something that most interns feel like doing at some point during their internships and I wonder how quickly Sagmeister stopped thinking this was a good idea? The way the typographic elements are produced is so powerful and shocking that it functions more as image than type. The pen is mightier than the sword but for some penmanship, it seems that the sword rules.

Design: Sagmeister Inc.

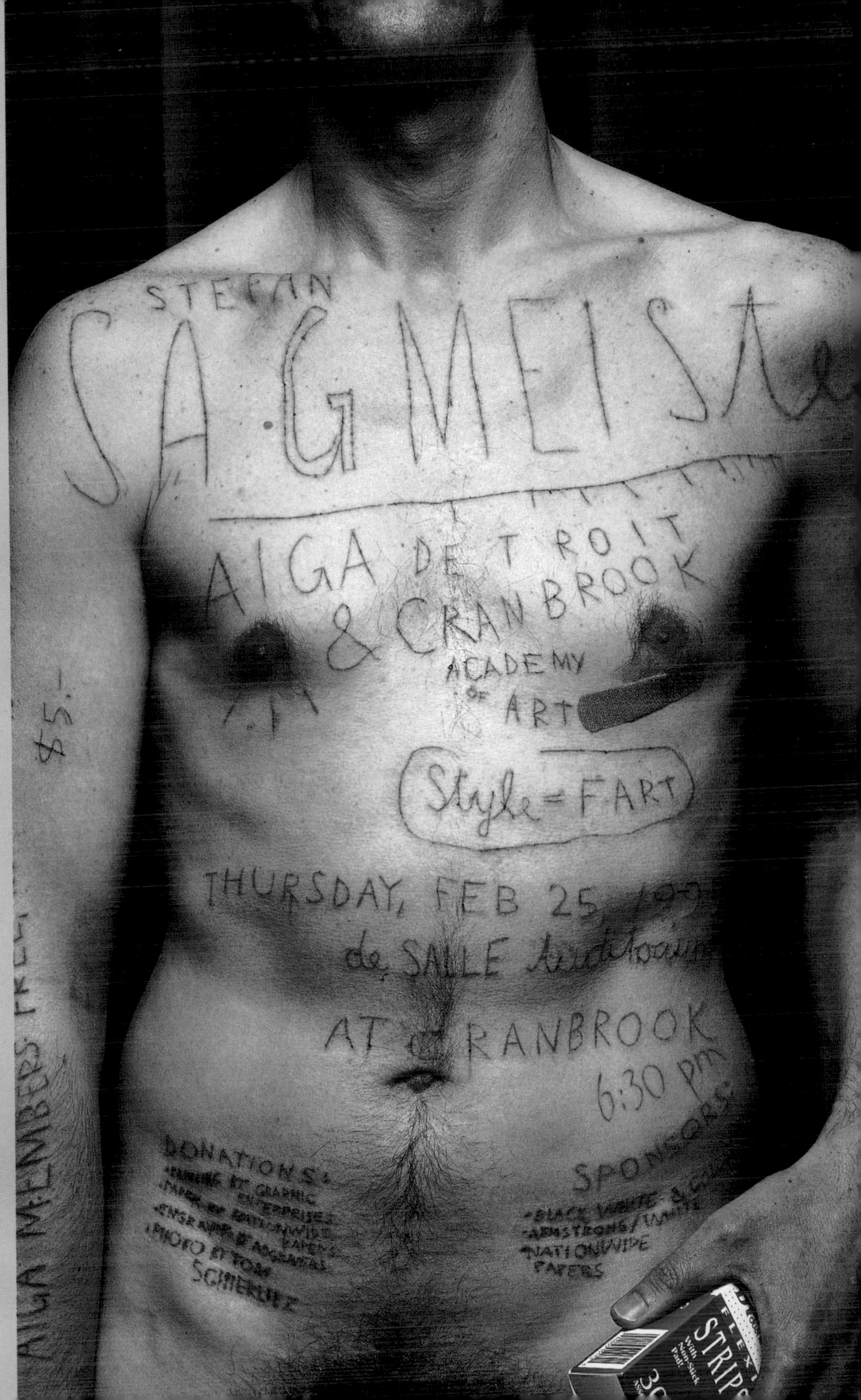

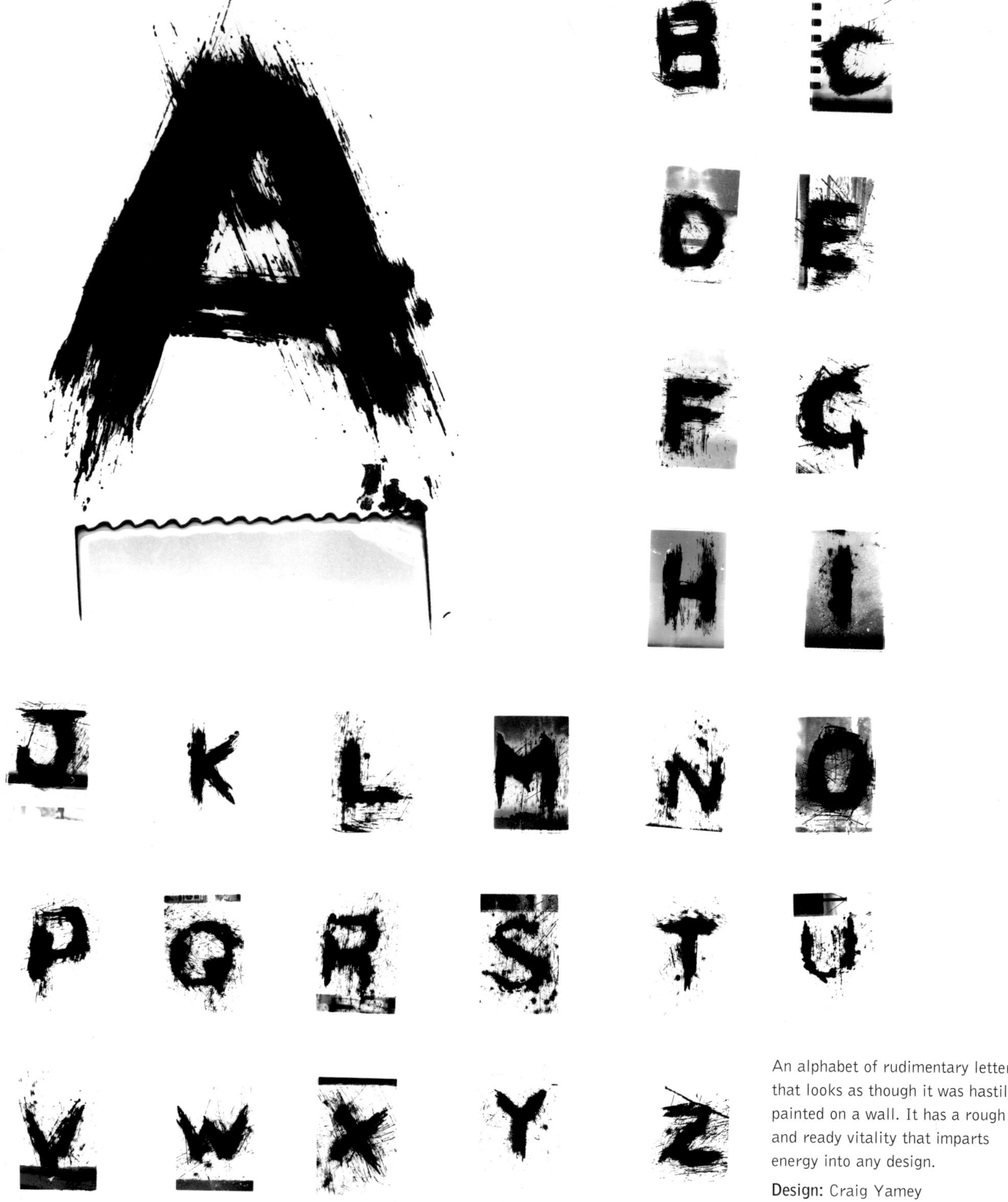

An alphabet of rudimentary letters that looks as though it was hastily painted on a wall. It has a rough and ready vitality that imparts energy into any design.

Design: Craig Yamey

Rectangular blocks or strips of tape? Either way, they are loosely arranged to form a colourful and interesting alphabet.

Design: Craig Yamey

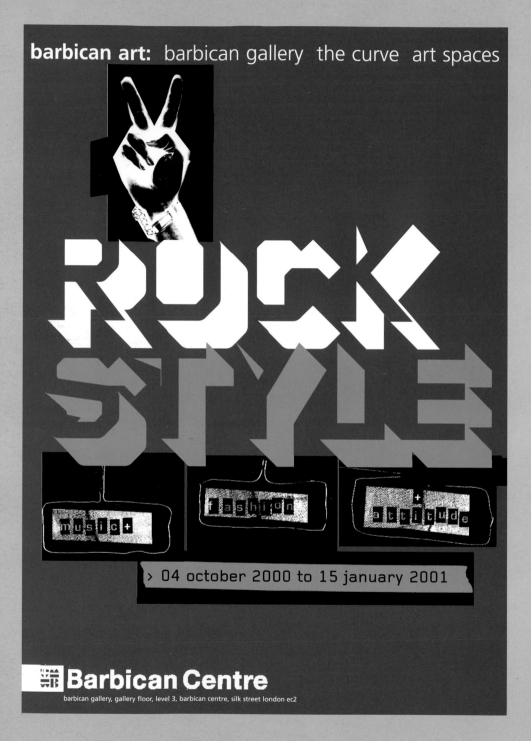

barbican art: barbican gallery the curve art spaces

ROCK STYLE

music + fashion + attitude

> 04 october 2000 to 15 january 2001

Barbican Centre

barbican gallery, gallery floor, level 3, barbican centre, silk street london ec2

Exhibition design and graphics for *Rock Style* exhibition at the Barbican Centre, London. The fanzine style of the design mimics the exhibition's content, with hand-drawn typography and collected ephemera forming an overall graphic style.

Design: Studio Myerscough

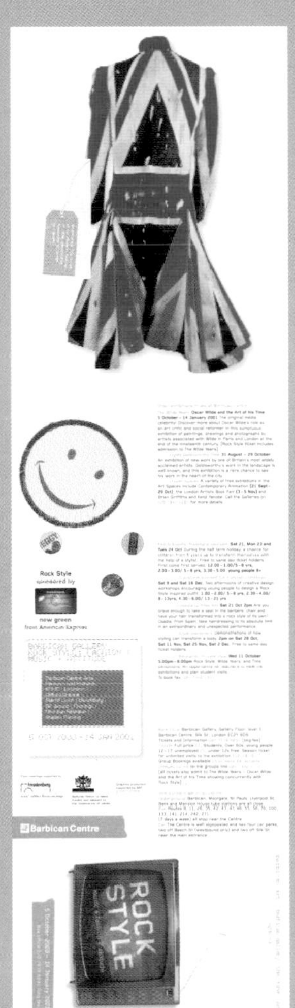
Rock Style
Barbican Centre
ROCK STYLE

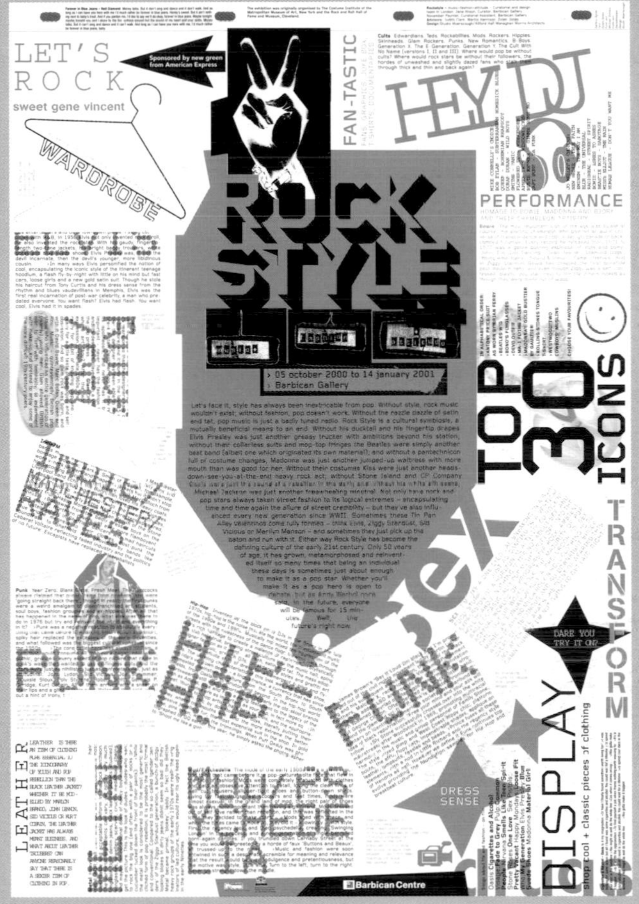
LET'S ROCK
sweet gene vincent
Sponsored by new green from American Express
WARDROBE
FAN-TASTIC
HEY DJ
PERFORMANCE
ROCK STYLE
05 october 2000 to 14 january 2001
Barbican Gallery
TOP 30 ICONS
TRANSFORM
DARE YOU TRY IT ON?
DISPLAY
shop cool + classic pieces of clothing
DRESS SENSE
PUNK
FUNK
LEATHER
Barbican Centre

classification systems

Typeface classification is one of the few occasions when it is appropriate to make judgements based on appearance. It is important to obtain an appreciation of how typefaces are classified, and the differences between them, in order to understand when best to use them. As there are many systems for classification this section will address the most commonly known classification classes, which may have several different names.

Loosely speaking, fonts are classified based on their characteristics. There are four basic categories of typefaces: Roman, Gothic, Script and Block (Sanders and McCormick, 1993). In general terms Roman is the class where we find all serif fonts; Gothic fonts are sans-serif; the Script category is for typefaces that mimic handwriting; and Blackletter is for fonts based on German manuscript handwriting.

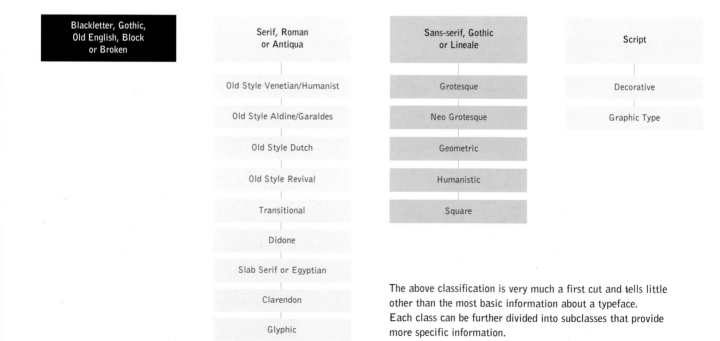

Blackletter, Gothic, Old English, Block or Broken

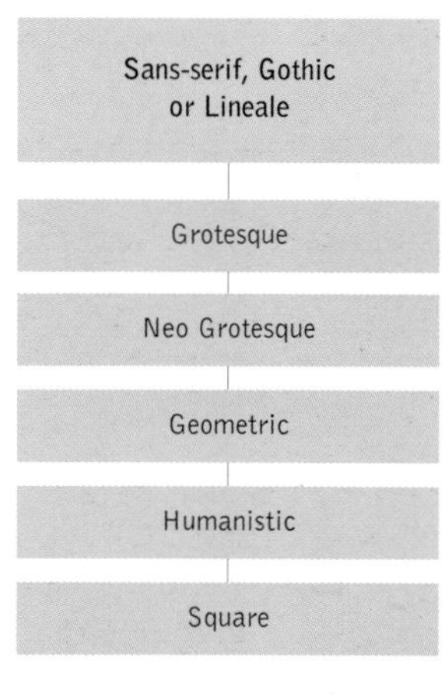

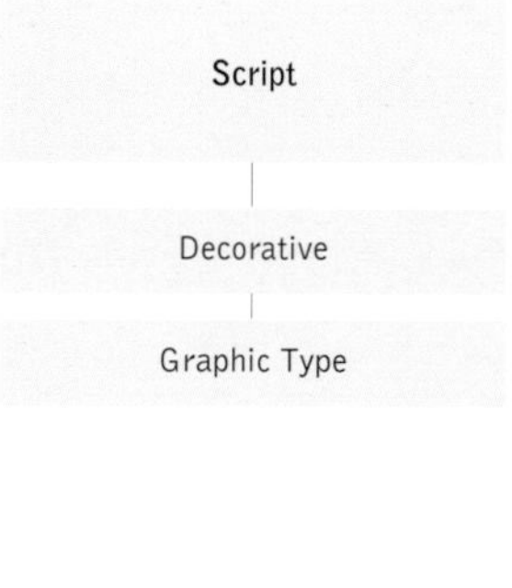

The above classification is very much a first cut and tells little other than the most basic information about a typeface. Each class can be further divided into subclasses that provide more specific information.

Blackletter is based on the heavy, ornate writing style prevalent during the Middles Ages. Due to the complexity of the letters they may be hard to read, particularly in blocks of text. They are commonly used for similar purposes as the Scripts, initial caps and on certificates. Recent research, however, found that legibility is linked to familiarity; and the sans-serif style of today would be equally illegible to Middle Age man.

Fraktur

Literally translated as broken writing, Fraktur was the prominent calligraphic style for centuries. Although no longer used for body copy this distinctive typeface conveys a feeling of historical importance.

Research has shown that the barely noticeable serifs greatly aid our recognition of the characters and help us to read by leading the eye across the line of text. For this reason body text is easier to read in a serif font.

Goudy Modern 1918 F W Goudy

Clear directional serifs create a legible font.

Sans-serifs, as the name suggests, do not have decorative touches that lead the eye and so, long passages in these typefaces are difficult to read. Their clean and simple design makes them ideal for display text such as headlines, captions and other non-body text uses.

Helvetica 1959 Max Miedinger

Typeface was formerly called Neue Haas Grotesk.

Script typefaces were designed to imitate handwriting

so that when printed the characters appear to be joined up. The writing implements they replicate range from a fountain pen to a paintbrush and as with handwriting, text should not be all in capitals. These fonts are commonly seen in short bursts such as on invitations, business cards and in advertisements.

Brody 1953 Harold Broderson

Very short descenders, with close fitting lower case letters.

Blackletter, Gothic, Old English, Black or Broken

ABCDEFGHIJKLMNOPQRSTUVWXYZ
abcdefghijklmnopqrstuvwxyz

Engravers Old English
Issued by the Monotype foundry.

ABCDEFGHIJKLMNOPQRSTUVWXYZ
abcdefghijklmnopqrstuvwxyz

Blackletter 686
Based on the earliest printing forms, which in turn were based on the scripture of books from Northern Europe.

Serif, Roman or Antiqua

Old style/Venetian

ABCDEFGHIJKLMNOPQRSTUVWXYZ
abcdefghijklmnopqrstuvwxyz

Schneidler 1936 Schneidler/Bauer/Neufville
Also known as Bauer Text.

ABCDEFGHIJKLMNOPQRSTUVWXYZ
abcdefghijklmnopqrstuvwxyz

Centaur 1929 Bruce Rogers
Derived from Janson's Roman.

Aldine

ABCDEFGHIJKLMNOPQRSTUVWXYZ
abcdefghijklmnopqrstuvwxyz

Sabon 1967 Jan Tschichold
Inspired by the designs of Claude Garamond.

ABCDEFGHIJKLMNOPQRSTUVWXYZ
abcdefghijklmnopqrstuvwxyz

Garamond 1499–1561 Claude Garamond
Based on earlier designs of Aldus Manutius.

Dutch

ABCDEFGHIJKLMNOPQRSTUVWXYZ
abcdefghijklmnopqrstuvwxyz

Janson 1937 Nicholas Kis
A typeface that has been misnamed, as it was believed to be cut by Anton Janson.

ABCDEFGHIJKLMNOPQRSTUVWXYZ
abcdefghijklmnopqrstuvwxyz

Caslon 1725 William Caslon
Numerous type foundries now issue a version of this popular font, originally styled on Dutch designs of the 17th century.

Old style/Revivals

ABCDEFGHIJKLMNOPQRSTUVWXYZ
abcdefghijklmnopqrstuvwxyz

Cooper Black 1924 O B Cooper
Distinctive 'blurred' serifs create a face that is both retrospective and contemporary. Unusual for its convex serifs.

ABCDEFGHIJKLMNOPQRSTUVWXYZ
abcdefghijklmnopqrstuvwxyz

Windsor 1903 Stephenson & Blake
A display type with beak-like serifs on most characters while the capital 'M' is slabbed.

Transitionals

ABCDEFGHIJKLMNOPQRSTUVWXYZ
abcdefghijklmnopqrstuvwxyz

Baskerville 1706–1757 John Baskerville
Ever-popular font, with a distinctive absence of a middle serif on the 'W'.

ABCDEFGHIJKLMNOPQRSTUVWXYZ
abcdefghijklmnopqrstuvwxyz

Perpetua 1928 Eric Gill
Unusually the accompanying italic to Perpetua is named differently; it is known as Felicity.

Didone

ABCDEFGHIJKLMNOPQRSTUVWXYZ
abcdefghijklmnopqrstuvwxyz

Bodoni 1790 Giambattista Bodoni

Originally cut over 200 years ago, the Bodoni typefaces have been recut by several foundries. This version was cut by Morris Fuller Benton for American Type Founders between 1908 and 1915.

ABCDEFGHIJKLMNOPQRSTUVWXYZ
abcdefghijklmnopqrstuvwxyz

Didot 1784 Firmin Didot

Standard typeface employed by French literature during the 19th century.

Clarendon

ABCDEFGHIJKLMNOPQRSTUVWXYZ
abcdefghijklmnopqrstuvwxyz

Cheltenham 1896 Morris Fuller Benton/Bertram G Goodhue

Designed with exaggerated ascenders and descenders following studies of legibility of typefaces that found readers scanned using the tops of letters.

ABCDEFGHIJKLMNOPQRSTUVWXYZ
abcdefghijklmnopqrstuvwxyz

Bookman 1925 Ludlow

Large x-height font retains legibility at smaller sizes.

Neo Clarendon

ABCDEFGHIJKLMNOPQRSTUVWXYZ
abcdefghijklmnopqrstuvwxyz

Clearface 1907 M F Benton
Originally designed as a display face.

ABCDEFGHIJKLMNOPQRSTUVWXYZ
abcdefghijklmnopqrstuvwxyz

Century Old Style 1906 M F Benton
Morris Fuller Benton was one of the most prolific type designers in the United States, designing in excess of 170 fonts.

Clarendon/Legibility

ABCDEFGHIJKLMNOPQRSTUVWXYZ
abcdefghijklmnopqrstuvwxyz

Corona 1941 Chauncey H Griffith
Designed for use in newspapers, this font has large counters to prevent 'fill in'.

ABCDEFGHIJKLMNOPQRSTUVWXYZ
abcdefghijklmnopqrstuvwxyz

Modern Bold Introduced by Stephenson Blake circa 1850
Quintessential English typeface with fine serifs and detailed hairlines. One of the few mid 19th-century typefaces still in use today.

Glyphic

ABCDEFGHIJKLMNOPQRSTUVWXYZ
abcdefghijklmnopqrstuvwxyz

Albertus 1932 Berthold Wolpe
Sloped bar widths create a distinctive typeface.

ABCDEFGHIJKLMNOPQRSTUVWXYZ
abcdefghijklmnopqrstuvwxyz

Lucian 1925 Lucian Bernhard
Exaggerated ascenders and a distinctive upper and lower case 'Q'.

Slab Serif/Egyptian

ABCDEFGHIJKLMNOPQRSTUVWXYZ
abcdefghijklmnopqrstuvwxyz

Aachen 1969 Colin Brignall
Designed as a header font with closely spaced lettering.

ABCDEFGHIJKLMNOPQRSTUVWXYZ
abcdefghijklmnopqrstuvwxyz

Lubalin Graph 1974 Herb Lubalin
Essentially a slab-serif interpretation of Avant Garde.

Sans-serif, Gothic or Lineale

Sans-serif/Grotesque

ABCDEFGHIJKLMNOPQRSTUVWXYZ
abcdefghijklmnopqrstuvwxyz

News Gothic 1908 M F Benton

In 1968 F Bartuska cut additional weights to compliment the original design.

ABCDEFGHIJKLMNOPQRSTUVWXYZ
abcdefghijklmnopqrstuvwxyz

Franklin Gothic 1904 M F Benton

Franklin Gothic is now available in italic, bold, wide and condensed, but has never been issued as a light.

Sans-serif/Neo Grotesque

ABCDEFGHIJKLMNOPQRSTUVWXYZ
abcdefghijklmnopqrstuvwxyz

Akzidenz Grotesk 1896 H Berthold

Popular with Swiss designers in the 1950s Akzidenz Grotesk was the inspiration for modern sans-serifs such as Univers and Helvetica.

ABCDEFGHIJKLMNOPQRSTUVWXYZ
abcdefghijklmnopqrstuvwxyz

Folio 1957 K F Bauer

A 19th-century sans-serif, also known as 'Caravelle', with the distinctive spurred 'G' and 'square' 'M'.

Sans-serif/Geometric

ABCDEFGHIJKLMNOPQRSTUVWXYZ
abcdefghijklmnopqrstuvwxyz

Metro No.2 Black 1929 W A Dwiggins
Distinguishable from the No.1 series by the splayed 'M', 'N', 'V' and 'W'.

ABCDEFGHIJKLMNOPQRSTUVWXYZ
abcdefghijklmnopqrstuvwxyz

Twentieth Century 1930 S Hess
Similar in its proportions to Futura.

Sans-serif/Humanist

ABCDEFGHIJKLMNOPQRSTUVWXYZ
abcdefghijklmnopqrstuvwxyz

Optima Bold 1958 Herman Zapf
The strokes thicken towards the ends creating a distinctive splayed appearance.

ABCDEFGHIJKLMNOPQRSTUVWXYZ
abcdefghijklmnopqrstuvwxyz

Gill Sans 1928 Eric Gill
Considered by many to be the most 'readable' sans-serif, probably due to it being derived from classical serif cuts.

Sans-serif/Square

ABCDEFGHIJKLMNOPQRSTUVWXYZ
abcdefghijklmnopqrstuvwxyz

Agency 1933 M F Benton
Square style font.

ABCDEFGHIJKLMNOPQRSTUVWXYZ
abcdefghijklmnopqrstuvwxyz

Eurostile 1962 A Novarese
Designed as a compliment to Microgramma, which had no lower case.

Script

ABCDEFGHIJKLMNOPQRSTUVWXYZ
abcdefghijklmnopqrstuvwxyz

Pushkin
Based on the handwriting of Russian poet Alexander Sergeevich Pushkin (1799–1837).

ABCDEFGHIJKLMNOPQRSTUVWXYZ
abcdefghijklmnopqrstuvwxyz

Coronet Robert Hunter Middleton
Ornate script font.

ONE FURTHER GENERAL CATEGORY NEEDS MENTIONING CALLED SYMBOL, DECORATIVE, DISPLAY, EXPERIMENTAL OR GRAPHIC THAT ENCOMPASSES TYPEFACES THAT CANNOT BE ASSIGNED TO THE OTHER CLASSIFICATIONS.

Stencil 1937 Gerry Powell
Utilitarian packaging-inspired typeface that comes only in upper case.

Symbol

Textile 1998 Elsner+Flake

Symbol font used for clothing label information.

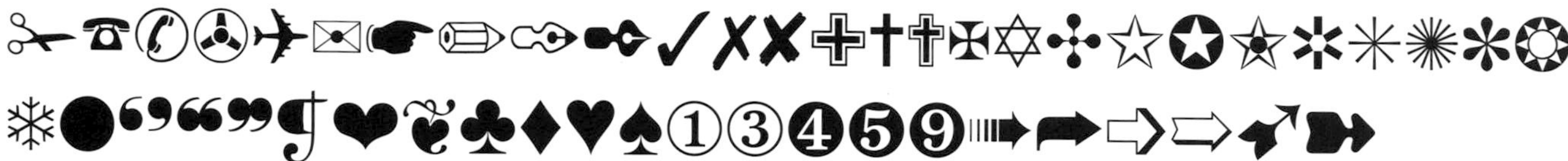

Zapf Dingbats 1978 Hermann Zapf

Designed to compliment contemporary typefaces, several traditional symbols are given a modern interpretation including the dagger and the pilcrow.

Decorative

ABCDEFGHIJKLMNOPQRSTUVWXYZ
ABCDEFGHIJKLMNOPQRSTUVWXYZ

Rosewood 1994 Kim Buker Chansler, Carl Crossgrove and Carol Twombly

Ornate circus-inspired decorative typeface.

ABCDEFGHIJKLMNOPQRSTUVWXYZ
abcdefghijklmnopqrstuvwxyz

Bell Bottom

Evocative of 1960's poster designs, this decorative display font is only suitable when used at larger sizes.

Experimental

ABCDEFGHIJKLMNOPQRSTUVWXYZ
abcdefghijklmnopqrstuvwxyz

Barnbrook Gothic Jonathan Barnbrook

Jonathan Barnbrook has issued experimental and cult fonts under the Virus banner since 1997.

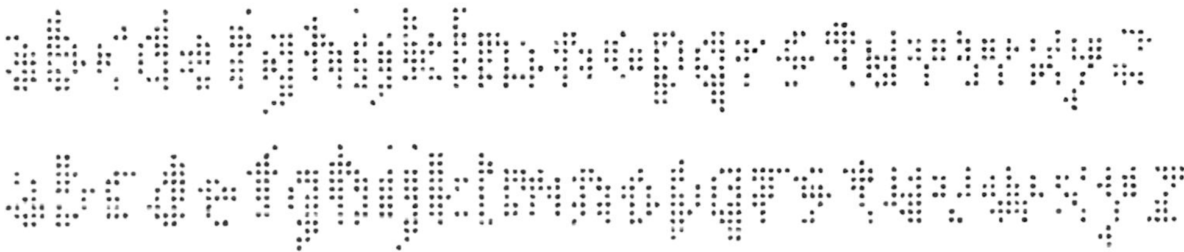

Flixel Just van Rossum

A font questioning the link between legibility and communication.

Graphic

ABCDEFGHIJKLMNOPQRSTUVWXYZ
abcdefghijklmnopqrstuvwxyz

AG Book Stencil 1985 Günter Gerhard Lange

Industrial crating stencil-inspired font.

ABCDEFGHIJKLMNOPQRSTUVWXYZ
abcdefghijklmnopqrstuvwxyz

American Typewriter 1974 Joel Kaden and Tony Stan

Font designed to replicate the appearance of hand-typed text.

Display

ABCDEFGHIJKLMNOPQRSTUVWXYZ
abcdefghijklmnopqrstuvwxyz

Bodoni Poster 1907 onwards G Bodoni
Verticals are hairline with serifs that are both straight and unbracketted forming a very mathematical typeface.

ABCDEFGHIJKLMNOPQRSTUVWXYZ
abcdefghijklmnopqrstuvwxyz

Avant Garde 1970 Herb Lubalin and Tom Carnase
Redrawn from the masthead of *Avante Garde* magazine.

Optical Character Recognition

ABCDEFGHIJKLMNOPQRSTUVWXYZ
abcdefghijklmnopqrstuvwxyz

OCRA 1968 ATE
Designed to meet the requirements of the European Computer Manufacturers Association (ECMA).

ABCDEFGHIJKLMNOPQRSTUVWXYZ
abcdefgh jk mnopqrstuvwxyz

OCRB 1968 Adrian Frutiger
Optical Character Recognition is used, amongst other things, for enabling text to be scanned and reformatted into live text files.

OCRB

Characters are shaped to be unmistakable, hence the exaggerated serif on the lower case 'i', and the curved tail of the 'l' – two letters that are easily confused. The font is also designed to be robust enough to cope with poor quality reproduction via fax transmission.

Faydherbe/De Vringer design studio firmly believes that combining text and images should equal more than the sum of their parts. For the Dutch design studio, typography has a visual role to play that is as important as its verbal communication role. The use of typography has a strong and distinctive visual element obtained by feeling what works dramatically to make an effect better.

These film posters were designed in the 1990s before the studio had computers. Type was selected and copied from typeface manuals from the 1920s and 1930s. The intention was to come up with type that no one else was using to give an original feeling to the work. **'Type is used more to add information now,'** says partner Wout de Vringer, **'rather than to make a piece look a certain way. There is a feeling that the image should do the work nowadays.'**

Typography is styled to provide extra meaning to the words. The dramatic angle and diminishing perspective in the 'Cinema Express' poster is intended to give the impression of speed. The angles in 'Film Architectuur' is to give a sense of building. With the use of four colour less prevalent than it is today designers tried to squeeze as much flexibility as possible from two-colour print runs by a combination of overprinting and separations.

Design: Faydherbe/De Vringer

10
t/m
30
december
1992
M·G·M Jaren '40
musicals

DE HAAGSE FILMSTICHTING
PRESENTEERT
CINEMATHEMA '89
VAN 3 T/M 30 NOVEMBER
de Europese Muziekfilm

DE HAAGSE FILMSTICHTING PRESENTEERT
CINEMATHEMA '8
film fashion
28 DECEMBER

DE HAAGSE FILMSTICHTING PRESENTEERT I. S. M. DE N.V. NEDERLANDSE SPOORWEGEN
CINEMA
EXPRESS
2|3 T|M 5|4|89
DE TREIN IN DE SPEELFILM

Cinematheek HAAGS FILMHUIS
presenteert:

EUROSCOPE
Festival
Europese Cinemascope Films
Reserveren na 13.00 uur
(zaterdag na 18.00 uur)
Spui 191
2511 BN Den Haag
(070) 365 60 30
3 nov
T/M
7 dec
1994

special characters

An alphabet alone is not enough to be able to structure textural information or communicate phonetic stresses and the infinite number of ideas and propositions that we want to. For this we need various special characters. Punctuation enables us to qualify, quantify and organise information; accents provide us with information about how a letter is stressed or sounded; and pictograms provide shorthand information such as currency units.

Punctuation

'	apostrophe
,	comma
( )	parenthesis
{ }	braces
[ ]	square brackets
-	hyphen
–	en dash
—	em dash
_	lowline/underscore
:	colon
;	semicolon
/	solidus
\	backslash
...	ellipsis
! ¡	exclamation
¿?	question mark
>	greater than
<	less than
« »	guillemets
'	prime
"	double prime
" "	double quotes
' '	single quotes

Points

˙	overdot
·	midpoint
.	period
•	bullet

Characters

+	addition
-	subtraction
x	multiplication
÷	division
%	per cent
‰	per million
#	octothorp/hash
=	equal
°	degree
°	ring

Accents

´	acute
	(á, é, í, ó, ú)
	(Á, É, Í, Ó, Ú)
`	grave
	(à, è, ì, ò, ù)
	(À, È, Ì, Ò, Ù)
¨	umlaut/dieresis
	(ä, ë, ï, ö, ü)
	(Ä, Ë, Ï, Ö, Ü)
ˆ	circumflex
	(â, ê, î, ô, û)
	(Â, Ê, Î, Ô, Û)
˜	tilde
	(ã, ñ, õ)
	(Ã, Ñ, Õ)
˘	breve
¸	cedilla
	(ç)

Pictograms

*	asterisk
¶	pilcrow
ß	eszett
Æ	aesc
¥	yen
£	sterling
$	dollar
€	euro
@	at
™	trademark
©	copyright
&	ampersand
†	dagger
‡	double dagger
§	section
Ω	omega
∞	infinity
☞	fist

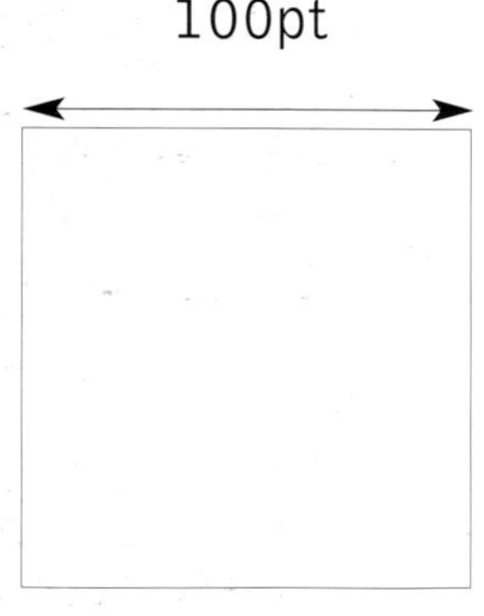

14pt

An em is a unit of measure equal to the width and height of the point size of the type being set. So 14pt type, uses an em of 14pts. The term originates from when type was cast in metal and the letter 'M' was cast on a square body. Nowadays, with computer-generated typefaces, the letter 'M' now has no relation to the em measurement.

An en is a measurement that follows the same origins as the em and is equal to half the point size of a typeface.

A hyphen is typically one-third of the length of the em. The typographic use of these characters varies widely and they are often confused. A hyphen is used to separate parts of compound words, to link the words of a phrase and to connect syllables of a word that is split between separate lines. Em rules and en rules are used to delineate nested clauses in a sentence. Em rules are typically preferred in the USA, with the letters of preceding and succeeding words closed up. The en rule is typically preferred in Europe with a space either side of it.

Knoël

frutiger's grid

Adrian Frutiger is prominent in the pantheon of typeface designers due to the many typefaces he has created but in particular the Univers family, launched in 1957 by Deberny & Peignot.

A key reason for its success was the numbering system he developed to identify the width and weight of each of the family's 21 original cuts. There are in excess of 50 members now following revisions and extensions to this family, some of which are shown on the opposite page. His achievement with Univers is not confined to providing a wide range of typefaces.

The diagrammatic presentation of the Univers typeface family by Frutiger provides a sense of order and homogeneity through the relationships of weight and width they have with each other. This grid provided a visual key and a standard that subsequent typeface designers have been able to use to devise and shape their own families.

This system has since been adopted by other type producers as can be seen with this example of Helvetica Neue.

Helvetica

Designed by Max Miedinger in 1959 for the Haas type foundry it became one of the dominant typefaces of the 1960s. This typeface was formerly called Neue Haas Grotesk.

Designed with an 'anonymous' character in the modernist style.

Helvetica Neue 95

Helvetica Neue 85

Helvetica Neue 75

Helvetica Neue 65

Helvetica Neue 55

Helvetica Neue 45

Helvetica Neue 35

Helvetica Neue 25

Adrian Frutiger is an internationally renowned typographer who as well as creating many typefaces has created house styles for various international organisations and is credited with creating the complete public signage system for the Charles de Gualle airport, Paris.

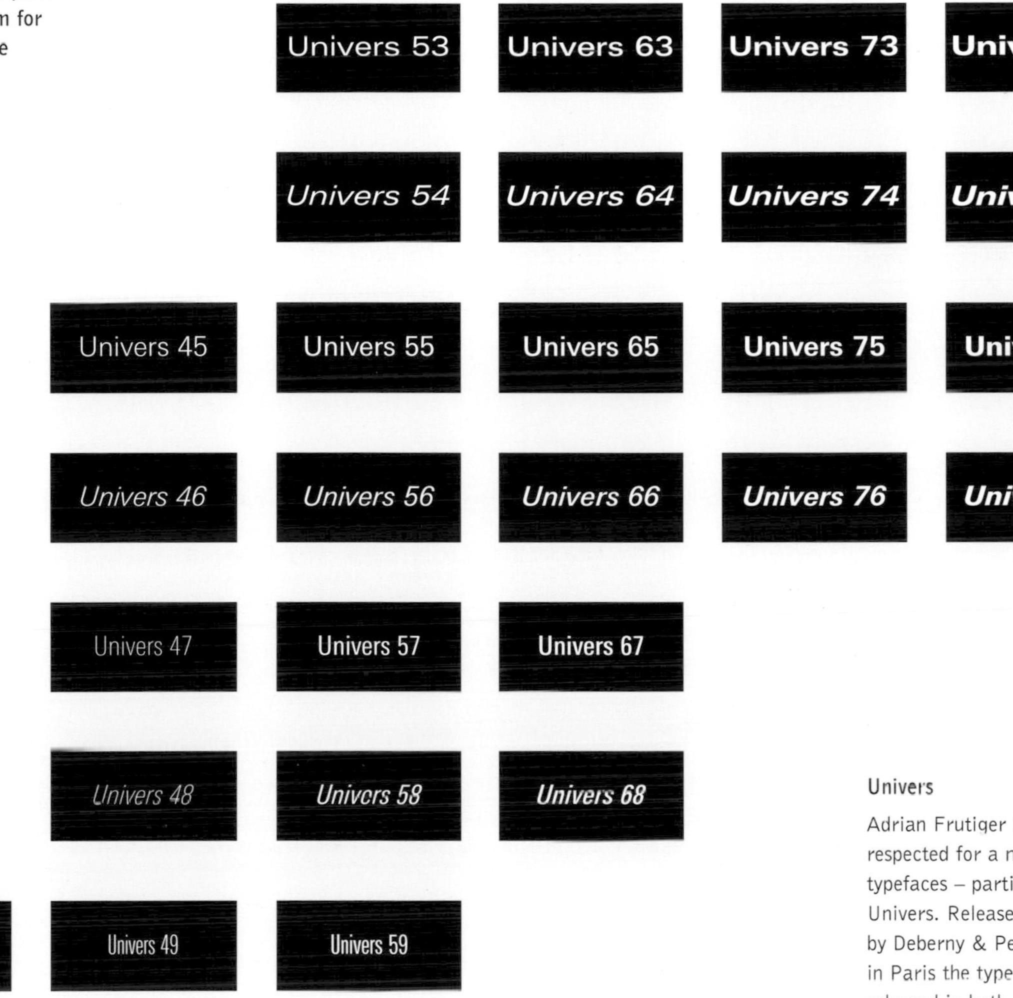

Univers

Adrian Frutiger is well respected for a number of typefaces – particularly Univers. Released in 1957 by Deberny & Peignot foundry in Paris the typeface was released in both metal and photo type.

Frutiger subsequently used this system for other typefaces; Serifa, Glypha, Frutiger, Avenir etc.

Other type manufacturers have since adopted this system as can be seen with Helvetica Neue.

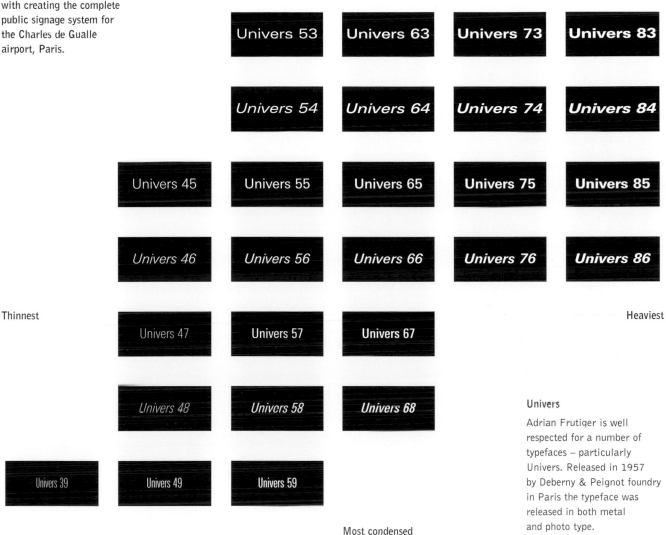

extended type families

An extended type family is all the variations of a particular typeface or font. It includes all the different weights, widths and italics. Examples of family names include Univers, Times Roman, Arial and Garamond. Many type families are named after their creator or the publication in which they were first used.

Type families are a useful design tool because they offer a designer a range of variations that work together in a clean and consistent way. To achieve clarity and a uniform feel to a piece of work, many designers restrict themselves to using only two type families for a project, meeting their requirements from the type variations these contain to establish the typographic hierarchy.

From the six examples of the Officina family on the opposite page you can pick out typefaces for use as titles, body text and captions, for example.

ABCDEFGHIJKLMNOPQRSTUVWXYZ
abcdefghijklmnopqrstuvwxyz 1234567890

ABCDEFGHIJKLMNOPQRSTUVWXYZ
abcdefghijklmnopqrstuvwxyz 1234567890

Rotis 1989 Otl Aicher
A font that offers many weights with interchangeable serifs.

The Sans The Mix

The Sans/The Mix 1994–1999 Luc(as) de Groot
Font(s) that offer a great range of weights and serif options.

ABCDEFGHIJKLMNOPQRSTUVWXYZ
abcdefghijklmnopqrstuvwxyz 1234567890

ABCDEFGHIJKLMNOPQRSTUVWXYZ
abcdefghijklmnopqrstuvwxyz 1234567890

ABCDEFGHIJKLMNOPQRSTUVWXYZ
abcdefghijklmnopqrstuvwxyz 1234567890

ABCDEFGHIJKLMNOPQRSTUVWXYZ
abcdefghijklmnopqrstuvwxyz 1234567890

ABCDEFGHIJKLMNOPQRSTUVWXYZ
abcdefghijklmnopqrstuvwxyz 1234567890

ABCDEFGHIJKLMNOPQRSTUVWXYZ
abcdefghijklmnopqrstuvwxyz 1234567890

Officina (top to bottom; Sans Book, Sans Book Italic, Sans Bold, Serif Book, Serif Book Italic, Serif Bold) 1990 Erik Spiekermann
Originally designed for use on office documentation and stationery.

type detailing

Typefaces vary in many ways. Some have serifs, some do not. Letter spacing is not the most obvious characteristic that springs to mind when specifying a typeface but in certain applications it is of prime concern. Letter spacing is the space that a letter occupies – a typeface is either monospaced or proportionally spaced.

Monospaced type

Each character in a monospaced typeface occupies the same width irrespective of its actual size. These typefaces were originally used on typewriters. They enable text that lines up in vertical columns to be easily produced such as for invoices. Courier is a common monospaced typeface in the personal computer age.

Monospaced
ffffffffff
. . . .
, , , , , , , , , ,

Proportionally spaced type

A system of proportional spacing was used by the Monotype and Linotype print foundries because it mimics the letter spacing of historical handset forms. Individual characters occupy a space proportional to their size.

Proportionally spaced
ffffffffffffffffffffff
....
,,,,,,,,,,,,,,,,,,,,,,

Lining numerals

The majority of typefaces contain a set of lining numerals, characters that have equal height and equal, or monospaced, widths. Monospaced characters allow numerals to be vertically aligned, which is important for tabular information such as accounts, and because they are the same height they are easy to read.

2,341,536,685.00
153,687,145.18
515,598.89

Old style numerals

Sometimes called lower case numerals, they have different heights that can make them more difficult to read.

2,341,536,685.00

Non-aligning numerals

These characters occupy widths proportional to their size making them unsuitable for presenting tabular information.

2,341,536,685.00
153,687,145.18
515,598.89

Type sizes

Type obviously gets bigger as you increase the type size, but because typefaces have different weights some appear to be bigger than others when they are at the same point size.

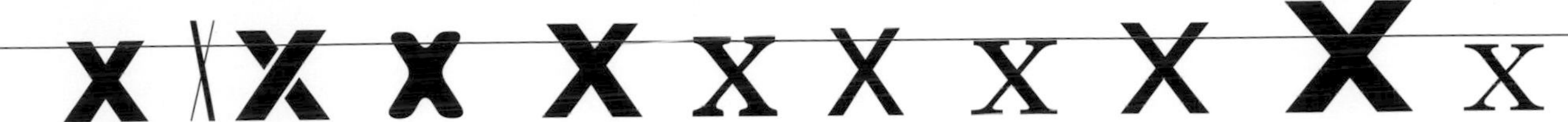

Meanline
Baseline
x-height

x-height

The x-height is not a fixed measurement. It is not even related to the point size of a given typeface. All the Xs above are set in 50 point type yet some are bigger than others. The x-height is a relative measurement that refers to the distance between the baseline and the meanline.

Palatino

Palatino

GENERATED SMALL CAPS

TRUE SMALL CAPS

Italics and obliques

The italic font for some typefaces is produced by inclining the Roman font. This is really an oblique (below). A true italic, such as Palatino, is essentially a redrawn typeface (above). Note the difference in the letter 'a'.

Helvetica Roman

Helvetica Italic

Small caps

True small caps have characters that are rendered at the same weight. Small caps generated by typesetting programs are not.

1/6 3/4 1/4 3/8

$^1/_6$ $^3/_4$ $^1/_4$ $^3/_8$

$\frac{1}{6}$ $\frac{3}{4}$ $\frac{1}{4}$ $\frac{3}{8}$

Fractions

Fractions can be presented in different ways. Fractions commonly appear as unset fractions when you type the numerals on your computer (above, top row). Em fractions (above, middle row) are created using superscript and subscript numerals separated by a solidus (slash). Nut fractions are normally pre-generated within a typeface (above, bottom row).

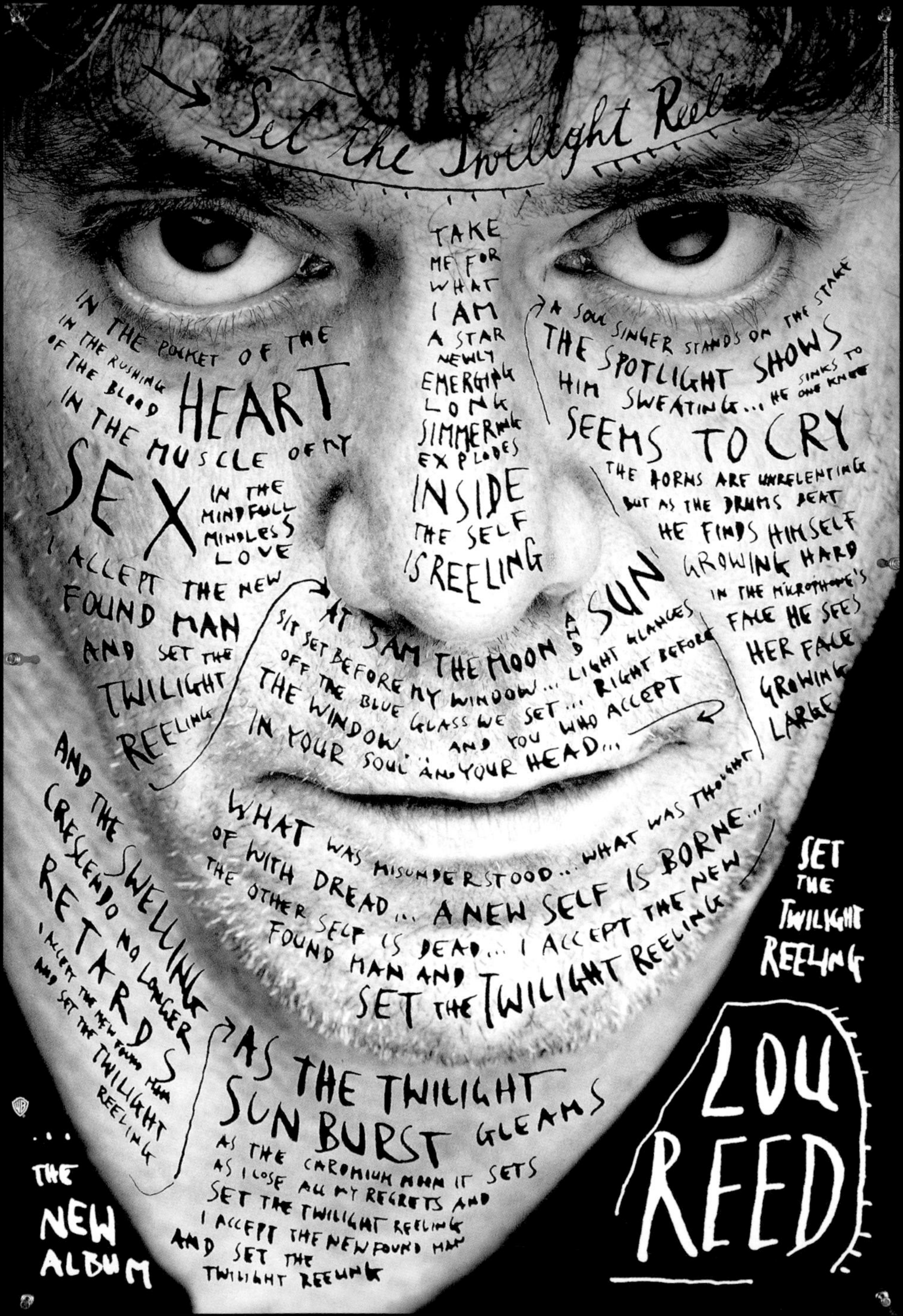

The songs on Lou Reed's *Set the Twilight Reeling* album have extremely personal lyrics. New York design studio Sagmeister Inc. took this as the starting point for its design for the album's cover by writing them directly over his face. The handwritten script, tailored to the contours of his face, adds to the impression of intimacy and almost looks as though it has been tattooed so that Lou Reed bares his soul visually as well as aurally.

Design: Sagmeister Inc.

See Type as image

ADVERTISING

DESIGN

THERE'S NOT MUCH DIFFERENCE BETWEEN ADVERTISING AND DESIGN. A TALK BY MICHAEL JOHNSON, JOHNSON BANKS

In this poster for a seminar discussing the similarities between Advertising and Design, the two words are overlaid to confirm how similar these disciplines really are.

Design: Johnson Banks

See Tracking

Formatting

The way a piece of text is formatted can result in many different and striking visual results as these examples show. From simply inserting a drop cap to utilising different weights of a font and the various types of indentation – running, hanging and off-a-point – to give structure, hierarchy or meaning, the techniques are simple but can have a dramatic impact on the way a piece of text is presented. Rules can also be used effectively to organise text and shepherd a readers' attention.

The way a piece of text is formatted can result in many different and striking visual results as these examples show.

From simply inserting a drop cap to utilising different weights of a font and the various types of indentation – running, hanging and off-a-point – to give structure, hierarchy or meaning, the techniques are simple but can have a dramatic impact on the way a piece of text is presented.

Rules can also be used effectively to organise text and shepherd a readers' attention.

Range Left, Ragged Right. 7pt type on 10pt leading. Set solid. Hard returns (above).

The way a piece of text is formatted can result in many different and striking visual results as these examples show.

From simply inserting a drop cap to utilising different weights of a font and the various types of indentation – running, hanging and off-a-point – to give structure, hierarchy or meaning, the techniques are simple but can have a dramatic impact on the way a piece of text is presented.

Rules can also be used effectively to organise text and shepherd a readers' attention.

Set with 1.5mm space after. Emboldened first paragraph (above).

The way a piece of text is formatted can result in many different and striking visual results as these examples show.

From simply inserting a drop cap to utilising different weights of a font and the various types of indentation – running, hanging and off-a-point – to give structure, hierarchy or meaning, the techniques are simple but can have a dramatic impact on the way a piece of text is presented.

Rules can also be used effectively to organise text and shepherd a readers' attention.

First line indent. Emboldened leaders (above).

The way a piece of text is formatted can result in many different and striking visual results as these examples show.

From simply inserting a drop cap to utilising different weights of a font and the various types of indentation – running, hanging and off-a-point – to give structure, hierarchy or meaning, the techniques are simple but can have a dramatic impact on the way a piece of text is presented.

Rules can also be used effectively to organise text and shepherd a readers' attention.

Hanging indent (above).

The way a piece of text is formatted can result in many different and striking visual results as these examples show.

From simply inserting a drop cap to utilising different weights of a font and the various types of indentation – running, hanging and off-a-point – to give structure, hierarchy or meaning, the techniques are simple but can have a dramatic impact on the way a piece of text is presented.

Rules can also be used effectively to organise text and shepherd a readers' attention.

Indent on point (above).

The way a piece of text is formatted can result in many different and striking visual results as these examples show.

From simply inserting a drop cap to utilising different weights of a font and the various types of indentation – running, hanging and off-a-point – to give structure, hierarchy or meaning, the techniques are simple but can have a dramatic impact on the way a piece of text is presented.

Rules can also be used effectively to organise text and shepherd a readers' attention.

Two-line count drop cap (above).

The way a piece of text is formatted can result in many different and striking visual results as these examples show.

From simply inserting a drop cap to utilising different weights of a font and the various types of indentation – running, hanging and off-a-point – to give structure, hierarchy or meaning, the techniques are simple but can have a dramatic impact on the way a piece of text is presented.

Rules can also be used effectively to organise text and shepherd a readers' attention.

With line after (40% offset) paragraph set to column width (above).

The way a piece of text is formatted can result in many different and striking visual results as these examples show.

From simply inserting a drop cap to utilising different weights of a font and the various types of indentation – running, hanging and off-a-point – to give structure, hierarchy or meaning, the techniques are simple but can have a dramatic impact on the way a piece of text is presented.

Rules can also be used effectively to organise text and shepherd a readers' attention.

With rule below set to text width (above).

~~**The way a piece of text is formatted can result in many different and striking visual results as these examples show.**~~

~~From simply inserting a drop cap to utilising different weights of a font and the various types of indentation – running, hanging and off-a-point – to give structure, hierarchy or meaning, the techniques are simple but can have a dramatic impact on the way a piece of text is presented.~~

~~Rules can also be used effectively to organise text and shepherd a readers' attention.~~

With strike through. Alternately tabbed (above).

The way a piece of text is formatted can result in many different and striking visual results as these examples show.

From simply inserting a drop cap to utilising different weights of a font and the various types of indentation – running, hanging and off-a-point – to give structure, hierarchy or meaning, the techniques are simple but can have a dramatic impact on the way a piece of text is presented.

Rules can also be used effectively to organise text and shepherd a readers' attention.

Centred (above).

The way a piece of text is formatted can result in many different and striking visual results as these examples show.

From simply inserting a drop cap to utilising different weights of a font and the various types of indentation – running, hanging and off-a-point – to give structure, hierarchy or meaning, the techniques are simple but can have a dramatic impact on the way a piece of text is presented.

Rules can also be used effectively to organise text and shepherd a readers' attention.

Range Right. Ragged Left. 4mm space after (above).

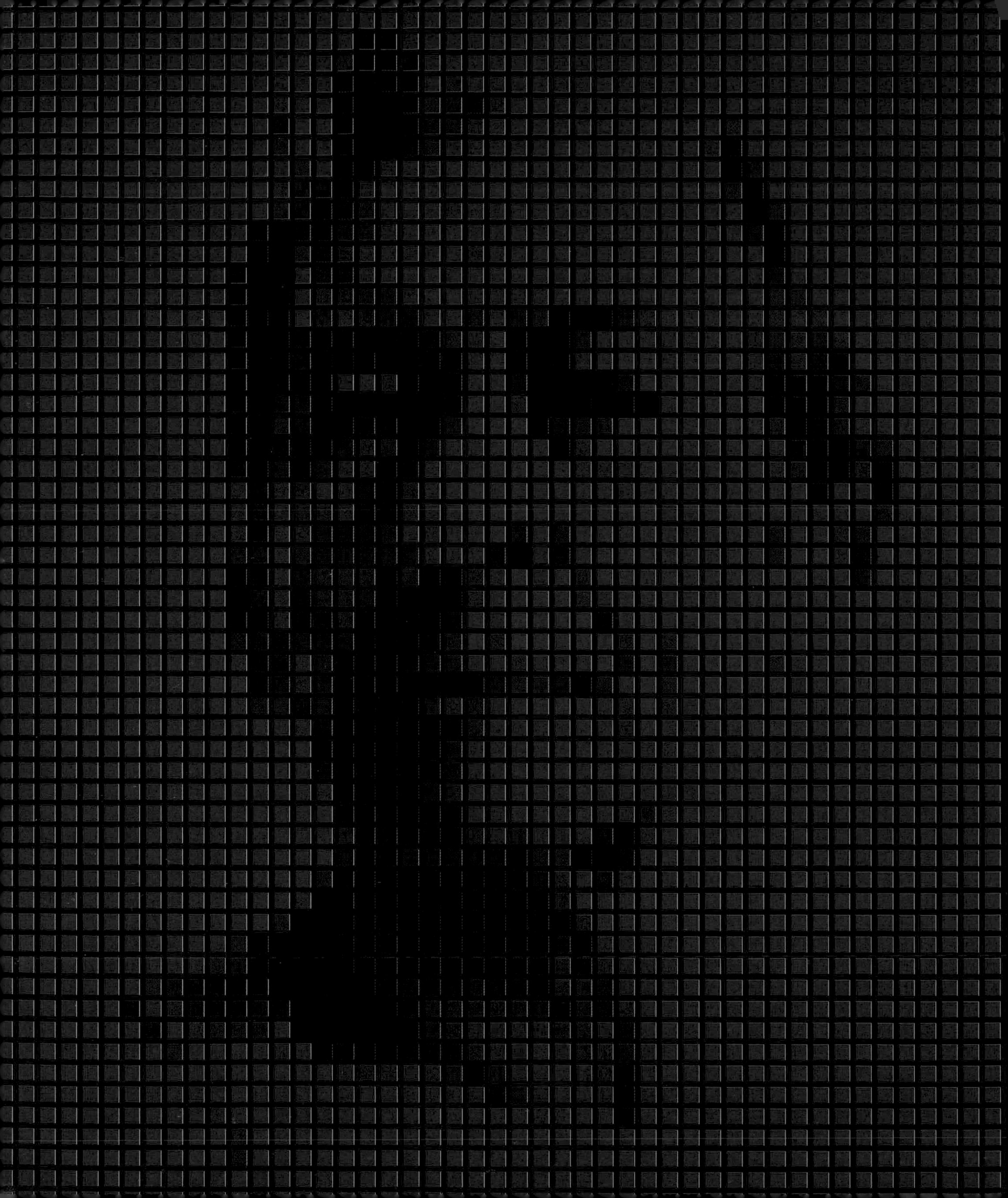

Image refers to the graphic elements that can bring a design alive. Whether as the main focus of a page or a subsidiary element, images play an essential role in communicating a message and they are thus a key part of establishing the visual identity of a piece of work. Images perform a number of functions from conveying the drama of a news report, to summing up and supporting an argument presented in the copy, or providing a visual break to an expanse of text or empty space. Images are effective because they provide instant communication of an idea or instruction, detailed information, or a feeling that the reader can comprehend very quickly. How would you describe the latest fashion trend in words? This is difficult compared to the relative ease of showing it in a picture.

Image usage is determined by many considerations including what the desired impact is, who the target audience is, the aesthetic of the project, the function the image will serve, and how adventurous or conservative the overall design needs to be. Image usage is perhaps the most exciting aspect of design as images can have a profound impact on the outcome and success of a piece of work due to the emotional reaction precipitated in the viewer. However, poorly used, images can detract from or counteract the message in the text.

Image placement and size, and its relationship with surrounding elements all affect the tone and impact of a design. This section will explore various techniques for image usage including cropping, cut outs, bleeds, computer software effects, and presentation in colour, black and white or duotone.

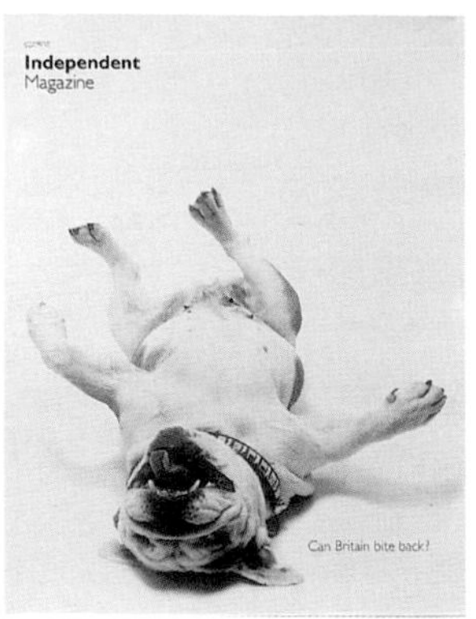

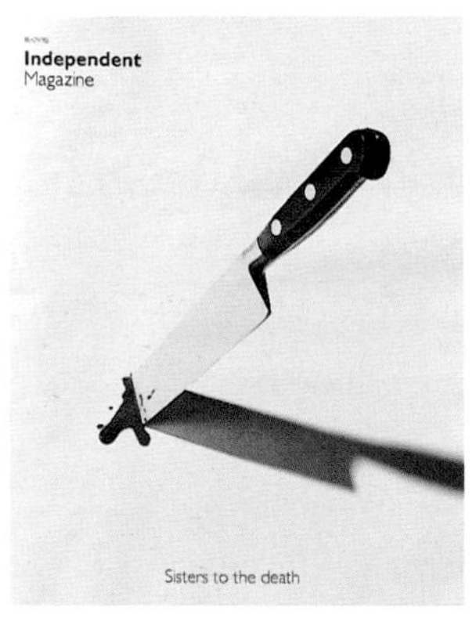

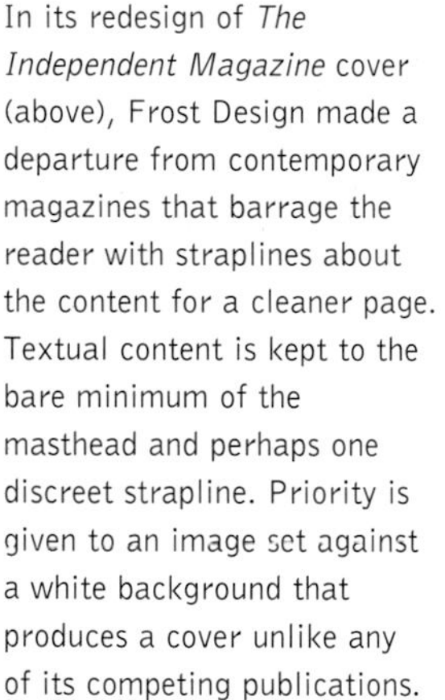

In its redesign of *The Independent Magazine* cover (above), Frost Design made a departure from contemporary magazines that barrage the reader with straplines about the content for a cleaner page. Textual content is kept to the bare minimum of the masthead and perhaps one discreet strapline. Priority is given to an image set against a white background that produces a cover unlike any of its competing publications.

Design: Frost Design

Frost Design's fondness for folded posters can be seen again here (right) in this poster about Keith Haring. Rather than simply reproducing an image of one of Haring's works, the studio used a photo of the artist in front of one of his works. Textual content is restricted to one side of the poster with the text columns defined by the folds in the poster.

Design: Frost Design

Frost Design keeps things simple (left) with its work for the Fourth Estate catalogue. The use of typography is sacrificed for a more natural, back-to-basics, handwritten lettering. NYC is a dramatic statement in itself pushed to the max by Frost Design (below). The lack of information on one side of the poster is countered by the reverse side, in text columns that form skyscrapers reminiscent of New York's skyline.

Design: Frost Design

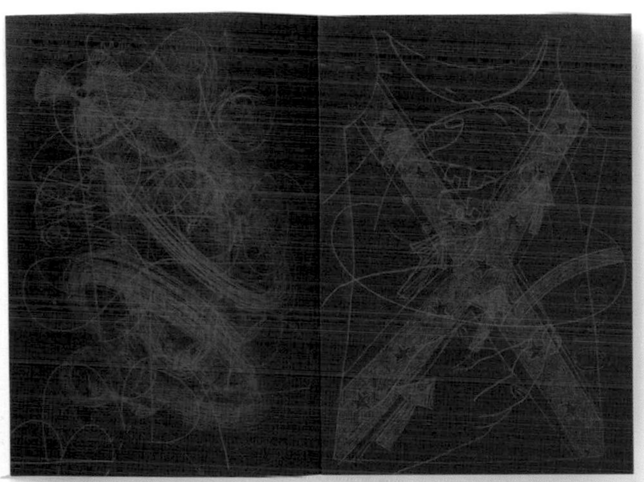

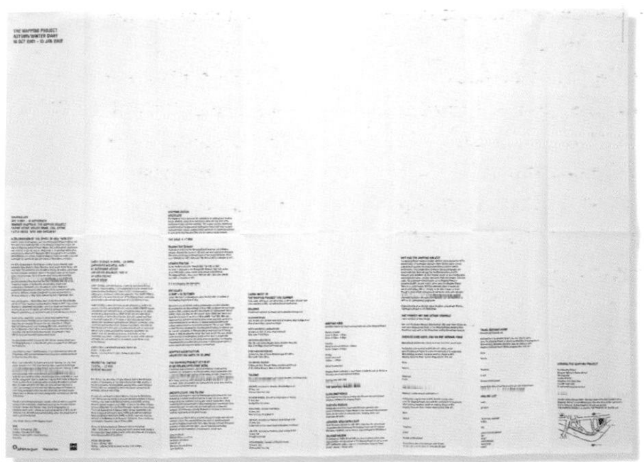

colouring images

A colour image is produced by separating it into the three trichromatic colours – cyan, magenta and yellow – and black, the process colours utilised in colour printing. Nearly all colours can be printed using these subtractive primaries in the four-colour printing process, using a separate printing plate for each colour to build the image as shown below. But the designer does not have to settle for the original colours of an image. Indeed, using some of the options that follow, the dramatic nature of an image can be changed and enhanced considerably.

Below are the CMYK colour separations needed to produce a full-colour image. Each colour film is made up of dots that when printed over the other films in registration produce the image (far left). The dots for each colour are aligned at different angles so that they overlap to produce the image. They are too small to see with the naked eye but the pattern they form is shown in the enlarged image (left). The printing process prints in the order CMYK and builds the image up in this way (below).

Cyan
(C)

Cyan and Magenta
(C+M)

Cyan, Magenta and Yellow
(C+M+Y)

Cyan, Magenta, Yellow and Black
(C+M+Y+K)

Original four-colour CMYK image

The basic photograph.

Greyscale image

A greyscale is an image formed by the shades of grey from black through to white.

In printing, a greyscale is reproduced using only a black halftone plate; tones are created through the 'white' of the paper.

Greyscale image with the picture converted to magenta

A greyscale, when saved as a TIFF (Tagged Information File Format) can be coloured directly in desktop publishing programs.

Greyscale image with the picture converted to 50% black and the background printing as 100% yellow

The background to the TIFF can be coloured independently from the image allowing rapid image manipulation.

Duotone image with equal parts of black and cyan

Duotone image of black and 100% cyan

Duotone image with equal parts of cyan and yellow

Duotone image with equal parts of magenta and cyan with opposite values

Tritone image with equal parts of black, red and orange

Quadtone image with equal parts of black, red, orange and yellow

Bitmap image with 50% threshold

A bitmap is formed by a pattern of pixels and records information as blacks and whites only.

Coloured bitmap

Bitmaps can be coloured in the same way as greyscale images

hulton archive

Brief

To design a brochure and supporting material for the Hulton Archive picture library with the use of colour to lead viewers away from the preconception that the company only supplies black-and-white photography.

Process

Black-and-white pictures were manipulated electronically and coloured to create a very different visual impact from the original image.

Original image

Solarised version

Original image

Image levels are adjusted to remove background noise, converted to a bitmap, and filled with 'gradient' colour fill

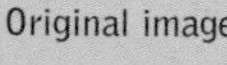

Original image

Levels and filters create striking results

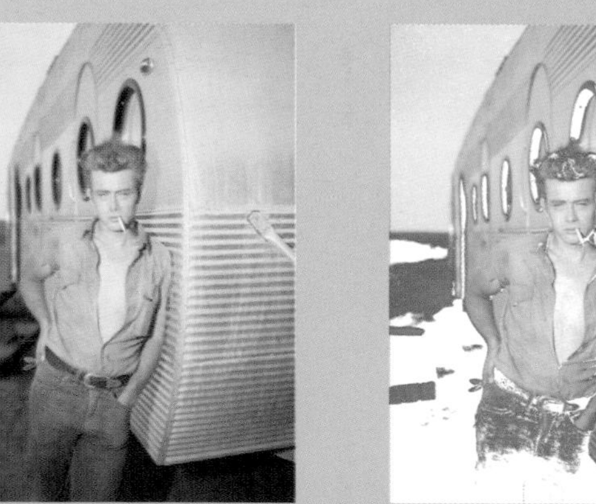

Original image

Sections of the image, selected by colour values are isolated and removed

Result

Colour and photo manipulation techniques combine to create a series of striking images that indicate some of the 'colour' possibilities for the use of black-and-white photography.

The images were used across a broad spectrum of media from postcards to brochures, and for display in an exhibition.

Colour and effects were used harmoniously with the subject matter to enhance the evocation of certain images. For example, the use of halftone dots to create a newsprint illusion for a picture of a young Fidel Castro (below, top right), or an image separated into 'channels' that are moved out of registration to give a psychedelic feel to Jimi Hendrix (below, bottom, second from left and far right).

Design: Gavin Ambrose

Screened shapes overlay the original image

Image of Frida Kahlo adjusted to look painterly

Greyscale image separated into 'channels' that are moved out of registration to overlap one another, and the top layer coloured

Greyscale colour halftone giving the illusion of newsprint image quality

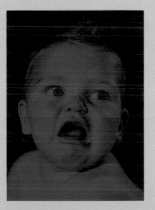

Doutone of red and black with the value of red set to full

Full-colour image separated into 'channels' that are moved out of registration to overlap one another

Full-colour image in halftone

Further 'channel' adjustment

illustration

Designer Andy Potts creates striking images fuelled by the random visual inspiration of imagery he sees in the everyday world such as: **'A bit of graffiti or print, an imperfect photo, signage, odd ephemera, textures or postcards, a good shot in a film or a piece of architecture,'** he says.

Potts usually begins by sketching his design on paper that he then scans into his computer, or maybe a photo or texture. On the computer he quickly works out a rough visual and blocks out the composition, the colours, and the shapes, positioning the sketches and so on until he is happy with the layout. **'It's a very disorganised but intuitive method,'** he says, **'fuelled by caffeine and stress until the right balance of elements is found.'**

Right: Healthy on the Inside

Editorial work can contain a strong idea that sends the designer off on visual tangents. This example for an article about prison fitness and notorious inmate Charles Bronson for the Saturday *Guardian* supplement, *The Guide,* clearly shows this. Using found photography and drawn elements, Potts created an image based around DIY weightlifting such as the use of a broom handle with filled plastic bags either end as weights. The main character is made from photographs of two people enhanced by drawn elements and lots of layer blending to achieve a painterly look, and images of concrete blended on to flat colours to add subtle textures for the prison wall.

Above: End of the Road

For the final issue of Internet magazine *Beast* (www.ths.nu/beast), Potts used a damaged Lomo photograph of the open road to convey the 'Goodbye' theme. Colour filtering was applied and the font was eroded to give it a handmade illustrative feel.

Below: Big Brother

Another illustration for *The Guide*, this time to accompany an article about electronic merchandising (including text messaging, interactive television and Internet marketing) for the Big Brother reality TV show. The 'target audience' image is both created and coloured by computer, with a hand-drawn logo on the shirt, against a background of found elements that are blended together to create a texture behind the Big Brother eye.

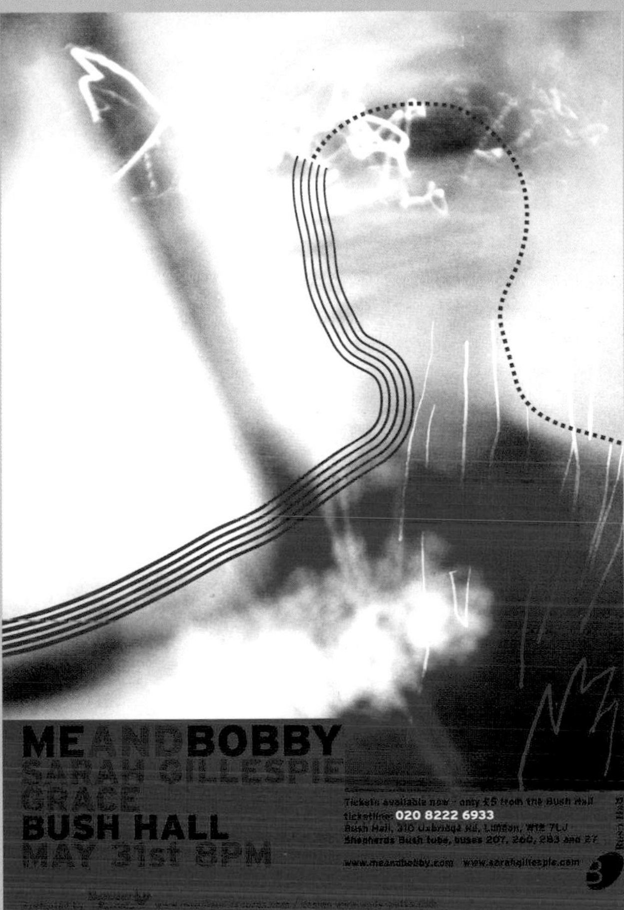

Above: Me and Bobby

A poster for a friend's gig. Potts took an abstract accidental photo taken with a Lomo which had a vague human shape and motion squiggles. He picked out the simple human with line work and added hand-drawn doodles and flame elements. **'I like the mood of this piece and see it as a successful departure from my usual style, relying as it does on a single photo and incorporating elements of graphic design and typography,'** says Potts.

Right: Spirit: Relationships

An illustration for the *Guardian Weekend* magazine's 'Spirit' section depicting the emotional stress of travelling couples. Photos with specific poses for the man and woman were worked into with various layers that were drawn upon and subjected to motion blur and paint daub filter effects on the skin, with postage watermarks scanned in for an airmailed postcard feel.

bouncers/shiners

When is black not black? Black is a colour that is not always what it seems when reproduced by the four-colour printing process. While it may do a great job of creating good shadow tone in full-colour images, when left on its own it looks pale and washed out. Where there are large areas of black in a design that is to be printed in four colours it is often advisable to use a cyan shiner. A shiner is typically a 50% or 60% cyan area behind the black that helps to improve the visual density and saturation. Cyan is the best of the other three process colours to use as a shiner as yellow and magenta result in a muddy black or one that looks artificially warm.

Black has a large part to play in the problem of bouncers. Bounce is a registration problem that can be avoided with the use of a 100% black that also contains amounts of cyan, magenta, and yellow. A four-colour black results in a much fuller and richer black as shown below and above, and having at least one shared colour between adjacent objects makes errors in registration less noticeable.

100% Black (K)

100% Black (K), 60% Cyan (C)

100% Cyan (C), Yellow (Y), Magenta (M) & Black (K)

Ink trapping is the adjustment of areas of coloured text or shapes to account for misregistration on the printing press by overlapping them slightly. It is required because the halftone dots that make up printed images overlap because they are of different sizes and at different screen angles, but is not necessary for photographic images. The colours are overlapped to prevent the appearance of white gaps where they are supposed to meet.

This also prevents undesired colours being formed when colours unintentionally overlap. Trapping is affected by how dry the original ink layer is and the ink film thickness of subsequent layers printed over it. The trap is normally created with the lighter colour, and it is either spread (enlarged) or choked (reduced) into darker colours to combine them in the area where they join.

Trapping is important on black text because the fineness (usually) of text means it is hard to register with surrounding colours. When trapped properly, the black is overprinted on the surrounding area. Trapping is used on black and very dark colours, as the change in colour is barely noticeable.

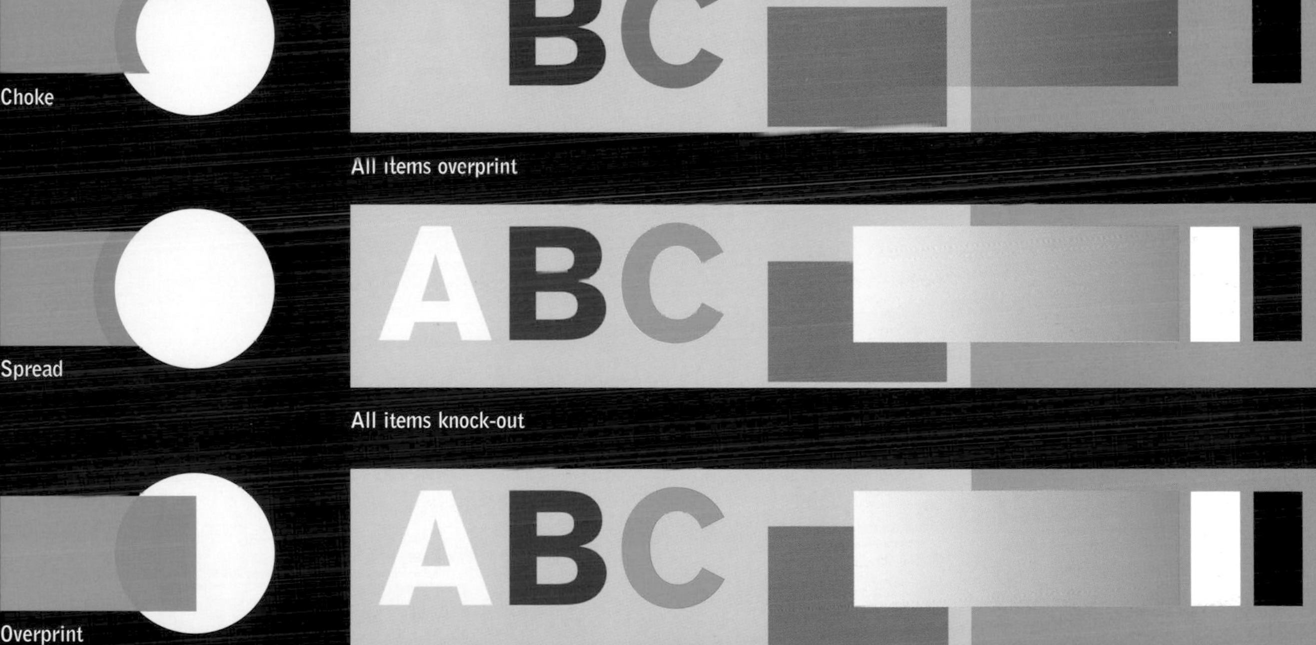

Choke

Spread

Overprint

All items overprint

All items knock-out

All items are left default. Type and brown square have 0.144pt trap, blend square and white square knock-out, black square overprints

A negative number in trapping setting will result in choke. A

languageimagetrap

Russell Bestley and Ian Noble of Visual Research utilised a striking visual identity in their poster designs for the Languageimagetrap lectures in 1999–2000 for the design and education research project called We Interrupt the Programme. In addition to the textual information that you would expect to find, such as when and where the events are taking place, the bulk of the poster area is occupied by images. The majority of these juxtapose a contemporary image with a detail from an old painting. A solitary word is emblazoned across each poster in a typeface that replicates stencilling and grabs the viewers' attention. The word is a short, sharp statement that obliquely combines with the images to provide a visual clue to the content of the lectures advertised. They are a deliberately odd mix, purposefully created to challenge the viewer to question the way image and language are used. The suggestion is of course, that the lecture will help provide interpretation along these lines.

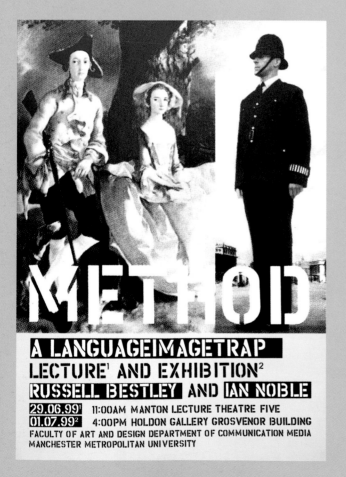

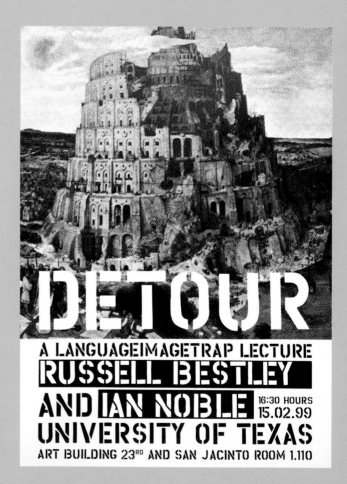

THE INDEX OF POSSIBILITIES WITHIN A MORE OPEN COMMUNICATION IS DETERMINED NOT BY A MONOLOGUE, BUT IN THE ACCEPTANCE THAT INTERVENTIONS MADE BY DESIGN CAN ACT AS A MEDIATING INFLUENCE AND ARE PART OF A LARGER REFLEXIVE PROCESS.
THE PROJECT AIMS TO EXPLORE OUR COLLECTIVE UNDERSTANDING OF THE PROCESSES AND RESPONSIBILITIES WITHIN GRAPHIC DESIGN, ITS RELATIONSHIP TO COMMUNICATION AND LANGUAGE, AND IMPORTANTLY THE INTENTION ON THE PART OF THE MAKER OR DESIGNER.

IMAGETRAP

WE INTERRUPT THE PROGRAMME IS AN INVESTIGATION NOT ONLY INTO THE DIALOGIC PRODUCTION OF MESSAGES AND THE MAPPING OF SHARED EXPERIENCE, BUT ALSO THE WAY IN WHICH IT IS POSSIBLE TO SEE GRAPHIC DESIGN AS A FORM OF SOCIAL COMMENTARY.

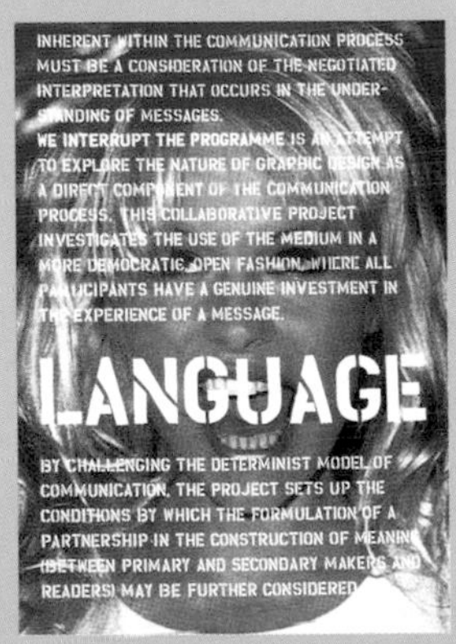

The posters (above and immediate left) serve a different purpose (to outline the aims of the project), but do so by maintaining the bold stencilled word outburst set over an evocative image that provides continuity throughout the poster series.

Design: Visual Research

colors

Brief

The brief was to redesign the bi-monthly *Colors* magazine sponsored by Benetton, published by La Fabrica in seven languages, with a worldwide distribution of over half a million. Something different was needed to compete in the increasingly crowded market for mainstream lifestyle titles.

Process

Pentagram partner Fernando Gutiérrez took over as art director of *Colors* in 2000 and made a thorough reappraisal of its guiding principles as he embarked on its redesign with editors Adam Broomberg and Oliver Chanarin.

Result

Gutiérrez created a content-based magazine that flies in the face of the glossy, luxury-fuelled maxims of other lifestyle magazines with content that introduces readers to communities around the world that exist on the margins of our consciousness and shows them as everyday people leading everyday lives. Talented young photographers were commissioned to document these communities and their environment to give a powerful expression of the real world. Each issue has two covers: one global and one local. The prominent, evocative visual language of *Colors* magazine is down to the guiding principle that static images are often far more resonant than the ephemeral moving images of television.

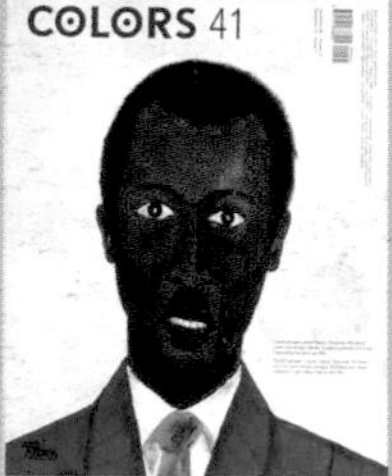

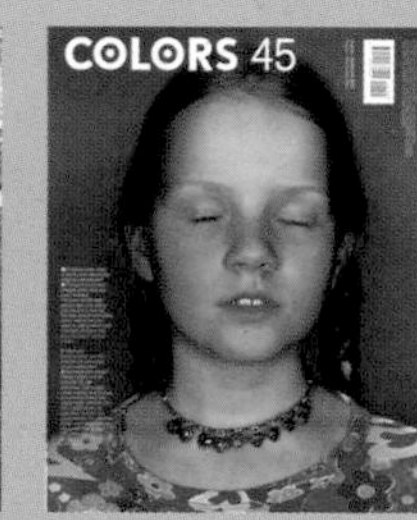

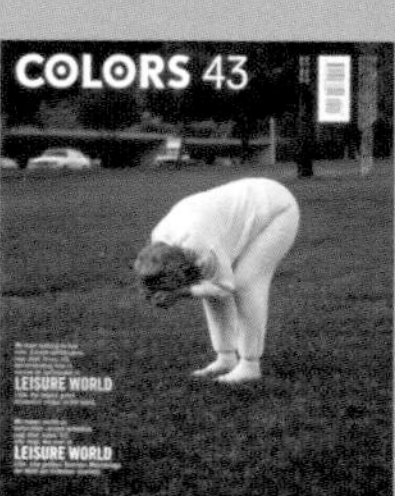

Above: These two groups of images show the very different local and global covers for six issues of *Colors*.

Right: Simple and straightforward layout is used to juxtapose the English text with one of the other seven languages that each issue is published in. The spreads are dominated by the large-scale visual content with the text relegated to a supporting member of the cast.

Design: Pentagram

I HAVE NO FEAR OF DEATH AT ALL, I HAVE ALREADY DIED TWICE

Virginia Russell, 69, a member of the Parapsychology Club, one of over 200 clubs in Leisure World, California, USA

ICH HABE KEINE ANGST VOR DEM TOD, ICH BIN SCHON ZWEIMAL GESTORBEN

Virginia Russell, 69, Mitglied des Clubs für Parapsychologie, einer der über 200 Vereine von Leisure World (Freizeitwelt), Kalifornien, USA

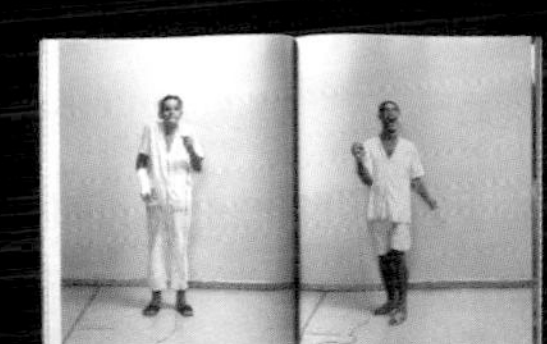

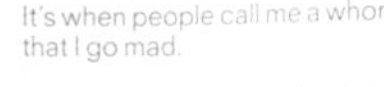

It's when people call me a whore that I go mad.
Es cuando la gente me llama puta que me vuelvo loca.

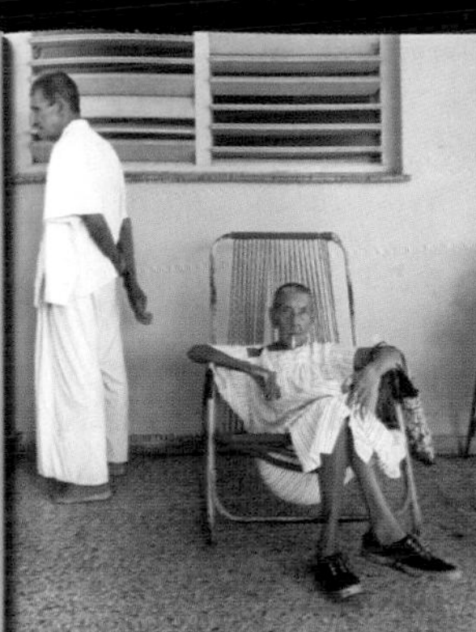

By juxtaposing images related by a common theme such as writing or football, Johnson Banks, in a series of posters for The British Council, showed that Britain was no longer just about warm beer and cricket. Adjoining the old and the new, such as playwrights Shakespeare and Stoppard, reflected the opinions held by people around the world about Britain that balance British pop stars, comedians or footballers with references to the country's history and traditions.

Design: Johnson Banks

Touring exhibition design and graphics for an initiative introducing the idea of sustainable cities. Drawing on the work of the group Urban Futures – Herbert Girardet, Pamela Charlick and Natasha Nicholson – the *Living Cities* exhibition seeks to promote understanding of sustainability.

Design: Studio Myerscough

>london living city
>building visions
>architecture week

herbert girardet/urban futures:rethinking the city >At the start of the new millennium cities and their resource use dominate life on earth. In the last 100 years, human numbers have grown fourfold, whilst both the world economy and urban populations and have grown about 15 fold. Today, half of us live in cities while most of the rest depends on urban markets for their economic survival. One species now uses about half of nature's entire annual production, and we are increasingly undermining the integrity of the global environment. We have to rethink how we run our urban economies, energy, transport and waste systems, and the way we construct our buildings. If sustainability was the main frame of reference for the way we plan urban spaces, structures and processes – how would things change? >Given the vast scale of urbanisation today, cities would be well advised to model their functioning on natural ecosystems. These are generally systems of permanence, whereas currently man-made systems are defined by high levels of entropy. Cities have a linear metabolism, consisting of the flow of resources and products through the urban system. Nature's own ecosystems have an essentially circular metabolism in which every output by an organism is also an input which renews the whole living environment of which it is a part. The web of life hangs together in a 'chain of mutual benefit'. To be sustainable, cities have to develop a circular metabolism, minimising waste discharges, and using and re-using resources as efficiently as possible. >Thinking differently is an important starting point in the process of remodelling our cities. The real challenge however is to act differently. People all over the world are working on how to make their cities more sustainable, in both environmental and social terms. This exhibition is intended to enhance that process in the city that started it all: London. It is, at present, a city of vast global dependencies. Its ecological footprint extends to an area the size of the UK, about 125 times its own surface area. If all the world's cities demanded such vast surface areas to supply themselves three planets would be needed rather than the one we have. >It makes sense for people to live in cities. They have the potential for great resource efficiency through closed-loop economies, diversity and mutuality. In the past, economic growth has meant automatic growth in the consumption of resources and services of all kinds. Sustainable development, in contrast, requires new solutions to ensure that economic well-being is founded on efficient use of resources, minimising pollution and waste. New energy systems can supplant technologies we inherited from the past. It is clear that many new local jobs can be created on the way. In the exhibition the main focus is on these areas where the potential for change is greatest. These sections form an agenda for constructing the future sustainable city. >The quest for sustainability requires a strengthening of local democratic processes. Methods such as neighbourhood forums, action planning and consensus-building should be widely used, because they usually lead to better decision making. Community groups, local and central governments are increasingly aware that efforts to improve the living environment must focus on cities and urban lifestyles. Eco-friendly urban development could well become the greatest challenge of the twenty-first century, not only for human self-interest, but also for the sake of a sustainable relationship between cities and the biosphere on which humanity ultimately depends.

act differently:**living city**

Cities, occupying 2% of the world's land surface, consume 75% of the world's resources and discharge 75% of the world's waste

London's total ecological footprint extends to around 125 times its surface area

Living City events

Mayoral Candidates Interviews
14 April to 04 May
decide who to vote for by viewing videos of the candidates policies on sustainability.
RIBA Architecture Gallery

Living City Forum
Tuesday 09 May
6.30pm
with Herbert Girardet, Patrick Bellew of Atelier Ten, Robin Murray of Ecologika and Dickon Robinson of Peabody Trust. Chaired by Paul Finch, Publishing Editor, emap, the event will outline practical steps to take forward possible outcomes of the Living City initiative

Education Sustainability Forum
Tuesday 16 May
2.30pm to 5.30pm
Event for technology and design teachers in architecture.
Contact: Pamela Edwards, RIBA Education

Green Kids Workshop
Saturday 10 June
11am
Bring the children to the Architecture Week family day at RIBA. This workshop, run by the Centre for Sustainability, is free.

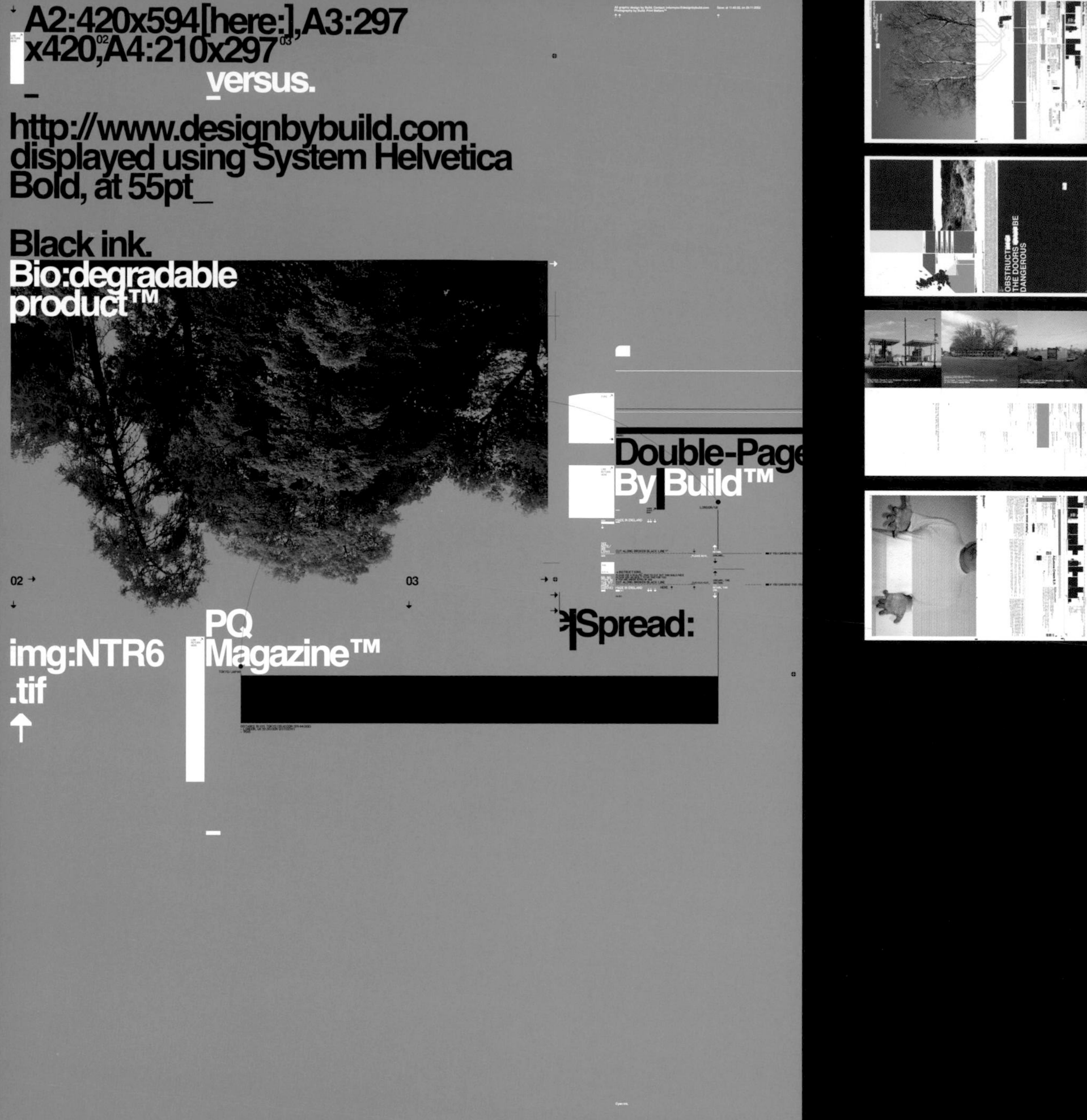

A2:420x594[here:],A3:297 x420,A4:210x297
versus.
http://www.designbybuild.com displayed using System Helvetica Bold, at 55pt_
Black ink.
Bio:degradable product™
02
03
img:NTR6 .tif
PQ Magazine™
Double-Page Spread:
By Build™
OBSTRUCTING THE DOORS CAN BE DANGEROUS

See Ink Trapping

>137

Michael C. Place, founder of Build makes no secret of the fact that he wants to keep exploring his own take on design. This he frequently does through designs that are a mixture of simplicity and complexity as can be seen here.

Design: Build

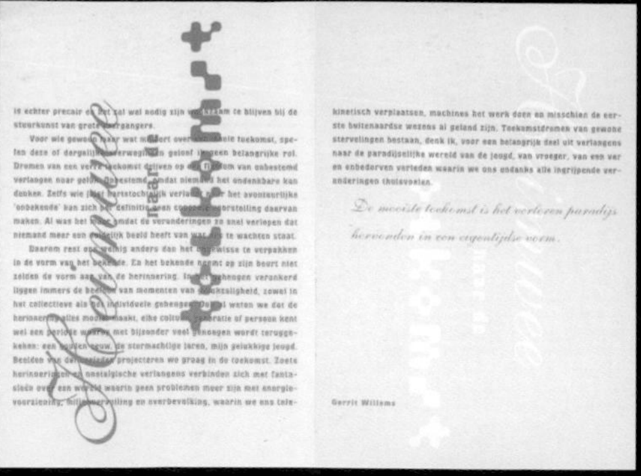

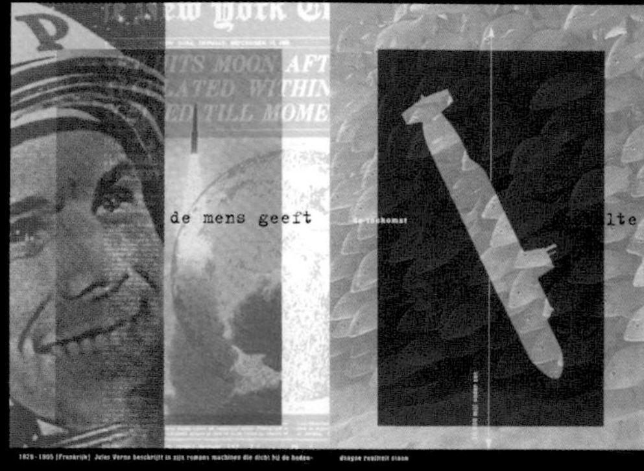

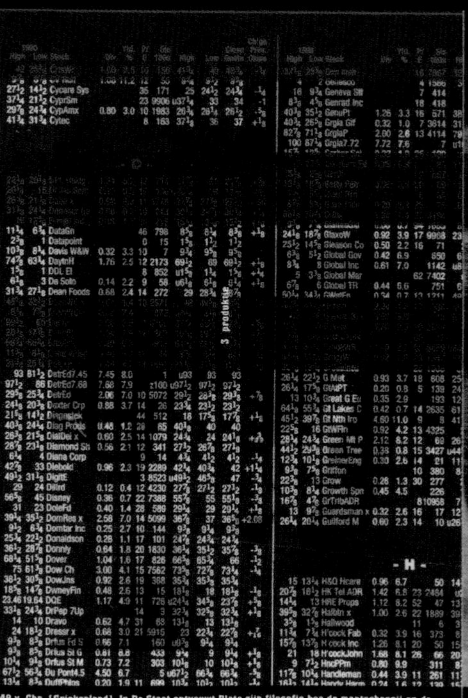

These images from Faydherbe/De Vringer illustrate how the layering and colouring of several images can be used to build up a stunning composite.

Design: Faydherbe/De Vringer

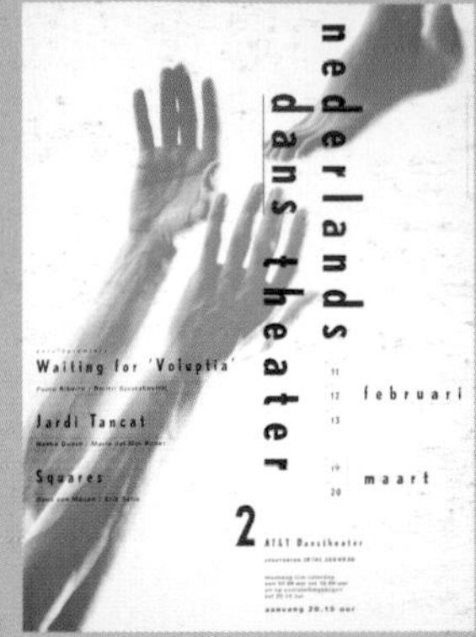

Design: Faydherbe/De Vringer

In these posters for Nederlands dans theatre created by Faydherbe/De Vringer we see extended arms and legs, a swirl of hair and an emotional embrace. Evocative images of the body, the tool of the dancer, cropped in unusual ways to zoom in and capture the drama of the movements of dance.

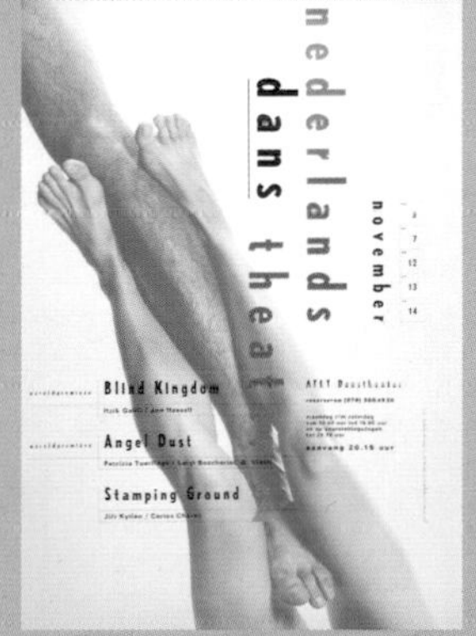

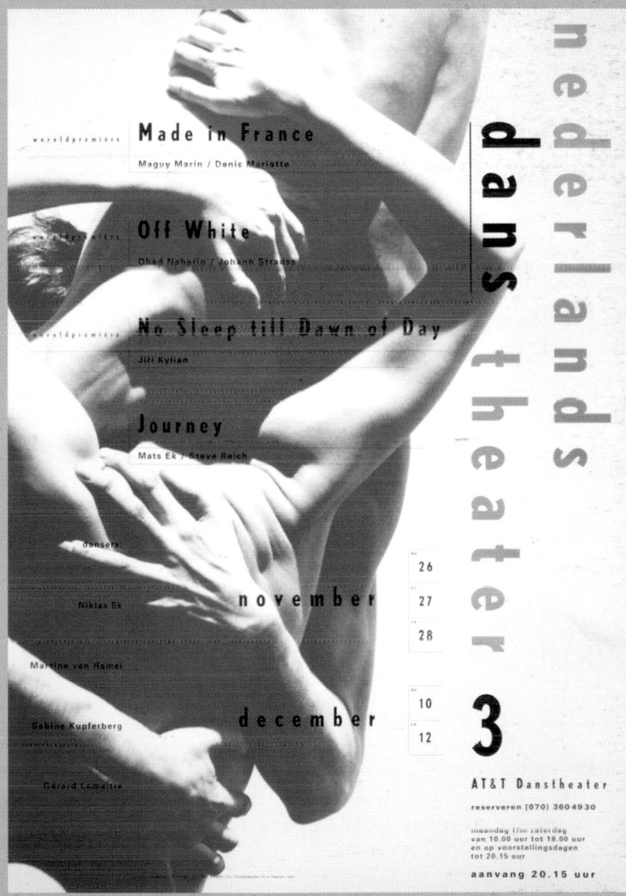

image manipulation

Image manipulation in the days before computers was an arcane alchemical art practiced in darkrooms or with an airbrush. Technology has relocated this role to the graphic designer and armed him or her with a vast array of software tools and effects, and the hardware to power them. The only limits are the creative abilities of the user.

From photo retouching to colouring, overlaying images to superimposing elements of one – such as texture – on the other, cut outs, shape alteration, and blending are some of the many possibilities. Rather than provide an exhaustive and marginally useful list of techniques, the following examples of imaginative image manipulation will give some idea of just how broad the possibilities are.

Left: Type and image superimposed upon each other create a visually arresting poster.

Design: NB: Studio

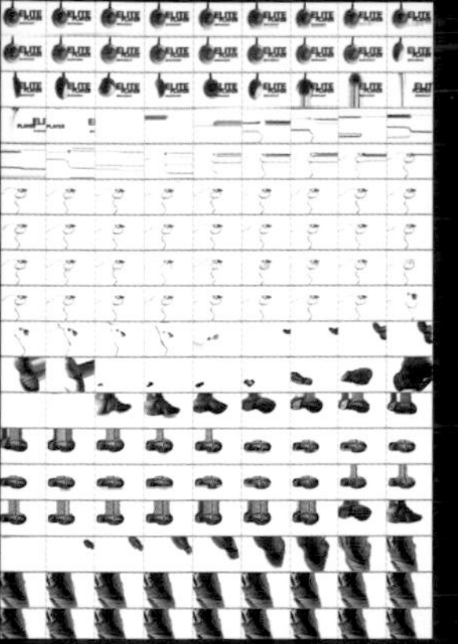
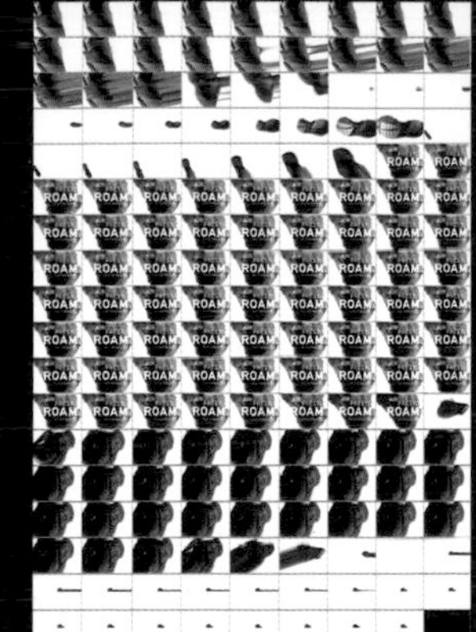

Left & below: Image manipulation is not restricted to static images as the sequence below shows, where the shape of a shoe is discreetly changed by breaking the image down into vertical lines that then gradually disappear before reforming as a watch.

Design: ImaginaryForces/ Matt Checkowski

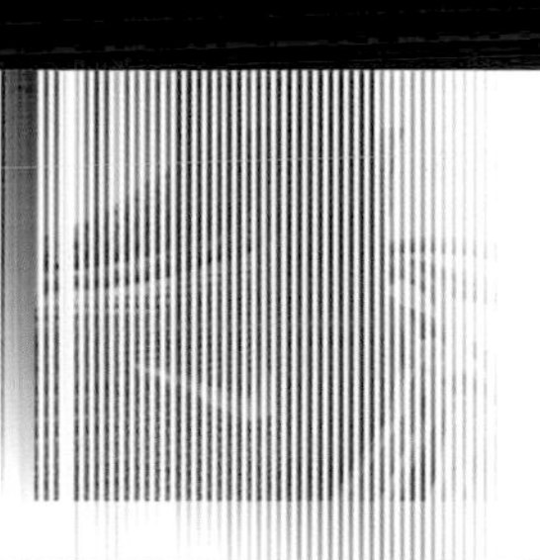
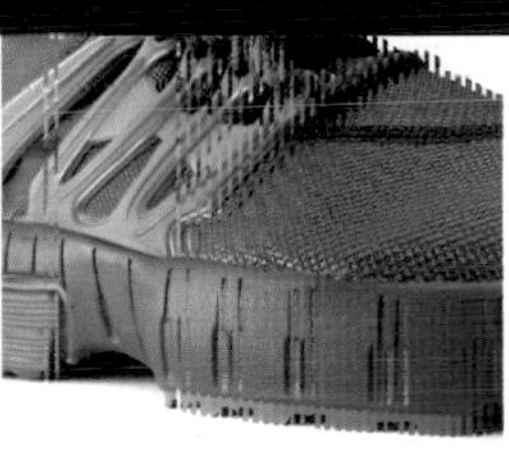

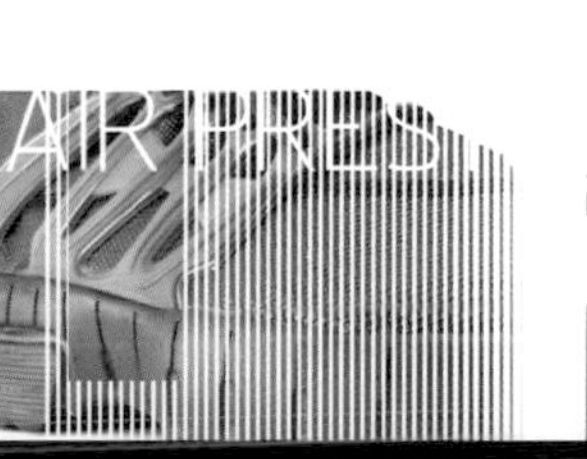

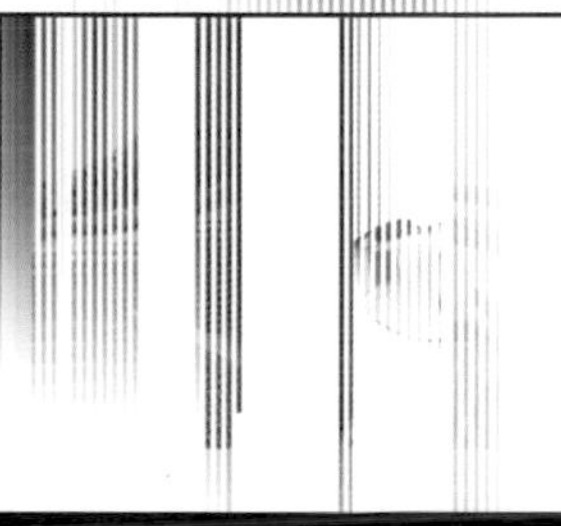

Below: Craig Yamey has used a collage of found elements including paint charts, newspapers, chewing gum wrappers, old sepia photographs and pages from a ledger in these designs, with photographic elements that have been cut out.

Design: Craig Yamey

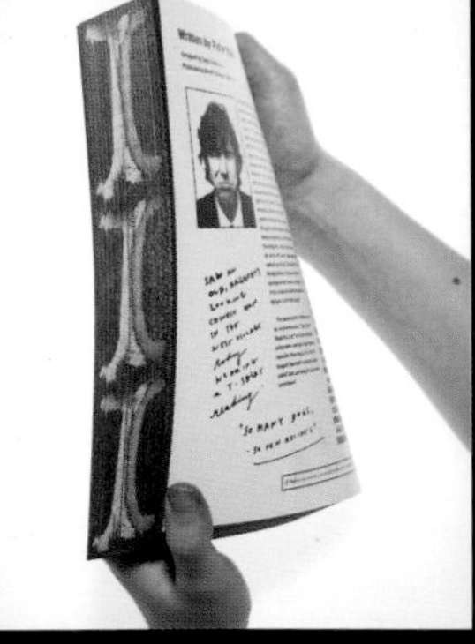

New York design studio Sagmeister Inc. chose to have a German shepherd dog as the cover star for a volume of its work entitled *Made You Look*. The paperback publication was designed with a transparent red slip-case. This functions to filter out some of the colours of the dog design, so that you see a docile German shepherd. But when the cover is removed and the complete dog image is revealed, it is in fact in mid attack.

The studio definitely has a hands-on sense of humour. The book has two images printed along the fore edge that are only revealed when the book is flexed. Flexed one way the book's title is revealed. Flexed the other, the dog gets something to eat.

Design: Sagmeister Inc.

Sagmeister used a similar concept in its design for a book about American photography for Amilus Inc. The only recognisable image on the outside surfaces of the book is the landscape revealed by flexing the pages. The curious image on the cover takes image manipulation to one extreme. It contains compressed versions of all the photographs in the book.

Design: Sagmeister Inc.

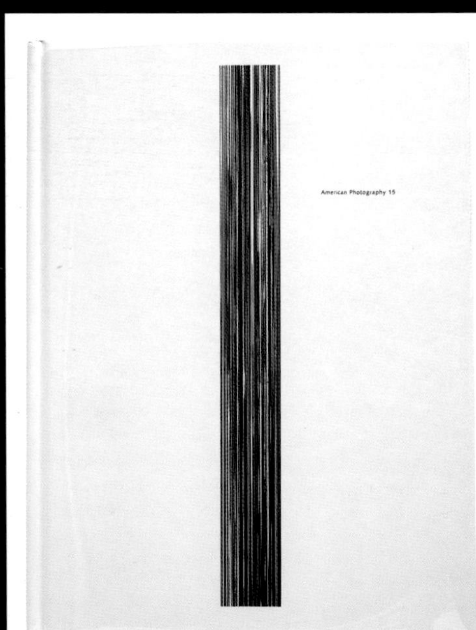

Asterik Studio of Seattle, Washington, USA, although a relatively young company that specialises in the design of record sleeves, is rapidly developing a reputation for innovative image manipulation.

As Don Clark, Creative Director, says: **'Music is our passion and art is our life. We wouldn't trade what we have for anything.'**

With every project having its own set of priorities and rules Asterik doesn't have a set way of approaching projects. **'Some clients have a specific idea of what they want, others don't have a clue,'** says Clark. **'Either way, we try to make sure the artwork developed for each release ties in with their music,'** he says.

The agency initially creates images that are evoked by the name of the record and then develops the artwork further. **'Some artists are very strict in what they want, and we develop their ideas further,'** says Clark. **'A lot of times though, an artist will give us complete freedom, which we tend to like a lot.'**

Design: Asterik Studio

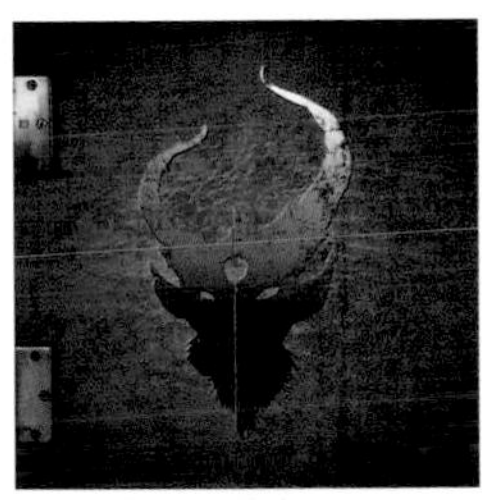

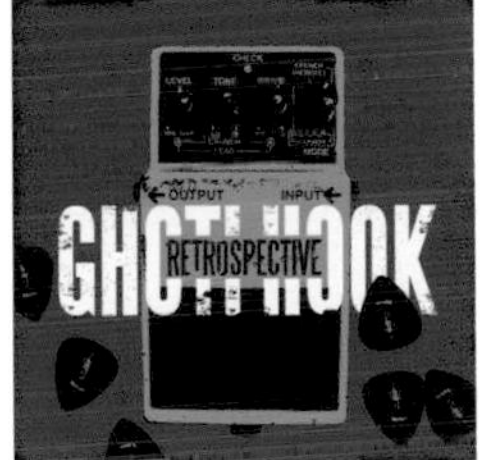

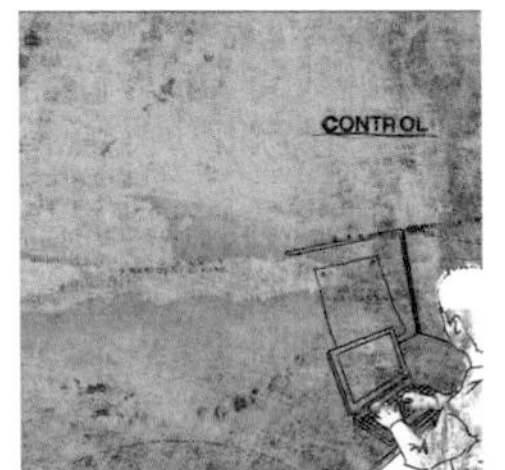

moving image

Fuelled by the growth and increasing power of technology, design houses are increasingly being asked by clients to produce designs for media other than print media. When a design will be viewed via the Web or video it presents the designer with the additional aspect of movement to use. Movement gives added dynamism to a design through the physical movement of the elements from which it is composed. We are now familiar with text bouncing around our screens when we surf the Internet. What does this mean for typography? The simple answer is that the same rules apply or are there to be ignored. Some designs will call for clarity while others will harness abstraction through movement.

Design: ImaginaryForces/Matt Checkowski

With Kurt Mattila, Checkowski created these pre-vision sequences for the feature film, *Minority Report.* Each pre-vision – a foretaste of a murder to come – was an integral moment in the film, combining special camera work, editing, and designing. All elements of the pre-vision needed to work in harmony to create compelling and innovative storytelling.

An example of the latter is the broadcast and stadium screen identity designed by Matt Checkowski for production company Imaginary Forces for the Portland Blazers NBA basketball team. As one of the most energetic and high-powered teams in the NBA, the Portland Blazers required an identity that captured the emotion they bring to the game while providing a framework that unified the franchise brand – including the introduction of a new logo – and could be extended across all media, from the giant LED display in the stadium, to the hi-def televisions in fans' homes.

The design has iconic red, black and silver graphic stripes, seemingly with a life of their own, that jump off the players' uniforms and form logos, transitions, crowd prompts, and team match-up screens. All elements, tracked from actual game footage, move dynamically leading to an identity that literally bounces to the beat of the basketball and shuffles to the movement of the players.

Design: ImaginaryForces/Matt Checkowski

Colour has become a permanent fixture in the field of visual communication in the last two decades. Magazines and even newspapers take advantage of four-colour printing and most companies now have the capability of producing colour documents in house due to the emergence of affordable personal computer printing technology. Colour provides added dynamism; it attracts attention and can be used to elicit emotional responses in the viewer. It can function to help organise the elements on a page, leading the eye from one item to the next, zoning elements or grouping items of a similar nature, coding certain types of information, and aiding the viewer to get the information they require.

Colour printing technology continues to increase the range of possibilities open to the designer. Hexachromatic printing (six colours compared to the four colours of the standard four-colour process) is becoming more widely available from printers extending the range of colours that designers can use without the need for special spot colours. Spot colours provide a vast palette for designers and have been added to with the development of spot varnishes and metallic effect pigments that continue to extend design possibilities.

Colour has different emotive or symbolic values depending upon where you are in the world, such as red for danger or stop in the Western world. The power of colour to alter the message of a design is one of the key reasons for its use, though cultural significance should not be ignored. This section will discuss the creative use of colour to increase visual appeal and maximise design impact.

In a world where four-colour printing has become established as a minimum requirement, Frost Design shows that black and white is still an effective 'colour' choice with these minimalist designs for Fourth Estate to depict things we are used to seeing in vibrant colour such as people's eyes, or a body.

Design: Frost Design

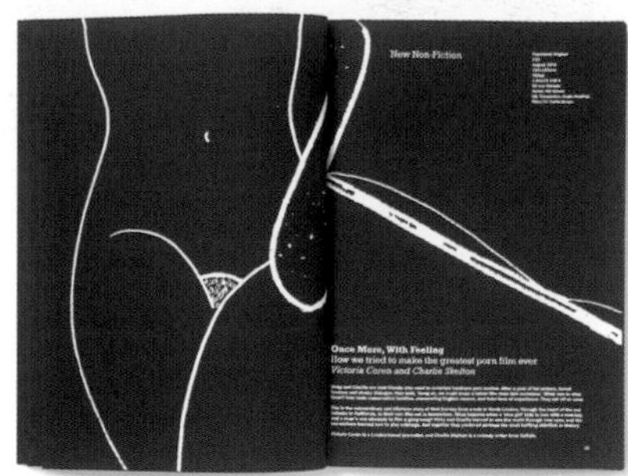

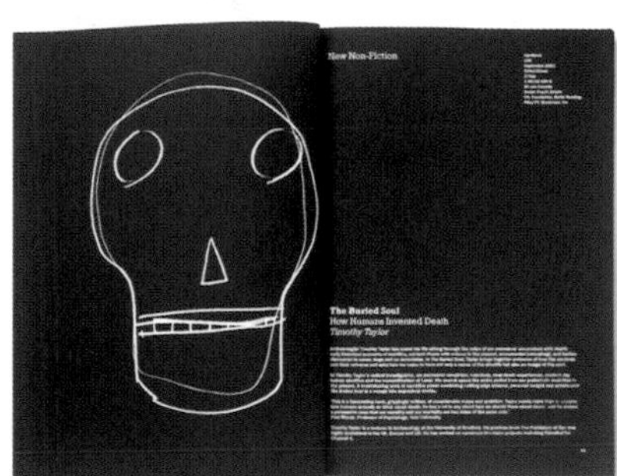

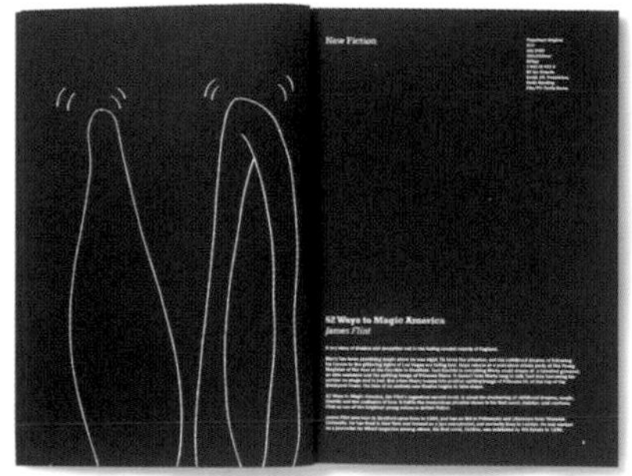

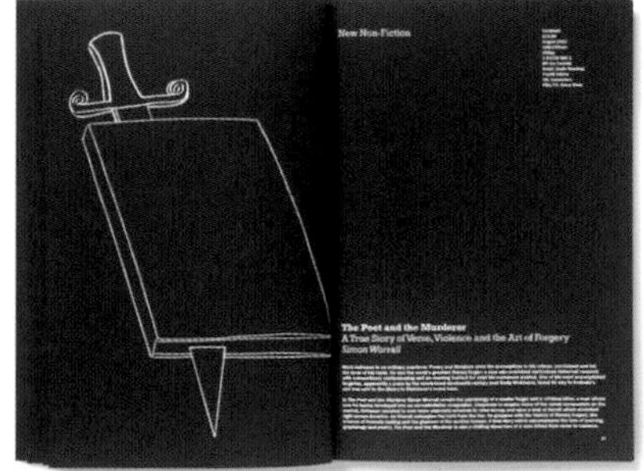

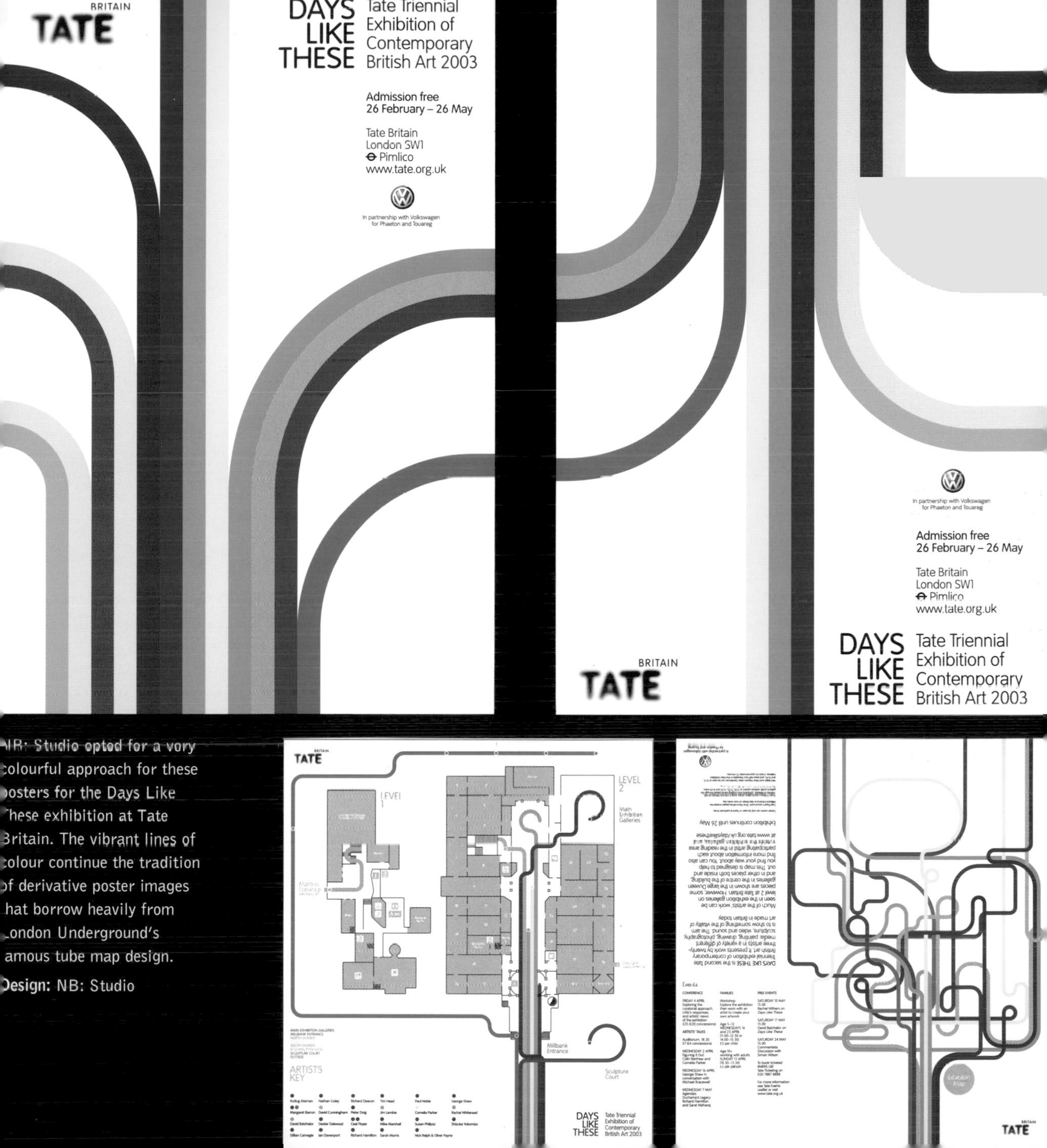

NB: Studio opted for a very colourful approach for these posters for the Days Like These exhibition at Tate Britain. The vibrant lines of colour continue the tradition of derivative poster images that borrow heavily from London Underground's famous tube map design.

Design: NB: Studio

four-colour tints

The reproduction of colour is created by screening the three trichromatic process colours cyan, magenta, and yellow – usually in 10% increments – that when combined with one or both of the other colours form all the permutations shown opposite. There are 1,000 tints available using the three process colours and a further 300 colours obtainable by combining a single process colour with black.

The three charts shown at the top of the opposite page demonstrate the 100 colour variations available by using a single process colour in combination with black. The remaining 11 charts are mixes of magenta and cyan in combination with varying increments of yellow.

The tint diagrams on the opposite page are designed to provide a clear visual indication of the true representation obtained by using four-colour tints.

It is important to be aware that these representations are only as accurate as the standard four-colour printing process and its limitations. The stock that this page is printed on will also affect the reproduction of the colour combinations, as will any stock you use.

The black and yellow chart below demonstrates how to determine the values of a chosen colour.

The top left-hand corner of the chart is 0% yellow with 0% black, hence nothing prints. The chart gives the range of colours at 10% increments of both yellow and black through to 100% yellow and 100% black in the bottom right-hand corner, which prints as a solid colour.

By drawing a line vertically and horizontally from a selected colour one can establish its component parts. In the example below, the selected colour is produced using 40% black and 60% yellow.

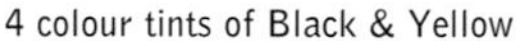

4 colour tints of Black & Yellow

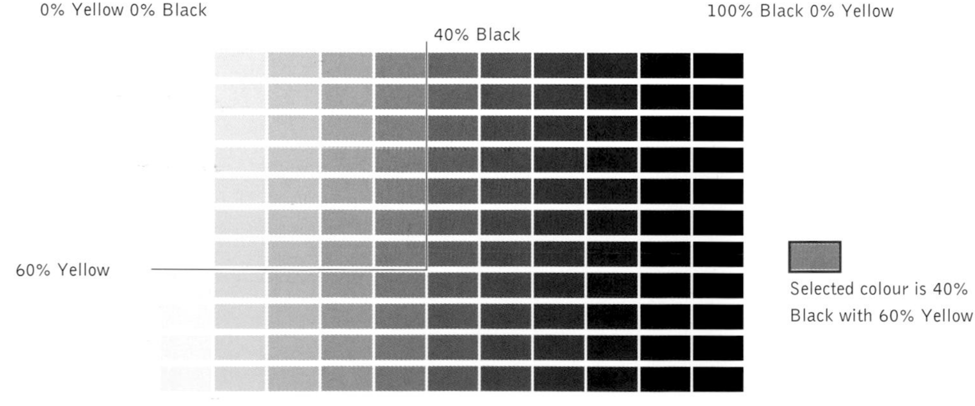

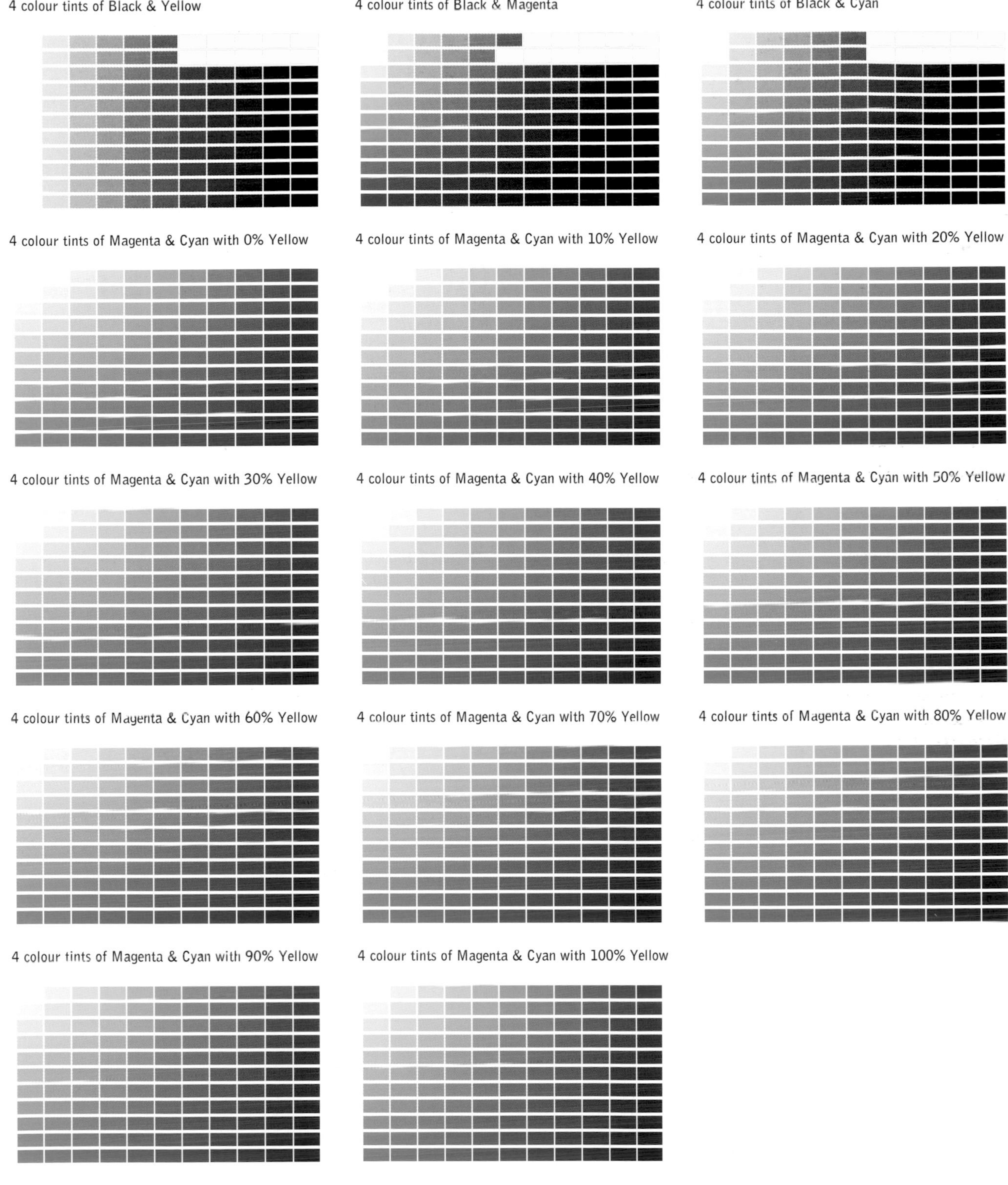
4 colour tints of Black & Yellow
4 colour tints of Black & Magenta
4 colour tints of Black & Cyan
4 colour tints of Magenta & Cyan with 0% Yellow
4 colour tints of Magenta & Cyan with 10% Yellow
4 colour tints of Magenta & Cyan with 20% Yellow
4 colour tints of Magenta & Cyan with 30% Yellow
4 colour tints of Magenta & Cyan with 40% Yellow
4 colour tints of Magenta & Cyan with 50% Yellow
4 colour tints of Magenta & Cyan with 60% Yellow
4 colour tints of Magenta & Cyan with 70% Yellow
4 colour tints of Magenta & Cyan with 80% Yellow
4 colour tints of Magenta & Cyan with 90% Yellow
4 colour tints of Magenta & Cyan with 100% Yellow

specials

The four-colour printing process uses the subtractive primary process colours – CMY (cyan, magenta and yellow) – that are applied via separate printing plates to create a colour image. The three primary colours are usually applied in the cyan, magenta, yellow order with black applied to add contrast.

This square was printed by the four-colour printing process. If you look closely you will see that it is made up of cyan, magenta, yellow and black dots. The four-colour process can produce nearly all colours by combining the three process colours in different ratios, which is achieved by the different sized halftone dots. Although this tri-colour process can produce a wide range of colours it has definite limitations, which means that a 'special' colour may need to be used.

The first PMS (Pantone Matching System) Printers' Edition was launched in 1963.

A spot colour is a premixed colour ink usually identified by a colour system e.g. PMS that is used for documents requiring few colours or specific colours. Spot colour is applied as a separate plate and will appear smooth when viewed closely.

Process colour uses four standard inks to produce many thousands of colours and is used for printing photographs and complex coloured images.

Printing costs vary depending on the number of inks used. Spot colour can be cheaper if fewer than four colours are used (process colour uses four inks).

Pantone has developed a six-colour printing process called Hexachrome that enhances the CMYK system by adding orange and green. The extended colour range enriches photographic reproduction and accurate simulation of all PMS spot colours.

This page was printed using a special or spot colour. If you look closely you will see that it is a solid colour and not made up of dots like the square on the opposite page, which was produced using the four-colour printing process. A special colour is one that cannot be made using the CMYK process colours and they include metallic, fluorescent and Pantone (PMS) inks that must be applied using additional plates. One common usage of special colours is for corporate logos. Although more expensive, the advantage is obvious, the design is printed in a precise, defined colour.

Pages 164, 165, 168, 169, 172, 173, 176 are also printed using PMS 812

understanding colour

Colour reproduction is based on the principles behind the three-colour vision of the human eye. The eye contains three different types of receptors that are each sensitive to one of the primary colours of light: red, green and blue. These are called additive primaries because when these colours are added together they produce white light. The standard four-colour process uses cyan, magenta, yellow and black inks as they can reproduce nearly all colours; but how is this achieved? A little colour theory will explain how the processes work.

Additive primaries

White light is made up of red, green and blue light, the additive primaries, so called because they are added together to produce white light. When only two additive primaries are combined they create one of the subtractive primaries as shown in the illustration (left).

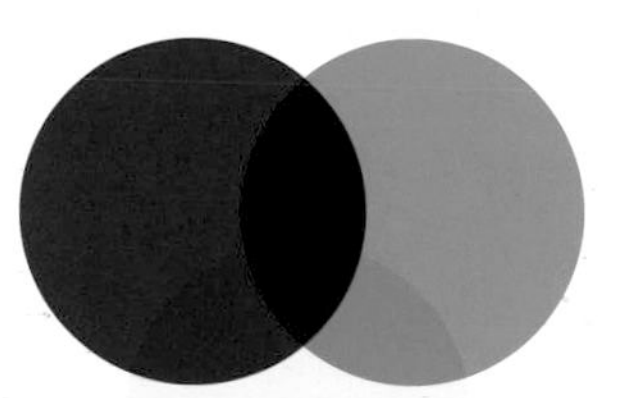

Subtractive primaries

Subtractive primaries work in the same way but when two are combined they make an additive primary and when all are combined they produce black.

White light is comprised of three main colours, the RGB additive primaries that when combined form white light. If you remove one of these colours a different colour is produced: blue and green minus red produce cyan, red and green minus blue produce yellow, and red and blue minus green results in magenta. As cyan, magenta and yellow are made by removing one of the additive primaries they are known as subtractive primaries.

What has this got to do with colour separation? You will notice that the subtractive primaries are the same as the process colours used in printing. To reproduce a full-colour image it is necessary to make a negative for each respective colour by photographing the original through a colour filter that has been matched to the standard CMY inks. These filters correspond to the RGB additive primary colours.

A red filter produces a negative record of all the wavelengths of red light reflected or transmitted from the image called the red separation negative. In effect this is a recording of the cyan component as the negative has subtracted the red light from the image, and the positive is a recording of the blue and the green, which is cyan. The positive is the cyan printer.

In the same way a green filter is used to produce the magenta printer and a blue filter is used to produce the yellow printer. Black is produced by another separation called the black printer that is necessary due to the limitations of the printing ink pigments.

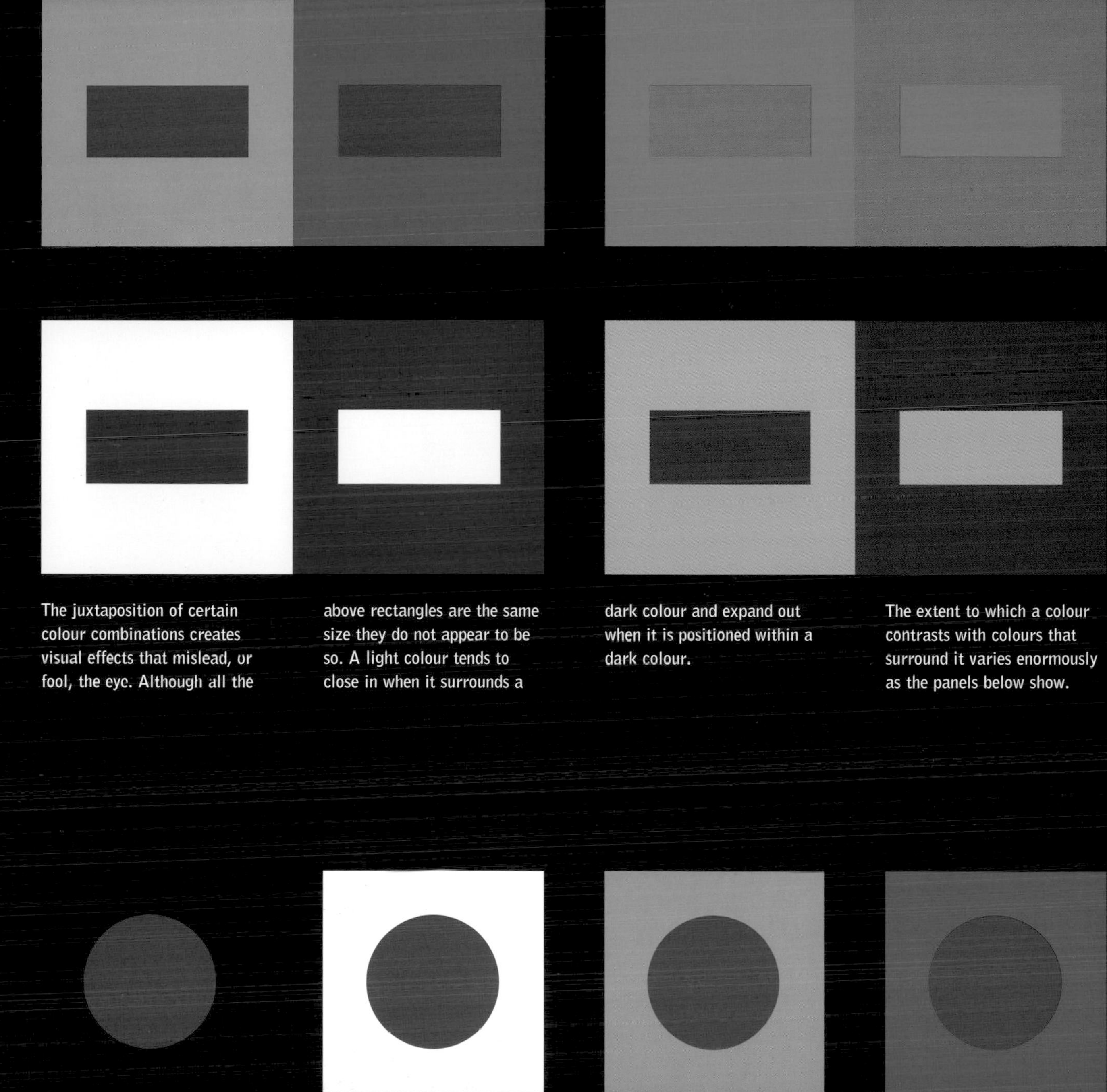

The juxtaposition of certain colour combinations creates visual effects that mislead, or fool, the eye. Although all the above rectangles are the same size they do not appear to be so. A light colour tends to close in when it surrounds a dark colour and expand out when it is positioned within a dark colour.

The extent to which a colour contrasts with colours that surround it varies enormously as the panels below show.

photodisc

To promote the possibilities of using stock photography beyond the mundane and obvious, Photodisc produced this marketing communication. Each image is composed of several examples of stock photography that have been subjected to various image manipulation techniques to radically alter their look, in effect making them unrecognisable but highly effective components of a larger man-made image. Each item details how the resulting image was achieved in effect, educating the users of stock photography and encouraging them to be more adventurous. For example the design top right informs the reader how to breathe new life into an old technique by rasterizing an image and using the 'create mosaic' feature.

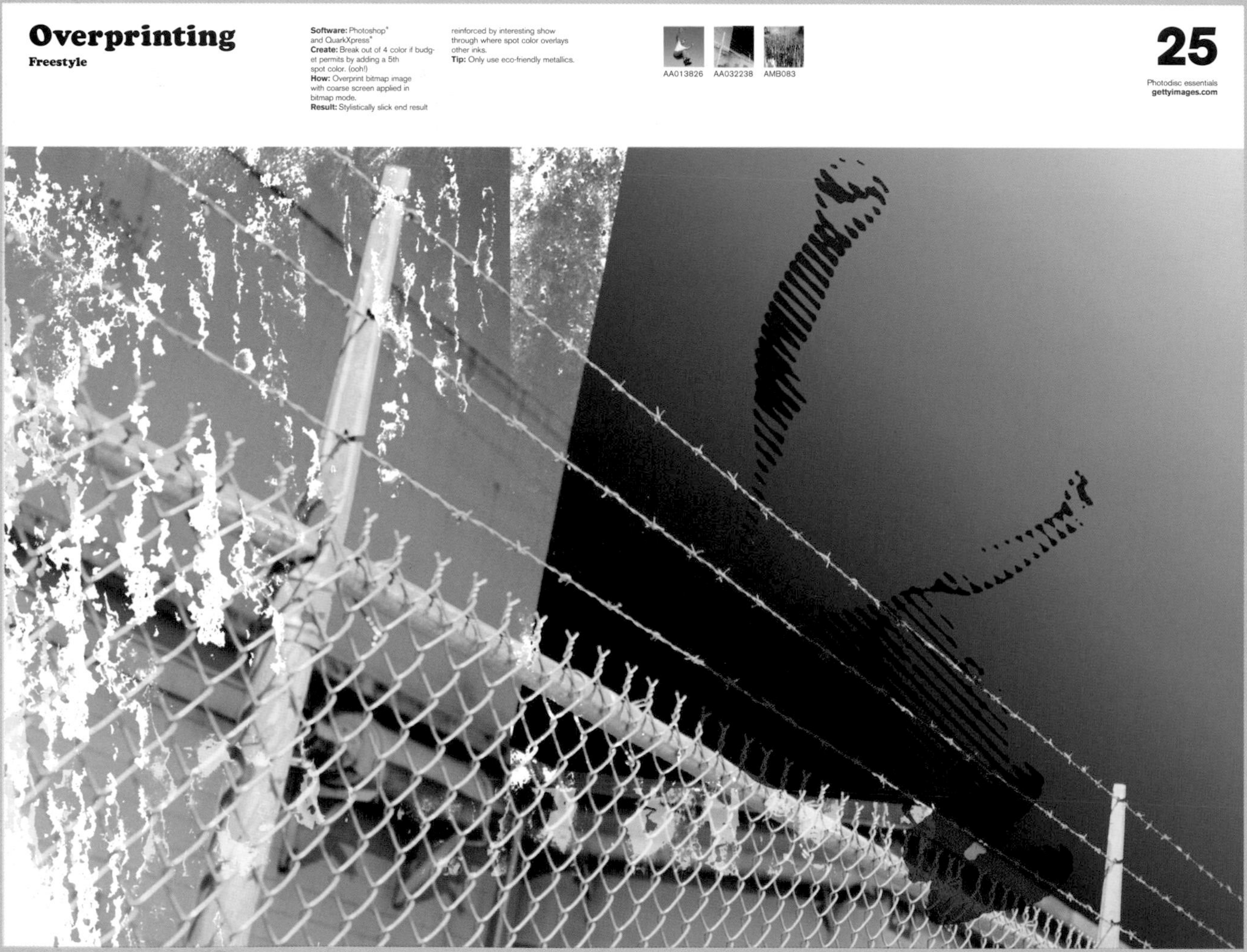

Overprinting
Freestyle

Software: Photoshop® and QuarkXpress®
Create: Break out of 4 color if budget permits by adding a 5th spot color. (ooh!)
How: Overprint bitmap image with coarse screen applied in bitmap mode.
Result: Stylistically slick end result reinforced by interesting show through where spot color overlays other inks.
Tip: Only use eco-friendly metallics.

AA013826

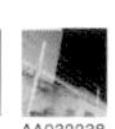
AA032238

AMB083

25

Photodisc essentials
gettyimages.com

Mosaic
Freestyle
Software: Illustrator® or QuarkXpress®
Create: Breathe new life into an old technique. Craft contemporary patterns using simple shapes.
How: By rasterizing image and using Create Mosaic feature in Illustrator. For a more organic pattern Step and Repeat squares and manually color.
Result: Modern graphic illustrations that stand out.
Tip: If you can read this you're too close!
AA050994 AA051178
29
Photodisc dynamics
gettyimages.com

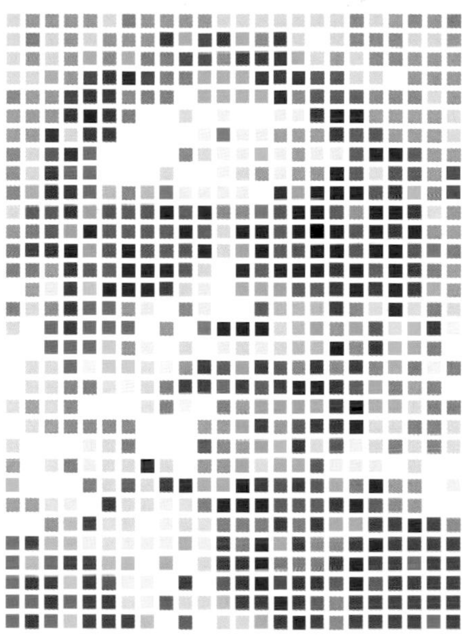

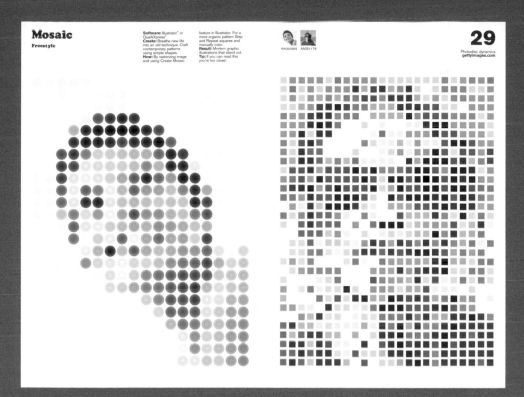

Photographic images can be broken down in many different ways as these images by Tobin Lush and Adrian Britteon at Getty Creative Studio show.

Left: The images are rasterized and turned into a mosaic that is then manually coloured.

Left: Overprinting in practice. The silhouette sits on top of the four-colour printing beneath.

Right: Image layers, colour gradients and the perspective tool combine to create an eclectic, eye-catching image.

Design: Getty Creative Studio

Perspective
Freestyle
Software: Photoshop®
Create: Dynamically altered landscapes, with a twisted perspective. You're only limited by your imagination. Our collection provides limitless possibilities.
How: Using image layers, color gradients and the perspective tool.
Result: Surreal suburbs. Altered states. The shifting cityscape.
Tip: Look around, there is wonder in what you're seeing.
AA030222 AA030921 LS017155 LS003671 AA023116
21
Photodisc dynamics
gettyimages.com

See Overprinting

colours

Colour is composed of different wavelengths of light, which means that an infinite number are possible. Computers can produce over 16 million colours and the human eye can distinguish more than that. Colour is the first thing we register when we assess anything and we have developed and been conditioned to make many associations with certain colours. This is called colour symbolism, but it is far from absolute. Reaction to colour will depend upon cultural associations, trends, age and of course individual preferences. In the West, white is associated with weddings while for Buddhists it is a mourning colour.

Boy

Girl

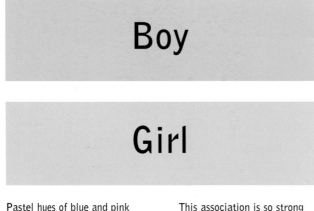

Pastel hues of blue and pink are associated with newborn children in Western cultures; pale blue for boys and pale pink for girls. This scheme is particularly used for clothing as dressed in this coding, the colours help identify the sex of the infant.

This association is so strong that when the colours and genders are switched there is a cognitive breakdown and something appears odd, wrong or even unacceptable. A similar reaction can be expected in other cultures and parts of the world if their colour usage associations are not considered.

The ability of colour to provide instant communication and recognition plays a major role in branding and not just for products as these two pictures illustrate. New York City is known as the Big Apple, but is that a yellow apple, a red one, or a green one? The city's famous nickname has no colour associated with it but its taxi cabs are a ubiquitous, easily recognisable symbol of the city.

London has its black cabs of course, but perhaps a more recognisable symbol of the city is the red telephone box. The strength of this symbolic association is highlighted by the fact that it is still made even though most red telephone boxes were withdrawn and replaced several years ago.

lue
holy colour for the
ewish faith

Red
Used in activities in China ranging from weddings to funerals as it represents celebration and luck

Orange
Used to represent Halloween in the USA

Blue
The Chinese link blue to immortality

Brown
In Colombia this is a colour that discourages sales

rown
he colour of
ourning in India

Purple
The colour of royalty in European cultures

Black
Used for mourning in Western cultures, associated with death, but also ultra cool, stylish and elegant

Green
Used for a hat it indicates a wife is being unfaithful in China

White
The colour for purity in Western cultures, used for wedding dresses

ellow
epresents happiness
nd joy in the West

Blue
A colour associated with protection in the Middle East, and indeed a 'safe' colour throughout the world

Yellow
A sacred and imperial colour in many Asian cultures

White
Mourning colour in Eastern cultures. It also symbolises death

Red
When used with white in Eastern cultures it means joy

rey
ymbolic of an
bsence of love or
oneliness in Western
ocieties

Blue
A sacred colour to Hindus as it is the colour of Krishna

Saffron
A sacred colour for the Hindu faith

Orange
Associated with the Protestant faith in Ireland

Green
Negative connotations in France and a poor choice for packaging

hite
ssociated with death
Japan, particularly
hite carnations

Green
Of high significance in Muslim countries because it is the colour of Islam

Red
Can mean stop or danger in Western cultures and also associated with Valentine's day and Christmas

Blue
Connected to soap in Colombia

Red
Used for wedding dresses in India as it is the colour of purity

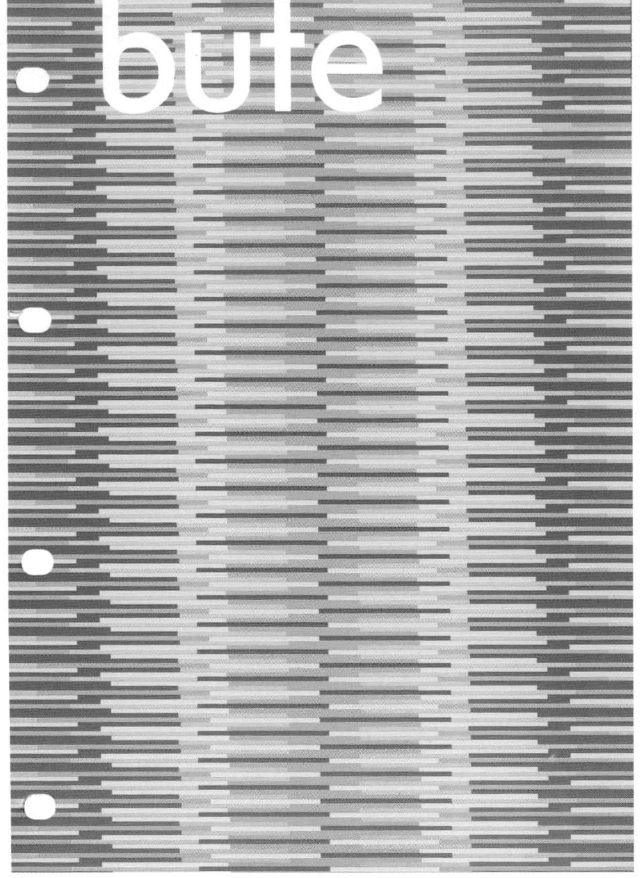

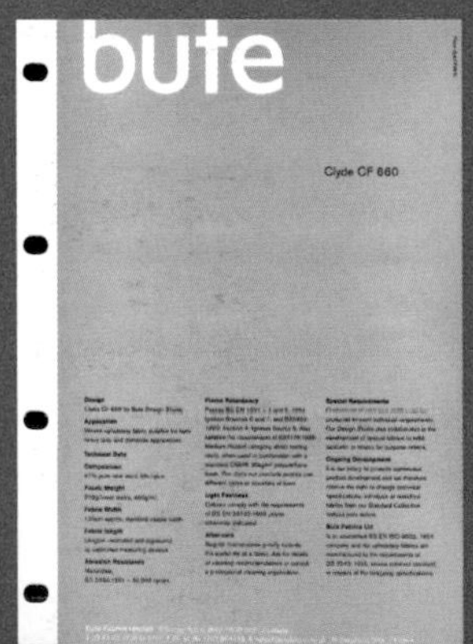

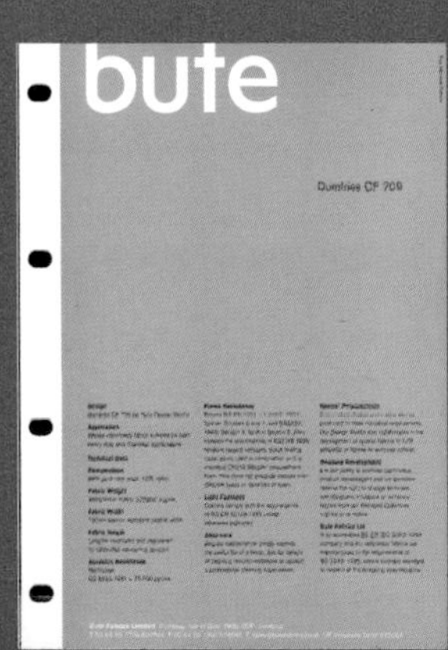

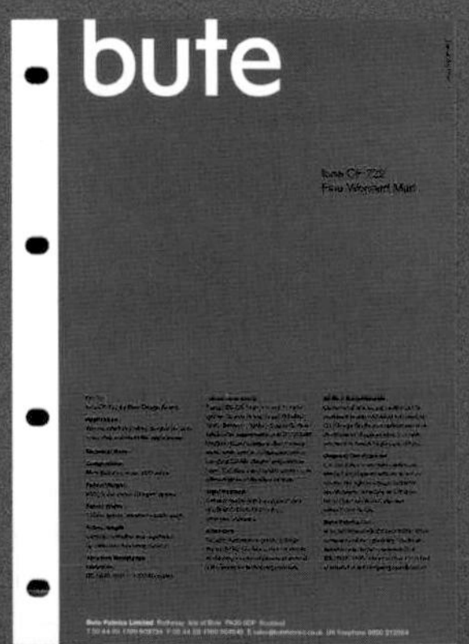

Identity and branding for Scottish textile manufacturer, Bute. Taking inspiration from the product the literature suite uses colour as a means of navigation. The simple silk-screened folder (top left) contains an intro card (top right), a brochure featuring the product (left), and a series of coloured gatefold fabric swatches (above).

Design: Studio Myerscough

MTV2–

Don't try this at home

or anywhere else.

Watch Txt Drugs n Rock n Roll.

Live Monday to Friday at 3pm.

2

mtv2europe.com

London agency dixonbaxi created a throw-away slogan approach for the rebranding of MTV2, a channel without fixed schedules or structures that sees itself as 'liquid TV'. To familiarise themselves with the target audience, partners Simon Dixon and Aporva Baxi hung out in London's Camden Town to gain insight on the current thinking of 16–25 year-old males.

The ident design they created is simple and disposable with purposefully crude typography that creates a dialogue with the audience in its own patois. It has attitude but doesn't take itself seriously, and because it is modular it can be easily and quickly refreshed to reflect the continuing changes to youth culture.

Type size, leading and kerning can all be changed by animation software to make the slogans literally pulse with life. Communication of the MTV2 brand is very much a low-key affair that reflects the target demographic's distrust of corporations and advertising.

Design: dixonbaxi

MTV2–

Makes me want to — smoke Blu-Tack.

Watch MTV2.

You may regret it.

2

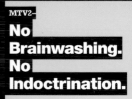

MTV2–

No Brainwashing. No Indoctrination.

Nope.

Watch Gonzo [with Zane].

5pm daily.

2

See Type detailing

>120

controlling colour

Colour is comprised of red, green and blue light at varying degrees of hue, saturation and brightness (HSB). Effective HSB manipulation allows accurate colour reproduction to be achieved by preventing any one element having undue emphasis. There may, of course, be occasions when a lack of colour harmony is required. Hue is synonymous with colour (red, green and blue are different hues), saturation or chroma is an indication of how pure or vivid a colour is, and brightness refers to its lightness, whiteness or tone. The following charts illustrate how adjustments to HSB values affect an image. However, it should be noted that effective and predictable colour control requires the calibration of software, test print devices and your monitor.

minimum hue

maximum hue

As hue refers to the actual colours of the image, changing the hue value dramatically changes the colours of the image.

minimum brightness

maximum brightness

Adjusting the brightness level alters how much light is used to produce the colour. The more light that is used the brighter the colour will be. However, as contrast diminishes towards the maximum and minimum levels a brightness level that results in good contrast is preferred.

minimum contrast

maximum contrast

Changing the saturation or contrast affects how vivid the colours appear. A desaturated image will appear grey as the vivacity of the colours has been reduced. A fully saturated image contains full colour values and may appear hyper-real. Balancing the amounts of red, green and blue will result in a less saturated colour.

Minimum hue &
maximum saturation

Maximum hue &
maximum saturation

increased saturation

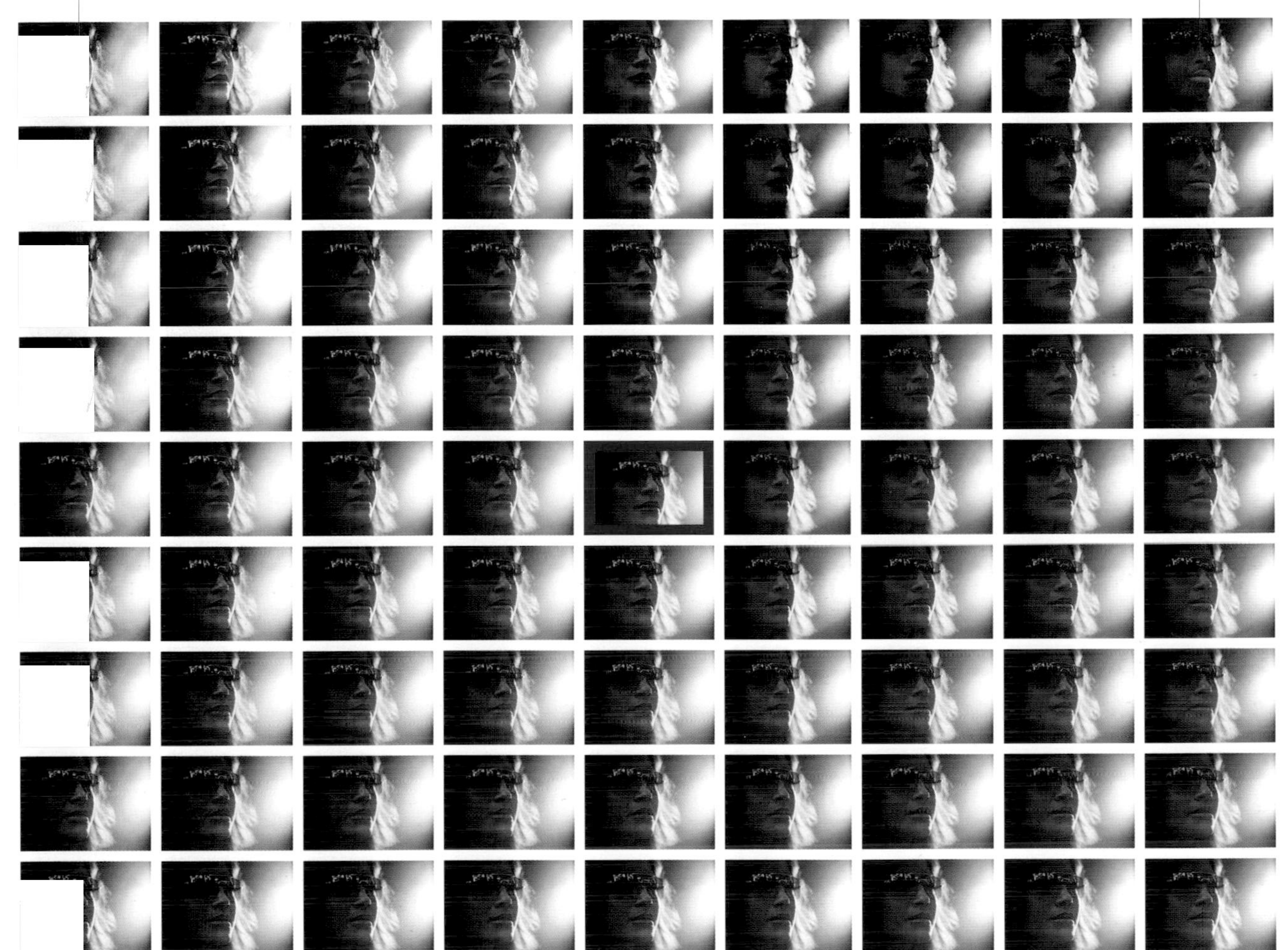

decreased hue

increased hue

decreased saturation

Minimum hue &
minimum saturation

Maximum hue &
minimum saturation

conclusion

THE SUBJECTS IN THIS BOOK ARE INTENDED TO HIGHLIGHT THE USE OF BASIC DESIGN FUNDAMENTALS AND TECHNIQUES. A THOROUGH UNDERSTANDING OF THE FUNDAMENTALS OF FORMAT, LAYOUT, TYPOGRAPHY, COLOUR, AND IMAGE EQUIPS THE DESIGNER WITH POWERFUL TOOLS WITH WHICH TO UNLEASH TREMENDOUS CREATIVITY. DESIGN IS A COMMERCIAL PURSUIT AND THE FUNDAMENTALS FACILITATE THE EFFICIENT USE OF DESIGN TIME WHILE KEEPING COSTS WITHIN BUDGET. INSPIRATION IS AT THE HEART OF CREATIVE ACTIVITY AND WE HOPE THAT THE COMMERCIAL PROJECTS FROM LEADING CONTEMPORARY DESIGN STUDIOS THAT ILLUSTRATE THE FUNDAMENTALS INSPIRE YOU.

WE WOULD LIKE TO GIVE SPECIAL THANKS TO EVERYONE THAT HAS CONTRIBUTED WORK TO MAKE *THE FUNDAMENTALS OF CREATIVE DESIGN* SUCH A VISUAL TREAT.

The Modern Poster

A REVIEW OF CONTEMPORARY POSTER DESIGN BY MICHAEL JOHNSON, JOHNSON BANKS

The Johnson Banks studio took a tongue-in-cheek approach for a poster to promote a review of contemporary poster design by creating a clean minimalist image that looks as though it is constructed of four separate posters, like for a billboard, that have somehow fallen out of alignment.

Design: Johnson Banks

glossary of terms

Accordion fold
Two or more parallel folds that open like an accordion.

Additive primaries
The red, green and blue components that together make white light.

Ascender
Part of a lower case letter that extends above the x-height of a typeface.

Baseline
The imaginary line upon which the bases of all capital letters and most lower case letters are positioned.

Baseline grid
The graphic foundation on which a design is constructed.

Bitmap
An image that is composed of dots.

Black printer
The film printing black in the colour separation process.

Bleed
A printed image that extends over the trim edge of the stock.

Body copy
Text that forms the main part of a work.

Body text
The matter that forms the main text of a printed book.

Bold or boldface type
A thick, heavy variety of type used to give emphasis.

Bouncers/shiners
A 50% or 60% cyan area behind the black that improves visual density and saturation.

Bowl
The curved portion of a type character.

Character
An individual element of type such as a letter or punctuation mark.

Chroma
The purity or intensity of a colour.

CMYK
Cyan, magenta, yellow and black, the subtractive primaries and four process colours.

Colour separation
Photographic filtration process to divide the colours of a continuous tone-coloured original into constituent colours.

Concertina fold
Paper folding method where each fold runs opposite of the previous one to obtain a pleated outcome.

Condensed type
Type that is elongated and narrow.

Continuous tone
Continuous shades in an image such as a photograph that are not broken up into dots.

Contrast
The level of tone separation from white to black.

Cool colour
Green, blue and other colours with a green or blue cast.

Cropping
Trimming unwanted parts of a photograph or illustration.

Cyan
A shade of blue, one of the subtractive primaries used in four-colour printing.

Deboss
As emboss but recessed into the substrate.

Descender
Part of a lower case letter that extends below the baseline.

Die cut
Special shapes cut in a substrate by a steel rule.

Display type
Large and/or distinctive type intended to attract the eye. Specifically cut to be viewed from a distance.

Dot gain
Spreading and enlarging of ink dots on paper.

Down stroke
The heavy stroke in a type character.

DPI (Dots Per Inch)
The resolution of a screen image or printed page.

Drop cap
Large initial at the start of a text that drops into lines of type below.

Dummy
Provisional layout showing illustration and text positions as they will appear in the final reproduction.

Duotone
A two-colour reproduction from a monochrome original.

Em
Unit of measurement derived from width of the square body of the cast upper case M. An em equals the size of a given type i.e. the em of 10 point type is 10 points.

Emboss
A design stamped without ink or foil giving a raised surface.

En
Unit of measurement equal to half of one em.

EPS (Encapsulated PostScript)
A picture file format for storing vector or object-based artwork, and bitmaps. EPS files can be resized, distorted and colour separated but no content alteration can usually be made.

Family
A series of fonts sharing common design characteristics but with different sizes and weights.

Foil stamp
Foil pressed on to a substrate using heat and pressure. Also known as heat stamp, hot stamp, block print or foil emboss.

Font
The physical attributes needed to make a typeface, be it film, metal, wood or PostScript information.

Format
The size/proportions of a book or page.

Four-colour printing
Full colour printing method using colour separation and CMYK inks.

GIF (Graphic Interchange Format)
A storage format suitable for images with flat areas of colour such as text and logos.

Golden section
A division in the ratio 8:13 that produces harmonious proportions.

Greyscale
A tonal scale that enables a printer to check tone reproduction.

Grid
A guide or template to help obtain design consistency.

Gutter
The space that comprises the fore edge, or outer edge of a page, that is parallel to the back and the trim. The centre alleyway where two pages meet at the spine and the space between text columns are also called the gutter.

Halftone
The simulation of a continuous tone by a pattern of dots.

Hue
A pure colour that does not include any black or white.

Imposition
The arrangement of pages in the sequence and position in which they will appear when printed before being cut, folded and trimmed.

Ink trapping
The adjustment of areas of colour, text or shapes to account for misregistration on the printing press by overlapping them.

International paper sizes (ISO)
A range of standard paper sizes.

Italic
A slanted variety of typeface often used for emphasis.

JPEG (Joint Photographic Experts Group)
A file format for storing photographic images. Contains 24-bit colour information i.e. 6.7million colours, using compression to discard image information. Suitable for images with complex pixel gradations but not for flat colour.

Justify
Formatting to space out lines of type uniformly to a fixed width.

Kerning
The removal of unwanted space between letters.

Layout
The placement of text and images to give the general appearance of a printed page.

Leading
Vertical space between lines of type measured in points.

Ligature
Tied type characters. Common ligatures are: fi, fl, ffi, ffl, and ff, and also the vowel pairs ae and oe.

Magenta
A shade of red, one of the subtractive primaries used in four-colour printing.

Majuscule
Upper case letter.

Matter
Copy to be printed.

Margin
The empty areas on a page that surround the printed matter.

Measure
The width of type, expressed in picas.

Metallic ink
A printing ink that gives a gold, silver, bronze etc. effect.

Minuscule
Lower case letter.

Moiré
A printing error where halftones appear as visible dots in the printed image.

Monochrome
An image made of varying tones of one colour.

Mosaic
A design made up of small pieces.

Oblique
A slanting typographic character also called solidus.

Optical character recognition
A process for scanning text and converting it into photoset matter without using a keyboard.

Original
Any matter or image for reproduction.

Pica
Unit of measurement equal to one sixth of an inch comprising 12 points.

Pigment
Material used as the colouring agent of inks and paint.

PMS
Pantone Matching System, a colour matching system.

Point
Unit of measurement equal to 1/72 of an inch used to measure type.

Primary colours
Red, green and blue, the primary colours of light, also called additive primaries.

Process colours
The subtractive primaries: cyan, magenta, yellow and black used for full-colour reproduction.

RA paper size
Untrimmed paper sizes in the international paper size series.

Registration
Exact alignment of two or more printed images with each other on the same substrate.

RGB
Red, green and blue, the additive primaries.

Rule
A line added to a page for emphasis.

Saddle stitch
A binding that uses a wire staple to fasten folded pages.

Sans-serif
Having no serif.

Saturation
The colour variation of the same tonal brightness from none to pure colour.

Screen angle
Relative angles of halftone screens in four-colour process reproduction to avoid moiré patterns.

Screen printing
The direct imprinting of a design on to the surface of a substrate, usually using paint.

Script
A typeface that imitates handwriting.

Serif
A small terminal stroke that accentuates the end of the main stroke of a letter.

Sheet
A single piece of paper.

Spot colour or special
A specially mixed colour.

SRA paper size
Untrimmed paper sizes for bleed work in the international paper size series.

Stem
The most prominent vertical, or closest to vertical, stroke in a type character.

Stock
The paper to be printed upon.

Stress
Variation in letter stroke thicknesses.

Substrate
A surface to be printed on.

Tagged Image File Format (TIFF)
A flexible method supported by many applications for storing halftones and photographic images.

Text
Written or printed matter that forms the body of a publication.

Tonal value
An image's relative densities of tone.

Typeface
The letters, numbers and punctuation marks of a typeface.

Type size
The size of type, measured in points between the bottom of the descender and the top of the ascender.

Upstroke
The finer stroke of a type character.

UV coating
Coating applied to a printed substrate that is bonded and cured with ultraviolet light.

Varnish
Coating applied to a printed sheet for protection or appearance.

X-height
The height of lower case letters such as 'x' with no ascenders or descenders.

contacts

Andy Potts
P. 134, 135
Tel: +44 (0)7817 159049
Email: info@andy-potts.com
Web: www.andy-potts.com

Asterik Studio
P. 151
3524 W. Government Way,
Seattle, WA 98199, USA
Tel: +1 206 352 3746
Email: info@asterikstudio.com
Web: www.asterikstudio.com

Atelier Works
P. 38, 39
The Old Piano Factory, 5 Charlton
Kings Road, London NW5 2SB, UK
Tel: +44 (0)20 7284 2215
Email: info@atelierworks.co.uk
Web: www.atelierworks.co.uk

Baba Design
P. 22
Bretislavova 12, Mala Strana,
Prague 11800, Czech Republic
Tel: +42 737 759 964
Email: info@baba-prague.com
Web: www.baba-prague.com

Blue Source.
P. 71
326 Kensal Road,
London W10 5BZ, UK
Tel: +44 (0)20 7460 6020
Email: info@bluesource.com
Web: www.bluesource.com

Build
P. 144, 145
Tel: +44 (0)7974 348494
Email:
informyou@designbybuild.com
Web: www.designbybuild.com

Clase
P. 21
Portaferrissa 7-9, 2n 2a 08002,
Barcelona, Spain
Tel: +34 93 301 00 83
Email: info@cla-se.com
Web: www.cla-se.com

Craig Yamey
P. 90, 92, 93, 149
56b Market Place,
London NW11 6JP, UK
Tel: +44 (0)20 8455 1805
Email: craigyamey@hotmail.com

dixonbaxi
P. 169
Tel: +44 (0)20 7864 9993

Faydherbe/De Vringer
P. 74, 75, 86, 87, 112, 113,
146, 147
2E Schuytstraat 76, 2517 XH Den
Haag/The Hague, The Netherlands
Tel: +31 (0)70 360 298
Email: ben_wout@euronet.nl

Forme London
P. 13, 16, 17
Frogmore Mill, London Road, Hemel
Hempstead, Herts HP3 9RY, UK
Tel: +44 (0)1442 241 244
Email: info@formelondon.co.uk

Frost Design
P. 14, 15, 128, 129, 156
The Gymnasium, Kingsway Place,
Sans Walk, London EC1R 0LU, UK
Tel: +44 (0)20 7490 7994
Web: www.frostdesign.co.uk

Gavin Ambrose
P. 21, 26, 27, 32, 33, 132, 133
Tel: +44 (0)1580 720 774
Email: gavin@dircon.co.uk

Getty Creative Studio
P. 164, 165
Getty Images Global Creative Studio,
17 Conway Street, London
W1T 6EE, UK
Tel: +44 (0)20 7554 2662
Email: tobin.lush@gettyimages.com
Web: www.gettyimages.com

ImaginaryForces
P. 149, 152, 153
530 W 25th St. 5th Floor, New
York, NY 10001, USA
Tel: +1 646 486 6868

Johnson Banks
P. 22, 60, 61, 123, 142, 173
Crescent Works, Crescent Lane,
Clapham, London SW4 9RW, UK
Tel: +44 (0)20 7587 6400
Email: info@johnsonbanks.co.uk
Web: www.johnsonbanks.co.uk

Lewis Moberly
P. 90
33 Greese Street,
London W1P 2LP, UK
Tel: +44 (0)20 7580 9252
Email: hello@lewismoberly.com

Matt Checkowski
P. 149, 152, 153
Los Angeles, CA, USA
Email: mche@sbcglobal.net

Mono
P. 77
Studio 2, Ground Floor, Panther
House, 38 Mount Pleasant, London
WC1X 0AP, UK
Tel: +44 (0)20 7833 4084
Email: info@monosite.co.uk
Web: www.monosite.co.uk

NB: Studio
P. 11, 18, 19, 25, 115, 148, 157
24 Store Street,
London WC1E 7BA, UK
Tel: +44 (0)20 7580 9195
Email: mail@nbstudio.co.uk
Web: www.nbstudio.co.uk

Pentagram
P. 36, 37, 52-55, 140, 141
11 Needham Road,
London W11 2RP, UK
Tel: +44 (0)20 7229 3477
Email: email@pentagram.co.uk
Web: www.pentagram.co.uk

Research Studios London
P. 80-83
94 Islington High Street,
London N1 8EG, UK
Tel: +44 (0)20 7704 244 5
Email: info@researchstudios.com
Web: www.researchstudios.com

Sagmeister Inc.
P. 23, 91, 122, 150
222 West 14 Street, 15a
New York, NY 10011, USA
Tel: +1 212 647 1789
Email: SSagmeiste@aol.com

Studio AS
P. 34, 35, 46-48
24 Ashburnham Place,
Greenwich, London SE10 8TZ, UK
Tel: +44 (0)20 8694 6882
Email: info@studioas.com

Studio Myerscough
P. 16, 40-43, 68, 69, 90, 94, 95,
143, 168
28-29 Great Sutton Street, London
EC1V 0DS, UK
Tel: +44 (0)20 7689 0808
Email:
post@studiomyerscough.demon.co.uk

Visual Research
P. 138, 139
57 Shadwell Road, Portsmouth,
Hampshire P02 9EH, UK
Email: visualresearch@hotmail.com